WHAT OT

This book makes my job easier. I'll have much more to talk about in my classes. Your book is informative, and I look forward to using it. I encourage ESL students to read it and use it as a reference.

Rachael Chen, English teacher
Taipei, Taiwan

Absolutely brilliant! This book has helped me to expand my understanding of the English language and culture. As a foreigner myself and student of American Politics, I do recommend it to those wanting to expand their understanding of idioms and expressions in a frugal and easy-to-read composition.

Jorge L. Mendoza, Graduate student of American Politics
University of California, San Diego

Thank you for writing this book. So many times, perhaps out of laziness or habit, we cause stress and distrust in life by using an obscure phrase or expression, when we could just as easily use words with our intent clearly stated. I expect that your readers will benefit greatly by learning the true meaning behind so many common expressions we take for granted. In addition, I hope many readers with English as their primary language will take seriously the importance of clarity in thought and speech. As "texting" and other technological shortcuts begin to dominate our communications systems, this will become increasingly important. Congratulations upon completing a most daunting task, and thank you for allowing me to add my comments.

Dorothy Miller, Literary Consultant
San Diego, California

I like the way this book goes beyond the American culture and covers many other countries' sayings, anecdotes and idioms in a very clear and concise language. This way, Reza brings us to the realization that people of different cultures and backgrounds share more or less the same thoughts and idioms on the same subjects. Reza's extensive work is definitely appreciated by me, and being an ESL instructor, I can use it as a valuable guideline in the curriculum of my class.

Angie Moeen, ESL teacher
San Diego, California

English Idioms And Expressions For Foreigners, *Like Me!*

I *Thought* I Knew English, But I Didn't Know *That!*

Reza Mashayekhi

East To West Publications
San Diego, California

English Idioms And Expressions For Foreigners, *Like Me!*
I *Thought* I Knew English, But I Didn't Know *That!* by Reza Mashayekhi

East To West Publications
P.O. Box 26546
San Diego, CA 92196 U.S.A.

ISBNs
  Softcover   978-0-9827736-5-9
  Hardcover   978-0-9827736-6-6
  Pocketbook 978-0-9827736-7-3
  E-book   978-0-9827736-8-0
  PDF   978-0-9827736-9-7

First edition 2011
Printed in the United States of America

             Library of Congress Cataloging-in-Publication Data
                    (Provided by Quality Books, Inc.)
Mashayekhi, Reza.
   English idioms and expressions for foreigners, like me!: I thought I knew
   English, but I didn't know that! / Reza Mashayekhi. -- 1st ed.
   p. cm.
   Includes index.
   ISBN-13: 978-0-9827736-5-9 (softcover)
   ISBN-10: 0-9827736-5-X (softcover)
   ISBN-13: 978-0-9827736-6-6 (hardcover)
   ISBN-10: 0-9827736-6-8 (hardcover) [etc.]
   1. English language--Idioms. 2. Figures of speech.
I. Title.
PE1460.M37 2011   428
                                 QBI10-600157
LCCN 2010932750

CONTENTS

ABOUT THE AUTHOR

Reza Mashayekhi was born and reared in Tehran, Iran. He later attended the University of Michigan, where he received a degree in aerospace engineering.

Reza has always been interested in learning the intricacies of the English language. This is why, alongside of his engineering work, he has taught English to non-English speakers. He has done this because he has wanted to expand his knowledge of English, and he has a good explanation for his reasoning.

"When you want to learn a subject, you approach it from your own perspective," he says. "Once you feel that you know enough about it, you typically move on to something else. When you *teach* a subject, however, you have to learn everything about it before you can satisfactorily answer all of the questions that are raised by the students."

Reza also consults with non-English speakers to prepare them for their public speaking events, or to help with their day-to-day conversational skills, both in the form of workshops and on a one-on-one basis.

Being a non-native speaker of English, living and working in the U.S., Reza's experience through the years and his interactions with his students and clients has led to the compilation of this book.

FOREWORD

A lack of or incomplete communication has been one of the major causes of conflict and bloodshed throughout history. While addressing major world conflicts is not the goal here, this book is an effective tool for helping to accomplish better communication between at least some of the people. It can help to reduce the possibility of unwanted, and sometimes devastating, consequences.

In 1990, a Boeing 707, from Colombia, crashed in New York before it could reach the airport. The investigation into the crash determined that the pilot's request for emergency landing had been misinterpreted. (See *Appendix*.) This miscommunication cost the lives of the 73 people who were on that aircraft.

In another tragic incident, in 1992, a foreign exchange student was accidentally shot to death when he inadvertently walked onto someone's lawn. He apparently didn't know what the homeowner meant when he yelled, "Freeze!" (See *Dedication*.)

These, of course, are extreme examples. Less serious incidents, however, are happening around us, all of the time. They have led to receiving lower grades at school, missing flights, losing business opportunities, having broken hearts, etc.

Although difficulties with idioms and expressions mainly involve non-English speakers and foreign students, people from different regions in English-speaking countries are not necessarily immune either. Even children, as they are growing up, encounter occasional surprises. Imagine the surprised look on a little child's face upon hearing this for the first time: "You can't play outside today; it's raining cats and dogs!"

This book has been compiled with the hope of eliminating some of these misunderstandings. The entries in this book are not usually found in dictionaries. Some are not even idioms or expressions. They are simply words or phrases that are used in daily conversation.

Because we're routinely using them, it's easy to forget that common expressions—such as: *He ended up with egg on his face,* or *He has a monkey on his back*—sound somewhat strange, especially if it's the first time you're hearing them. So, if you're talking to someone, and you get the feeling that you're not getting through to them, maybe you should use one of our substitutes!

What has been compiled here will help non-English speakers, especially foreign students. It can also help native English speakers by showing them alternative ways of saying things, if necessary. Who knows, some parents may find it useful, too!

Reza Mashayekhi
San Diego, California

ACKNOWLEDGEMENTS

I cannot thank them enough, but I will try. I'll start with author and designer Dawn Farson, without whose encouragement this book would still be just another one of many ideas in my head, and author and music instructor Suellen Fast, without whose help and ideas it would still be just another file on my computer.

Wendy Appel, Manuel Arambul, Ana Arteaga, Chris Belton, Matt and Aase Bence, Melanie Dellas, John Descano, Marc Emmelmann, Bahram Fariba, Dragan Giurici, Ana Goebel, Tommy Gonzales, Melanie Heisey, Kanae Hirano, Dilek Koksal, Zvart Malkhassian, Kesha Palmer, Vicki Quarders, Elizabeth Rose, Ron Peterson, Tyson Simon, Jheri St. James, Crossby Vargas, and Yolande Witkin helped so much with ideas, research, explanations, and marketing.

April Nelson did the proofreading and editing of the entire book, which was no small job.

The interior layout and design was done by *Scribe Freelance*.

Alina Fairy did the beautiful job of cover design.

Azita Mousavi, of *azitaart* in San Diego, and Sarah Arakaki and Kacie Paik, both graduates of the University of California, San Diego, did the wonderful job of creating the illustrations.

Mojgan Mehran did the still photography.

Also, this is probably the place to mention author and publisher Dan Poynter, whose many publications showed me the way to publish this book without relying on a big publishing company. Dan's publications have helped numerous authors to put their ideas into print.

Please see the Appendix for contact information for some of the above professionals.

ABOUT THE BOOK

Whether or not you are a native English speaker:
The information here will help you to better communicate with others. It doesn't matter if you're a student, teacher, tourist, businessman, employee, or an employer; this book will help.

You will find:

- Easy-to-understand meanings and equivalents for:
  Idioms.
  Phrases.
  Expressions.
  And some commonly used sentences.

- Typical examples showing how the expressions are used.

- The likely origins of some of these expressions.

- Illustrations that serve two purposes:

  1. They add some humor to an otherwise serious reference book; and
  2. They illustrate how some expressions could be misinterpreted by someone who is hearing them for the first time.

- And, finally, some interesting expressions and proverbs from other languages and cultures, which show how people of the world have more things in common than we tend to realize.

This book is not about English grammar. It's about being able to communicate more effectively. *Best of all, it's good for all language levels.*

If English is NOT your native language:

Use this book to better understand what you hear, read, or even say.

If English IS your native language:

Use this book to say things more clearly so that others will understand you better.

It's important to know that some idioms and expressions may have different meanings under different circumstances. If what you see here does not satisfactorily explain what you've heard or read, please let us know.

Finally, we've tried to keep it clean. Obscene words are either excluded or only partially spelled.

Please let us know if we've missed anything.

* * * * * * * * * *

WARNING-DISCLAIMER

This book contains definitions and equivalents of commonly used phrases, idioms, and expressions of the English language and should be used as a general guide to facilitate communication. In order to make sure that the correct message is conveyed, if you're dealing with sensitive issues, you should consult other sources to receive second or third opinions. The author and publisher of this book do not assume any liability or responsibility to any person or entity for any loss or damage caused, directly or indirectly, as a result of using the information presented in this book.

CLUES TO USE!

Please read this entire section at least once!

When you refer to *The List* of idioms, phrases, and expressions, please remember the following:

- **Also:** means:
  The following idiom or expression has the same meaning, or is very similar, but is not necessarily included in this book.

- **Also see:** means:
  The following idiom or expression has the same meaning, or is very similar. It, too, is listed in this book.

- **Compare to:** means:
  The following idiom or expression has a somewhat different meaning. It, too, is listed in this book.

- The *hidden meanings* of idioms, phrases, and expressions are provided in this book, but the more obvious (literal) meanings are not.

  Example: In defining *Coming from behind,* we don't mention *Approaching from behind.*

  Example: In defining *Hot potato,* we don't say *A potato that is hot.*

- The entries in *The List* have been tabulated alphabetically in their most common form.

  Example: If you're looking for the meaning of: *It was raining cats and dogs,* you should look in *The List* for: *Raining cats and dogs.* (Of course, you may also look in *The Index* for one of the key words: *Rain, Raining, Cat,* or *Dog.*)

- Single words that are defined in dictionaries are not included here, unless they have unique applications.

Dedicated to the memory of

Yoshihiro Hattori

Yoshihiro Hattori was a Japanese foreign exchange student in the United States who lost his life due to an apparent misunderstanding over language.*

It seems that he did not know what a frightened and armed homeowner meant when he said "Freeze!"

A message from the Hattori family:

We hate the word "freeze," which was used when our son was shot to death. We desire the time when America will be safer, and the word "freeze" will disappear.

Masaichi and Mieko Hattori,
Yoshihiro's parents

*For more information about this tragedy, please visit:

http://articles.orlandosentinel.com/1992-10-20/news/9210200470_1_baton-rouge-peairs-haymaker

http://www11.plala.or.jp/yoshic/index.html

http://www11.plala.or.jp/yoshic/y-frame-eng.html

The List

A bird in the hand is worth two in the bush.	Don't risk it. Don't risk losing what you have. Don't be greedy. Be content with what you have. You know what you've got, but you don't know what you'll get.
A camel is a horse designed by a committee.	Decision making by a committee is not an efficient process.
A comeback	A smart aleck kind of response. A good verbal rebuttal to an insult. A smart (and somewhat arrogant) kind of response. Also: Comeback line.
A day late, and a dollar short!	Too little, too late! It's not enough. Besides, it's too late!
A dollar a pop	A dollar each. Similarly, $65 a pop, five cents a pop, etc
A drop in the bucket	Insignificant. A very small amount. Q. *Did you get a raise?* A. *Yeah, but it's a drop in the bucket. I want more!*

A five-hundred-member-strong club	A club with 500 members. (This is an example. Any organization and any number could be used.)
A handful	Difficult to handle. Not very easy to control or take care of.
	Q. *Would you please take care of my dog while I'm gone?* A. *No thanks! She's a handful.*
A hole in the head	Something that's definitely not needed.
	When someone says: *I need it like I need a hole in the head,* they mean to say (with a lot of emphasis), *I don't need it!*
	Q. *Do you want to buy my limousine? It's very cheap.* A. *Right now, I need a limousine like I need a hole in the head!*
A leg to stand on	A support. Supporting material. Available influence or power.
	When someone says: *He doesn't have a leg to stand on,* they mean something like:
	He doesn't have enough data to support his theory. *He doesn't have an alibi to help him in his defense.*
A little time in the desert	Time spent away from others.
	When someone says: *She needs a little time in the desert,* they mean something like:
	We've seen too much of her. She should go away (disappear) for a while!
A place of one's choosing	One decides where. A place that one chooses.
	Similarly, a time of one's choosing, an activity of one's choosing, etc.

A pretty penny   A lot of money.
Very expensive.

Buying a house in Tokyo costs a pretty penny.

Also:
A bundle.
A fortune.
A lot of dough.
An arm and a leg.

A question of   About something.
something

A question of economics means:

About economics;
A matter of economics;
It has to do with economics; etc.

Similar:
A question of taste, ethics, freedom, etc.

A reach   A difficult thing.

When someone says: *This is a reach for me,*
they mean something like: *It's difficult for me to
do something like this. I don't know if I can.*

Also:
A stretch.

Gulls on land, storm at the sea. *(Portuguese.)*
Sea bird by solid ground, storm coming ahead. *(Venezuelan.)*
> *When things are not in their proper
> place, there may be trouble somewhere.*

A shot in the arm   A boost.
A helpful deed.
Something that gives new energy to a person
who is weary emotionally, mentally, physically,
financially, etc.

Q. *Did you get a year-end bonus?*
A. *Yes, and what a shot in the arm it was! I
was just about to file for bankruptcy, but
now I don't have to.*

A shot in the dark   This is about doing something with the hope that it will work. There is no way to predict whether or not it will be successful.

We're not having any success, so let's talk to your dad. Maybe he can help us, maybe not. Anyway, it's a shot in the dark.

A thing of the past   Obsolete. Dead and gone.
Something that has no use any longer.

Thanks to Craig Newmark and his Craigslist, paying a lot of money for a small ad in a local or global publication is now a thing of the past.

Flatter the sea, but stand on earth when you do so. *(Greek.)*

A ways off   In the distance.
A long way off   In the distant future.

When someone says: *A new entertainment system is a long way off,* they mean something like: *We won't see a new entertainment system for a long time.*

Q. *Is your brother ready to start all over again?*
A. *Considering the fact that he's lost everything, he knows that having a normal life again is a long way off.*

Above board   With honesty.
Without tricks.

Q. *Do we really need to do exactly as the contract says?*
A. *Yes, I want everything to be above board!*

Above the fray   Being above commotion, confusion, etc.
Having nothing to do with the usual things, especially bad things, corruption, etc.

Used with verbs such as stay, remain, rise, etc.

A. *The senator's campaign manager is arguing with the reporters all of the time!*
B. *Yes. She lets the manager do the fighting, but she stays above the fray herself!*

Ace in the hole
Origin: Gambling

Big secret help.
A winning factor kept hidden.

She is our ace in the hole. With her at our side, I'm sure we're going to win this thing. But keep it to yourself for now.

The prosecutor had an ace in the hole: an eyewitness!

Background:
This may have its origin in the game of poker where you have an ace with the face down, until it's time to show it.

According to someone

As someone says.
Per someone's statement.

When someone says: *According to my brother, you're not innocent,* they mean something like: *He says you're not innocent.*

Achilles heel

A seemingly small, but actually crucial, weakness.
A very significant weakness in an otherwise very strong person or idea, etc., that can result in complete failure

Her biggest Achilles heel is the number of people who don't think she is qualified to be their representative.

Background:
According to Greek mythology, Achilles was invulnerable all over his body except in the area of his heel. He died from an arrow that had been shot into his heel.

Across the board

All levels, all categories, all employees, etc.

Everybody's happy as they raised salaries across the board.

Acting in a certain capacity

Having certain responsibilities.
Working in a certain capacity.

He's acting in a professional capacity. He can't just take off and go on a ski trip with you!

Acting somebody
Acting something

Temporary *somebody* or *something* as in:

Acting vice president;
Acting director of public relations; etc.

I'm the acting chairman, not the chairman. I'm acting as the chairman. I'll be temporarily performing the duties of the chairman until we have a permanent one!

Tell me who your friends are, and I will tell you who you are!
(Assyrian, Persian, Spanish, Turkish, etc.)

Adding insult to injury

Making things even worse.

I got a ticket for parking in the wrong place. Then, to add insult to injury, they towed my car while I was talking to the policeman!

Also: Rubbing salt in the wound.

Compare to: Kick in the teeth.

Addressing something

Not ignoring it.
Talking about it.
Taking care of it.
Paying attention to it.

Admission on one's part

A person admitting to something.

This is an admission on my part, means:

I'm admitting it;
I'm saying I did it; etc.

After the fact

After something has happened.

You've already signed the contract. You can't change it after the fact!

Your honor, the evidence was planted at the scene after the fact!

Age before beauty

Older person first, prettier person next.

This is used (mostly by older men) when younger or prettier women let older men do something first, or hold the door for them, etc. It is used as a humorous compliment.

Ahead of the curve	Ahead of the others.
Ain't	Isn't. Is not. Aren't. Am not. Are not.
Ain't that the truth!	I really agree. That is the truth. That is exactly the truth.
Airhead **Air head**	Stupid. Ditzy, empty-headed, no brain. *She's an airhead. She can't even spell her own name!*

A lie has no legs. *(English.)*
In lies, one has short legs. *(Croatian.)*
Lies have short legs. *(Czech, German.)*
Lies have short feet (or memory). *(Armenian.)*
> *A lie cannot get too far; the truth will come out.*

Airing one's dirty laundry	Exposing one's private matters. Also: Airing one's dirty laundry in public.
AKA **a/k/a**	This is an abbreviation for: **A**lso **K**nown **A**s. *Let me introduce you to Bill, a/k/a the Love Machine!*
Albatross around one's neck	A punishment. (In the old days.) A burden that is difficult to get rid of. A burden to remind the guilty person of his crime. Also see: White elephant.
Alive and kicking	Alive. Healthy. Alive and healthy.

All bets are off.	Rules don't apply any more. All agreements are canceled. A. *And one more thing, I also want a 20 percent raise every year.* B. *In that case all bets are off! We've never talked about an automatic raise before.* Compare to: No holds barred.

The carpenter's door is loose. *(Arabic.)*
The cobbler's children go barefoot. *(English.)*
    About those who take care of other people's problems but neglect their own family.

All but	Almost, nearly all, as in: *The chairman's visit was all but certain. I'm surprised he canceled it!* Everyone (or everything) except, as in: *All but the morons stayed home during the heavy snow.*
All hands on deck	Everyone needs to help. Everybody be ready (to get started). *We have so much to do. Come on everyone! All hands on deck!* **Background:** This was originally a seaman's term. When turbulent seas caused a boat or ship to be in danger, the captain would call *All hands on deck!* It is now a general term.
All out **All-out**	Full force. With all available resources. *All-out war, all-out effort, etc.*
All talk and no action	This is said about people who: Give lip service. Make promises but never keep them. Talk a lot, but don't really do anything.

Continued on the next page.

All talk and no action

Continued from the previous page.

Q. *What do you think of the new manager?*
Sounds like he'll do a lot for us!
A. *Don't be so sure. I know him from before,*
and I know he's all talk and no action!

All the same

Still.
However.
In spite of.
Regardless.
Nevertheless.

It was a long trip, but a nice one all the same.
She may have acted stupidly as they say, but
she's a gifted performer all the same.

Making no difference, as in:

Democrat, Republican, they're all the same.
If it's all the same to you, I'd rather stay home.

From a thorn a rose emerges and from a rose a thorn. *(Greek.)*
Children don't necessarily take after their parents.

All too easy

Too easy.
Very easy.

All walks of life

When you say *People from all walks of life were*
in attendance, it means:

All kinds of people were there.
All professions and classes were represented.

All's well that ends well.

If it ends well, it's okay.
The important thing is that it ends well, no
matter what else happens.

Along party lines
Political

In line (in agreement) with one's own party,
even if it means going against the will of the
people who elected them.

When you say: *The senators are voting along*
party lines, you mean:

They are voting for their own party's agenda;
Democrats for Democrats, and Republicans for
Republicans.

Along the lines of	Something like that.
	When someone says: *Sohaila said something along the lines of quitting school,* they mean:
	She said she doesn't want to go to school anymore, or something like that.
	Also: Something to that effect.
America's Finest City	This is a nickname for the city of San Diego, although not many people in other cities agree with it!

A pear will fall to its root. *(Turkish.)*
A splinter doesn't jump far from a log. *(Serbian.)*
The pear falls exactly underneath the pear tree. *(Albanian.)*
The apple doesn't fall far from the tree. *(English, Greek, Slovak.)*
                                      Children take after their parents.

Amounting to something	Becoming successful, having a meaningful life:
	Q. *Dad, do you think I'll ever amount to anything?*
	A. *Of course, son. You're smart, you work hard, and you have a good teacher, me!*
	Being the same as, or similar to, something:
	A. *I give up. I'm not going to work on this project anymore.*
	B. *If you ask me, don't stop. In my book, quitting amounts to failure!*
	A. *They say they want to train us, but they are really threatening us.*
	B. *That's right. This "training" session is really amounting to intimidation!*
And counting	Still going on. There will be more.
	Layoffs total 45,000 and counting.
And something to match	If someone says: *She has beautiful eyes and a smile to match,* they mean something like:
	Her smile is equally as beautiful as her eyes; Her smile matches her beautiful eyes; etc.

And then some	And even more. Even more than that. Q. *This lady was nice to offer us food. Did you pay her for the food?* A. *I've been very generous to her. I've paid for the food, and then some!*
Animal magnetism	Sex appeal. Attractiveness in a rough way.
Anyone's guess **Anybody's guess**	No one knows. No one knows for sure. When someone says: *The answer is anybody's guess,* they mean: *No one knows the answer.* When someone says: *What she'll do is anyone's guess,* they mean: *We don't know what she'll do.* Also: Your guess is as good as mine!

A woman and the sea are the same in anger. *(Greek.)*

Anyway you cut it **Anyway you slice it**	Anyway you do it. Anyway you look at it. For a little humor: *Anyway you look at it you lose. Ask Mrs. Robinson!*
Appealing to people	Attractive to people. Something that people like. Related: *If something appeals to you, you like it.*
Are you cool?	Are you okay? Is everything okay? Have you chilled out? (After an argument.)
Are you with me?	Do you understand? Another meaning: Do you agree with me? Related: You're either with us, or against us!

Around-the-clock	Continuously.
Round-the-clock	Twenty four hours a day.
	We've been working around-the-clock to meet our deadline, I mean ALL of the time!
	Also:
	24/7.
	Twenty-four hours a day, seven days a week.

If wishes were horses, beggars would ride. *(English.)*
If they had planted "if," a tree would have grown in its place. *(Persian.)*
If the word *if* wasn't there, my father would be a millionaire. *(German.)*
If children's prayers were answered, there wouldn't be a single teacher alive. *(Persian.)*

Various plays with the word *"if."*

As God is my witness!	I swear to God!
	God is my witness.
	God knows I'm telling the truth.
	As God is my witness, I'll do my best to defend you!

As good as dead	Dying.
	Not active.
	Will be dead.
	Heading in the direction of being dead.

If you say: *He's as good as dead,* it could mean any of the following:

He's dying;
He's not active;
He'll die very soon;
He will be killed very soon;
If I see him again, he'll be in trouble, etc.

Note: Also applies to plans, projects, etc.

As luck would have it	As it turned out.
	The way it happened.
	As luck would have it, I had left my wallet at home. So I couldn't buy the jacket!

- Have you seen Joey? I'm late for my meeting, and I need my report.

- He must be around. I've told him to burn a few copies of the report for you.

For a definition, see:

- **Burning a copy**

As much as the next person (guy)	The usual amount. The same amount. The normal amount. *Don't get me wrong. I love watching political debates as much as the next guy. I just don't like this one.*
As of some time	Depending on how it is used, *As of some time* means "until," or "starting." *As of yesterday, we had not received a notice! (Until yesterday.)* *As of yesterday, we're not friends anymore! (Starting yesterday.)*
As sure as Bob's your uncle	Sure. You can be one hundred percent sure. Q. *Are you sure this is going to work?* A. *I've done it before, and, as sure as Bob's your uncle, it'll work for you, too.* Also: There you have it! Compare to: Bob's your uncle.
As we speak **Even as we speak**	Right now. At this very moment.

When you pick up the stick, the robber dog knows. *(Armenian.)*
When you pick up the stick, the stealing cat gets alert. *(Persian.)*
When they shouted, "Pumpkin thief," he touched his shoulder to check. *(Indian.)*
  Guilty people are always on guard, looking over their shoulder.

As well **As well as**	Too. And. Also. In addition to. *I'll buy some food as well as some gas.* *I'll buy some food, and some gas as well.*
ASAP	This is an abbreviation for: As Soon As Possible. *We need some help ASAP!*

Asleep at the wheel **Asleep at the switch**	Missing the problem signals. Not doing one's job (properly). Not being aware of what's going on.

Q. *We're about to go bankrupt. Why isn't the management doing anything?*
A. *They must have fallen asleep at the wheel!*

Avoid those who constantly praise you. *(Swahili.)*
He who knows to praise sure knows to slander. *(Albanian.)*
Do not believe that a person who lies *for* you will not also lie *to* you. *(Arabic.)*
One who tells you about someone else's business will tell someone else about yours. *(Swahili.)*

Asset, liability   Asset is a positive point, an advantage, a good thing to have, as in:

Welcome to our company. Having you on our team is a great asset!

Liability is a negative point, a disadvantage, a bad thing to have, as in:

When someone says: *He'll be a liability for us,* they mean:

His presence will hurt us more than it will help. If we keep him, it won't be good for our image.

Assuming you are right   If you're right.
Let's say you're right.
Supposing you're right.

Similarly:
Assuming it will rain; assuming we still have time; etc.

At a moment's notice   Quickly.
Very fast.
At any time.

Don't worry! Just call me and I'll be there at a moment's notice.

Firemen need to be ready to respond to an alarm at a moment's notice.

At arm's length
Origin: Legal

At a distance.

When someone says: *He's been allowed to manage the project at arm's length,* they mean: *His control over the project is limited.*

In law or real estate:
At arm's length refers to a transaction between parties who are not related to each other.

Also used in terms of relationships:
She's been hurt so many times, she is keeping him at arm's length emotionally.

At best, at worst

The best and the worst possibilities expected in a certain situation.

If someone says: *At best they won't say hello, and at worst they'll call the police,* it means something like: *The best thing they might do to me is not say hello, and the worst thing is they'll call the police to kick me off the field!*

The day you decide to leave your house naked is the day you run into your in-laws. *(Swahili.)*

At each other's throats

Verbally fighting.
Arguing very angrily.

A. *I thought they were going to kill each other.*
B. *I know, they were really going at each other's throats!*

Similar:
Duking it out.
Going at each other. Letting each other have it.

At large

As a whole, as in:
The city at large.

Not specific to a certain area, as in:
The representative at large.

Free, not in captivity, as in:
The killer is no longer at large. He has been arrested.

At odds with	In disagreement with.
At sea	Confused.
All at sea	A. *I don't really think he knows what he's doing.* B. *No, he doesn't. Let's face it, he's at sea again!* Similar: At a loss. Also see: Out to lunch.

Out of sight, out of mind. *(English.)*
Out of the eye, out of the heart. *(Dutch.)*
Absence makes the heart forget. *(Parts of Africa.)*
He who leaves the eye will leave the heart. *(Persian.)*
Eyes that don't see each other, forget about each other. *(Greek.)*
If people don't see you, they'll forget you.

At someone's expense	When someone says: *They're vacationing at DeWitt's expense,* they mean: *DeWitt is paying for it.* When someone says: *They're laughing at Hamid's expense, or at the expense of his feelings,* they mean: *They're making fun of Hamid.* When someone says: *We're publishing books faster at quality's expense, or at the expense of quality,* they mean something like: *We're publishing more books, but with lower quality.*
At someone's mercy **At the mercy of someone**	Under someone's control. When someone says: *We're at April's mercy,* they mean something like: *It's April's decision;* *She'll call if she wants to;* *We'll have to do what she says;* *What we do, or what will be done to us, is all up to her; etc.*

At the end of the day	In the end. When it's all over. All things considered. Considering everything. *At the end of the day YOU have to decide what you want to do with your life, not me!* Also: When it's all said and done.
At the risk of	Taking the risk of. Running the risk of. If you say: *At the risk of offending you, here's what I think,* you probably mean: *I hope you don't mind, but I think you're wrong;* *I may be offending you, but I think you're a moron;* *I hope I'm not upsetting you, but I think you're crazy; etc.*
At the top of one's voice **At the top of one's lungs**	Very loud. The loudest voice with which one can talk or sing. Q. *How's your neighbor doing? Are you glad you're living next door to an opera singer?* A. *No, I'm going crazy. She's always singing at the top of her lungs!*

A doctor's mistake is God's writing. *(Greek.)*

AWOL *Military*	This is an abbreviation for: **A**bsent **W**ith**O**ut **L**eave. When someone says: *He's AWOL,* it could mean any of the following: *No one knows where he is.* *He has left without permission.* *He's absent without approval to leave.* Note: This is a military term, but it is being used outside the military as well.

Back in the day   A long time ago.
Years, maybe decades or generations, ago.

Q. *Isn't it funny that your mom still sends handwritten letters to her friends?*
A. *Yeah. Actually, back in the day, that was the only way to communicate!*

Back of the barn   This has a sexual connotation.

When you say: *They've been to the back of the barn,* you mean something like:

They're more than friends;
They know each other very well;
They have (had) a sexual relationship; etc.

Back on one's feet   Back to one's normal condition with respect to health, finances, etc.

I've been down with the flu, but I hope to get back on my feet soon.

He lost everything due to the economy, but he hopes to find a job and get back on his feet again.

You look prettier when you're quiet. *(Spanish.)*
Don't speak if you can't improve on the silence. *(Spanish.)*
If talk is made of silver, then silence is made of gold. *(Arabic.)*

Back story
Back-story   Not the main story.
The story in the background.

I'd like to know more about Batman's back story. I already know what he does. I want to know what made him who he is.

Back to square one   Starting over again.
Re-doing everything from the beginning.

A. *Hideko, the test results don't look good!*
B. *Well, I guess it's back to square one, right?*

Also:
Starting from scratch.

Backhanded compliment	An insult. An insult that sounds like a compliment at first.
	Your wife is so charming that I don't want to believe what people say about her!
Backhanding *Origin: Sports*	Hitting with the back of the hand. Returning a shot with the back of the hand.
	After he made a joke at her expense, she playfully backhanded him on the arm.
Backing down	Yielding after being aggressive at first. Changing one's position or decision under pressure.
Backseat driver	Someone who complains about how badly other people do things, but won't do anything about it himself, or herself, similar to a person in a car who's not driving but corrects the driver and/or tells the driver what to do.
Backstabber **Back stabber** **Back-stabber**	A person who: Attacks you unfairly behind your back. Hurts you when you're not expecting it. Befriends you but betrays you to others behind your back. Assures you of his or her support, but does not support you when you need it.
Bad blood	Friction. Hostility. Bad history.
	Q. *Why can't those two get married?* A. *There's bad blood between their families. They won't let them.*
Bad news	When you say: *Stay away from her, she's bad news*, you might mean one of the following:
	She does drugs; She's a bad influence; She writes bad checks; She regularly misses school; She might get you in trouble; etc.

Bad seed	Really bad.
Bad to the bone	Completely bad, pure evil.
	Not just bad on the surface but all the way through to the bone.
Bailing (out)	Quitting.
	After only one week on the job, he bailed (out).

Lentils are still in the market, and the Brahmin is beating his wife for not cooking them properly. *(Indian.)*

Bailing (out) on someone	Leaving them.
	Abandoning them.
	My wife has bailed out on me!
Bailing someone out	Helping, as in:
Origin: Legal	*I'm tired of bailing you out of your problems. Next time, call someone else!*
	Related:
	Helping someone out of jail by paying the bail money.
Bait and switch	Telling a lie at first, and changing one's word later, in order to cheat someone.
	They're using a bait-and-switch strategy. They get you interested in their plan with a low interest rate, but tell you about the hidden fees later, at which time they encourage you to accept their plan with a higher interest rate!
Balancing act	Multi-tasking.
	Doing, or trying to do, more than one thing at a time.
	A. The government needs to do a lot about health care, jobs, the war, recession, etc.
	B. They will need to do a real balancing act if they don't want to fail.
Ball is in your court.	It's up to you.
Origin: Sports	It's your turn.
	It's your decision.

Bang for one's buck	Value for one's money.
	When someone says: *You get the most bang for your buck here,* they mean something like:
	Our prices are the lowest; *Here you get more for what you pay;* *Your dollar goes a long way in this store; etc.*
Bar none	No exceptions.
	When someone says: *This restaurant has the best steak in town, bar none,* they mean something like: *It has the best steak in town without any exceptions.*
Bare knuckle fight **Bare knuckle race** *Sports*	A fight with no rules. A fight where anything is allowed.
	Also see: All bets are off. No holds barred.
Bargaining table	Negotiation. A place for negotiations.
	When someone says: *They're still at the bargaining table,* they mean something like:
	There's still hope; *They're still talking;* *They haven't stopped negotiating;* *They haven't come to a decision yet; etc.*

The sun won't stay behind the cloud. *(Armenian.)*
The sun shines even when it is cloudy. *(Albanian.)*

There's always hope.

Bases in baseball *Sports*	First, second, and third base refer to various stages in the game of baseball. Home run, or home base, is the ultimate stage.
	All of these terms also refer to various levels of success in any activity, where *first base* refers to *minor success,* and *home run* refers to *achieving a goal in a big way.*

Continued on the next page.

Bases in baseball   *Continued from the previous page.*

All of these terms also refer to various stages in a romantic or sexual relationship, where *first base* refers to *kissing,* and *home run* refers to *full sexual intercourse.*

When someone says: *He didn't get anywhere, not even to first base,* they mean something like: *He wasn't very successful in his business,* or, *He didn't even get to kiss her!*

Taking rye to Kerman. *(Persian.)*
Carrying water to the sea. *(Dutch.)*
Carrying owls to Athens. *(German.)*
Carrying coal to Newcastle. *(English.)*
Taking water to the Danube. *(Hungarian.)*
Crossing the stream to get water. *(Danish.)*
About doing something that is a waste of time.

Be as it may
Be that as it may

However.
Although that may be true.

A. *I think John means well.*
B. *Be that as it may, he's an idiot!*

Be put under
Medical

Be sedated or drugged into unconsciousness.

Q. *Why didn't you tell them they were operating on the wrong knee?*
A. *I was put under! I didn't know what was going on.*

Bean counter

An accountant.
A financial officer.

Beating a dead horse

Repeatedly talking about something.
Talking about something that has already been decided.
Wasting one's time talking about something that won't change.

Q. *Can we talk about my trip now?*
A. *Come on, stop beating a dead horse! We have already decided that you're not going.*

Beating a rap
Origin: Legal

Getting out of a bad situation without being punished.

Q. *Didn't they arrest him for stealing from his mother?*
A. *Yeah, but somehow he beat the rap and avoided going to jail.*

Also see:
Getting away with something.

Beating around the bush

Speaking indirectly.
Not saying what's on one's mind.

Of course I've asked her about her plans, but she always beats around the bush. She never gives me a straight answer.

Also:
Dance around the issue.
Dance around something.

The pot calling the kettle black. *(English.)*
The donkey called the rooster bigheaded. *(Greek.)*
The ragged says to the naked: Why don't you get dressed? *(Portuguese.)*

Beating someone to it

Doing something before someone else gets a chance to do it.

Q. *Did you pick up the free tickets?*
A. *I was going to, but my so called friend beat me to it.*

Also:
Beating someone to the punch.

Beating the heck out of someone

An exaggerated, but polite, way of saying:

Beating someone up seriously.
Really beating someone at a game.

The following mean the same thing but are not polite:

Beating the hell (or the ho-ho's, or the bejesus, or the sh-t, or the crap) out of someone.

Beating the odds
Origin: Sports, Gambling

Winning despite low probabilities.
Succeeding despite low expectations.

It's difficult but I know that she can do it. She'll beat the odds and surprise everyone.

Related:
The odds are against it, means: *It's very risky.*
The odds are in its favor, means: *It isn't very risky.*

He even has bird's milk. *(Greek.)*
For some, cows die; for others, bulls give birth. *(Portuguese.)*
A wealthy, or lucky, person can have anything.

Beauty is in the eye of the beholder.

People have different opinions.
Beauty means different things to different people.

A. *I don't know what he sees in her. She's as ugly as a bulldog.*
B. *He thinks she's the most beautiful creature alive. Truly, beauty is in the eye of the beholder!*

Also see: Different strokes for different folks.

Been around the block

Experienced. (Could be positive or negative.)

I think you should listen to your older brother. He's been around the block. (Positive.)

I don't want my son hanging around with that girl sitting over there. She's obviously been around the block. (Negative. It refers to sexual promiscuity.)

Been there, done that!

I've tried it already.
It has been done before.

Before one could say ...

Quickly.
Very fast.

He is the fastest locksmith I've ever seen. He unlocked the door before I could say: This is the door!

Begs the question Makes you wonder.
Raises the question.

> Q. *The teacher's decision yesterday begs the question: Did she consider all of the facts?*
> A. *I've asked myself the same question. I don't think she considered everything!*

Also: Beg the question.
Begging the question.

Behind closed doors In private.
Private matters.

Toshiro wanted all family matters to stay behind closed doors. His wife didn't; she decided otherwise!

Behind the eight ball

Sports

In a tough spot.
In a difficult situation.

Background:
From the game of pool, where, if you're behind the eight ball, you will be in trouble.

Being a burning candle for someone Showing the way.
Benefiting people.
Helping someone.
Saying a prayer for someone.

If I can't be a burning candle for those who count on me, then what's the use?

Being above doing something If someone says: *Susan feels she is above being a secretary,* they mean something like:

Susan thinks being a secretary is beneath her, or is not good enough for her, etc.

Compare to:
Not being above doing something.

Being carded

Getting carded

Being checked for identification.

If someone says: *She was carded at the door,* they mean: *Someone checked her identification card when she arrived.*

Being critical of ... Criticizing someone or something.
Not approving someone or something.

The opposition is being critical of the government's latest economic plans.

Walls have ears; doors have eyes. *(Thai.)*
Walls have mice; mice have ears. *(Persian.)*
Birds listen to day-words, and rats listen to night-words. *(Korean.)*
Be careful. Someone might be listening!

Being decent. Being properly dressed.
Having one's clothes on.

Being even with someone Not owing them anything.

A. *Thanks for the ride. I'll make it up to you.*
B. *No, we're even. You bought me lunch the other day.*
A. *Are you sure?*
B. *Yes, I don't owe you anything, and you don't owe me anything!*

Compare to: Don't get mad, get even!
Getting even with someone.

Being framed
Legal

If someone says: *Boris was framed,* they mean something like:

He didn't do what they say he did.
Someone arranged things to make him look guilty.
Someone gave false testimony (lied) to make him look guilty.
Someone planted (put) evidence somewhere to make him look guilty.

Similar:
Being set up.

Being let go Getting fired.
Being dismissed from a job.

Q. *What happened to Jenny?*
A. *They found her sleeping on the job. She was let go this morning.*

Being up to something

Planning to do something sneaky, as in:

I don't usually see you at the office on weekends, but you're here today! What are you up to?

Ricky is up to something. I can tell by the way he stops talking whenever I come around. He's hiding something. He's up to no good!

Being able or willing to do something, as in:

Q. Are you up to going to the movies?
A. No, not today. Let's do it tomorrow.

In the land of mad people, there are insane rituals. (*Nepalese.*)

Believe you me!
Believe me you!

Believe me!

Also: You better believe it!

Below the belt
Origin: Sports

Not fair.
Not by the rules.
Excessively mean.

Q. Did you hear what your opponent said about your background yesterday?
A. Yes. It was below the belt, not worthy of him, and definitely not appreciated.

Compare to:
Cheap shot.

Bending someone's ear

Talking to someone for a long time.

Also:
Talking someone's ear off.

Bending the rules
Breaking the rules
Origin:
Legal, Political

Doing things that are against the rules.
Changing the rules a little to suit your needs or the needs of someone you want to help.

If you want the work to be done fast, we need to bend some rules!

We don't usually take orders without a small deposit. I'm going to bend the rules in your case, however, because you've been our client for a long time.

- I feel for her. She's been burning the candle at both ends for a while now.

- She must be good at it. I tried it once, and I got wax all over the carpet!

For a definition, see:

- **Feeling for someone**
- **Burning the candle at both ends**

Beside oneself

Excited, emotional, upset, etc.
Stunned to the point of coming out of your body and being beside your own self.

She was so excited to see her baby again, she didn't know what to do. She was beside herself with joy!

Not to be mistaken with *besides* which means *in addition to.*

Q. Why aren't you coming with us?
A. I'm too tired. Besides, it's too late.

Beside the point

Not the issue.
Something else.
Not what we're talking about.

Q. Did you also want to talk about my trip?
A. Yes, but that's beside the point. That is not really why I called you.

Better half

One's spouse, girlfriend, boyfriend, etc.

Q. Where is your better half?
A. Oh she couldn't come, but she sent her regards.

Also: Significant other.

Better off

Doing better.

Q. Do you feel better now that she's gone?
A. Yes, I'm much better off without her.

Better part of

Most of.

I spend the better part of the year in California; We were sleeping for the better part of the lecture; etc.

Betting a cup of coffee

This is about being (or not being) sure about something.
When someone says: *I wouldn't bet a cup of coffee on that rumor,* they obviously don't trust that rumor.

Note: Anything of little value could be used in place of coffee.

Betting one's bottom dollar	Being very sure about something.
	You can bet your bottom dollar I'll be at that race next week. Count on it!
Between a rock and a hard place	Being in a position where one doesn't have any good choices available to choose from.
Between the devil and the deep blue sea	When someone says: *I'm between a rock and a hard place*, they mean something like:
	I can't do anything; I don't know what else to do; etc.

He who is bitten by a snake fears a lizard. *(Parts of Africa.)*
Whoever gets burnt by hot milk blows on the cool yogurt. *(Greek, Turkish.)*
A person once bitten by a snake will be scared by an old rope. *(Parts of Africa.)*
One who's been bitten by a snake is afraid of a black-and-white rope. *(Persian.)*
He who has scalded himself on milk weeps when he sees a cow. *(Spanish.)*

Between the two of us	The two of us together.
	Between the two of us, we make a lot of money!
Beyond a shadow of a doubt Legal	Without any doubt.
	Q. *Did they really find her innocent?* A. *Yes and, what's more, they found her innocent beyond a shadow of a doubt.*
BFF	This is an abbreviation for:
	Best Friends Forever.
	It is used by the younger, Internet and texting generation.
Big Apple	This is a nickname for New York City.
Big brother	The government.
	Be careful, big brother is watching us! They are listening to our phone conversations, too!

Big mouth **Blabber mouth**	A person who can't keep a secret, or talks more than he should, or exaggerates a lot, etc.
Big shoes to fill	Hard to replace. *I've known your former director, and I know these are big shoes to fill but, as your new director, I'll try to do my best.*
Big shot **Big wheel**	An important person. *Q. How's your uncle doing?* *A. He's doing alright. He's a big shot now, which is how I got this job!*

Don't open a wall of your house. *(Thai.)*
Don't air your dirty laundry in public. *(English.)*
Washing one's dirty laundry must be done as a family. *(French.)*
Home affairs are not talked about on the public square. *(Parts of Africa.)*

Don't talk about private matters in public.

Big timing	Being too busy for others. Ignoring or avoiding others, especially if you're in a more important position than you were before. *He's been big timing me since he's become the president!*
Bill of goods *Origin: Legal*	A plan or list of promises, especially one that's not honest. *A. The new mayor was promising a lot of things before, but nothing is happening now!* *B. Can't you see? He sold us a bill of goods just to get himself elected.*
Bitch slapping	Slapping with the open hand. Slapping not meant to hurt, but meant to humiliate and to show authority and to put the slapped person in his or her place. Compare to: Jack slapping.

Biting off more than one can chew Trying to do more than one is able to do.

This is probably too big of a mortgage for me to handle. I may be biting off more than I can chew, but I'm going to do it. Besides, I'll be getting a raise soon!

Also see: Over one's head.

Biting the dust Dying.
Failing, breaking apart.
Falling down when wounded or dead.

A. *We are really getting old.*
B. *Oh, I know. Every now and then another one of our friends bites the dust!*

Q. *Do you know what time it is?*
A. *Sorry! My watch battery just bit the dust.*

Bless you!
God bless you! An expression used when someone sneezes.
An expression of gratitude used to show well-wishing.

Similar:
Bless your soul!
May God bless you!
God bless your soul!

Note:
In response to sneezing, the German word *Gesundheit* is also used.

Half-filled pots splash more. *(Indian.)*
Noisy is the can that contains nothing. *(Filipino.)*
Hollow barrels sound the loudest. *(Dutch, Slovak.)*
Empty vessels make the most noise. *(Danish, English.)*
    A loud person does not necessarily know more than others and is not necessarily more correct than others.

Blessed with something Fortunate or lucky to have a special skill, or gift, or position, or home, etc.

Q. *Do you think she has a great voice?*
A. *Oh, yes! She's blessed with one of the greatest voices ever.*

Blessing in disguise

A good thing that you don't recognize at first. Something that initially appears to be unfavorable but turns out to be beneficial.

My having the flu was a blessing in disguise. That's how the doctor found out about my heart problem!

A. *I'm sorry I couldn't come to meet you today. I think I have the flu.*
B. *Well, if you do, it's a blessing in disguise because there was a shooting at work.*

Also see:
Silver lining.

Blowing hot air

Exaggerating.
Talking about nothing.

A. *Your friend says he's becoming a company executive.*
B. *He's blowing hot air. Don't take him seriously.*

Also:
Full of hot air.
Pompous windbag.

Don't look for noon at two o'clock. (*French.*)
Don't complicate the issue.

Blowing in the wind

This has different meanings for different people.

Being present or clear.
Being in a state of motion.
Being in a place that nobody knows.

The answer's blowing in the wind. It's there for everyone to see.

Blowing one's own horn

Bragging about oneself.
Praising one's own accomplishments.

Tooting one's own horn

I'm not trying to blow my own horn, but admit it, I was really good!

Blowing out of proportion	Making something seem more serious (or important, or spectacular, etc.,) than it actually is.

> A. *I'm sure this was a minor accident but, the way your son explained it, I was really worried.*
> B. *I know, he has a habit of blowing things out of proportion.*

Blowing out of the water	Really surprising someone. Completely destroying someone or something.

A good day is apparent in the morning. *(Swahili.)*
A good year is apparent from the spring. *(Persian.)*

Blowing someone's mind	Being amazing.

It will blow your mind, means:

It's great;
You'll love it;
It's unbelievable;
You'll be so surprised; etc.

Also see: Knocking someone's socks off.

Blown to smithereens	Blown to very small pieces. Also: Blown to bits.
Blue in the face	Angry, excited, exhausted, etc. Exerting yourself to the point of depriving yourself of oxygen and turning blue.

She'll argue until she's blue in the face, means:

She'll argue for a very long time.

Bob's your uncle!	It's done. You're done. Your job is done.

> Q. *How do I know I'm doing it right?*
> A. *Just follow the instructions carefully, and Bob's your uncle!*

Compare to: As sure as Bob's your uncle.

Body language	The way people act physically.
	Q. How can you tell she's happy? I certainly can't!
	A. Well, I've known her for a long time. I know her body language.

A good word will bring out the rat from the hole. *(Maltese.)*
He pulls a snake out of the nest with his tongue. *(Persian.)*
With a soft tongue, you can pull a snake out of its nest. *(Armenian.)*

Boiling down to ...	Coming down to ...
	Basically meaning ...
	Removing all of the extra things and giving the main idea or point or the heart of the matter.
	When someone says: *It all boils down to them not liking us,* they mean something like:
	Considering everything, they don't like us; The conclusion is, they don't like us; etc.
Bone headed	Stupid.
	Simple.
	Also: Knucklehead.
Bone of contention	Reason for conflict.
	The subject of a disagreement.
	She had previously worked for another company, which was a bone of contention between her and her new boss, until he explained the history for the tension between them.
	Background:
	This apparently comes from the fact that when a bone is thrown to dogs it causes a fight among them.
Booya! Booyah! Boo-yah! Boo-yeah!	This is an expression showing extreme joy and excitement due to a success of some sort, and can mean any of the following:
	Yes! Yeah! All right! Hell, yes! Awesome!

Bottom line	In the end. The end result. The main point. When someone says: *The bottom line is that you have to pay,* they mean something like: *You have to pay, no matter what.* *All things considered, you have to pay.*

The illiterate person is like an uncarved piece of wood. *(Greek.)*
The more you strike the steel, the more beautiful it becomes.
(Albanian.)

Bottoming out **Bottom falling out**	Failing badly. A thing you've been working on completely getting destroyed. Also the uncertainty due to worries about such great failure. A. *I hope I'm wrong, but I have a feeling that the bottom is falling out of the economy.* B. *You bet. The bottom is falling out of everything!*
Bottoms up!	This phrase is used when people drink and it means: *Cheers!* *Let's drink to that!*
Brain drain	Mentally exhausting, as in: *Reading a physics book is a brain drain, especially for my brother!* Migration of top minds, as in: *Our top scientists and engineers are leaving us to work at larger companies for higher pay. A sad case of brain drain.*
Bread and butter	One's main source of food. One's basic source of income. Q. *You're not quitting your job, are you?* A. *Of course not. It's my bread and butter. I don't have a rich uncle, you know!*

Breaking bread	Eating. Sharing food. Eating together. Sharing your belongings with others. Spending quality time with them, close enough to eat with. Making others comfortable by sharing things with them.
Breaking in	Training someone, as in: *It'll take a few days to break in our new secretary.* The initial period of usage, as in: *I'm not supposed to drive my new car too fast during the recommended break-in period.* Entering a place without permission or authorization, as in: *There was a break-in at our company headquarters earlier today.* Also see: Breaking into a place.

No answer is also an answer. *(German.)*
He who is quiet agrees. *(Dutch, Spanish.)*
Silence is the sign of agreement. *(Persian.)*
    Taking someone's silence as a sign of agreement.

Breaking into a place *Legal*	Any illegal entrance by force. Going into a place forcefully and without a key, by breaking a door or window, etc. Also: Breaking and entering. Compare to: Breaking in.
Breaking the mold	Doing something in a new way, as in *I broke the mold when I showed up at work in my slippers. Later, of course, I was fired!* Eliminating duplication, as in: *They broke the mold when they made her. She is so unique!*

Breath of fresh air   A refreshing change.
A change that is welcome.

   A. *This new girl at the office is like a breath of fresh air. She has such a nice personality!*
   B. *Are you sure it's her personality, and not her miniskirt that has attracted you?*

Those who've lost dreaming are lost.
The more you know, the less you need.
Keep your eyes on the sun, and you will not see the shadows.
We are all visitors to this time, to this place. We are just passing through. Our purpose here is to observe, to learn, to grow, to love. And then we return home.
Aboriginal Australian

Bridging the gap   Finding a solution.
Making a compromise.
Making a connection where a big difference exists.

Bring it on!   I'm ready when you are!

Bringing down the house   Causing enthusiastic applause.
Being very good at what you do.

Bringing in a clean broom   Starting over with intention to do good.

Bringing to
Medical
Bringing someone into consciousness.
Waking someone up after they were passed out or drugged.

   Q. Were you out?
   A. Yes, I think I was out for several minutes before they brought me to.

Compare to: Coming to.

Bro   Brother.
Male friend.

Broken man   A real loser.
A man who really, really feels he's a failure.

Also a man who has suffered a huge loss or is in deep grief.

Brotha, sista
Brothah, sistah
One way of referring to an African American man or woman by another African American.

Bruised ego
Hurt feelings.
Someone's pride being hurt.

Brushing something off
Being dismissive.
Not taking it seriously.

My cousin doesn't accept criticism. He simply brushes it off.

It's no use crying over spilled milk. *(English.)*
Thinking first is an asset; regret later is useless. *(Indonesian.)*
Don't say the first thing that comes to your mind. *(Parts of Africa.)*
If you speak the word, it shall own you. If you don't, you shall own it. *(Arabic.)*

About the need for thinking
before doing or saying something.

Bucket list
A list of things someone wants to do before he or she dies.

Also see: Kick the bucket.

Bull's eye
Origin: Sports
The small circle in the center of a target.

When someone says: *He has a bull's eye on his back,* they mean something like: *He is an easy target.*

Also:
When you want to tell someone that you think he's right about something, you say: *Bull's eye,* which is another way of saying: *Yes, you're right on target on the issue.*

Bum's rush
A rush.

There was a bum's rush to get the job done yesterday.

Burden of proof
Legal
The task of proving something.

The burden of proof for my brother's innocence is on me. I'll do my best. He's my kid brother, you know.

Burning a copy	Making a copy. (Mostly applies to CDs and DVDs)
Burning bridges	Cutting off connections. Terminating relationships.

If you burn your bridges behind you, you cannot go back!

When someone says: *Stop burning bridges with your friends,* they mean something like:

Don't cut off your relationships with them because, if you need them again, they won't be there.

Burning rubber	Driving very fast. Taking off quickly. Accelerating so fast that you leave (burned) tire marks on the road.

Faster, faster! I want to see you burn rubber!

Also see:
Putting the pedal to the metal.

Better is a wise enemy than an insane friend! *(Greek.)*
A good enemy is better than a bad friend! *(Jewish/Yiddish.)*
A wise enemy is better than an unwise friend! *(Azerbaijani.)*

Burning the candle at both ends	Working too hard. Overextending oneself. Doing too many things at once.
Burning the midnight oil **Burning the late night oil**	Studying or working very late. Q. *Are you ready for the final exams?* A. *No, I guess I've got to start burning the midnight oil again!*
Bursting at the seams	Too fat. Falling apart. Someone who really wants to (or needs to) say something, but they can't.

Compare to: Coming apart at the seams.
Slang, but incorrect: *Busting* at the seams.

Burying one's head in the sand

Hiding one's head in the sand

Ignoring the surroundings.
Being embarrassed for doing a stupid thing.
Not wanting to be aware, or pretending not to be aware, of what's going on.

Q. *Mindy's daughter is on drugs. Why doesn't she do something about this?*
A. *She'd rather bury her head in the sand. She can't face the truth.*

How come you are going barefoot on the thorns? *(Greek.)*
Why are you getting into this difficulty unprepared?

Butterflies in stomach

A sign of being nervous.

It was time for me to give my first lecture, but I had butterflies in my stomach and just couldn't move.

Buttering the bread

Making things more interesting.

We're buttering the bread for our employees and giving them more benefits and vacation time.

Also:
Sweetening the lemonade.
Sweetening the deal (or the pot.)

Okay, I'll sweeten the deal by giving you a free sixth night if you stay at our hotel for five nights in a row. How about that?!

Also see: Up the ante.

Buttoning up

Keeping quiet.
Not saying a word.

I want you to button up about this meeting. No one is supposed to know about it, got it?

Buying in bulk

Buying as a wholesaler.
Buying in large amounts.

Q. *How much for the pencils?*
A. *Do you want a few, or are you buying in bulk? If you buy in bulk it'll be cheaper.*

Excuse me sir, do you have some midnight oil?

For a definition, see:

- **Burning the midnight oil**

Buying something	Believing or accepting something.

When someone says: *No one's buying your story,* they mean: *Nobody believes you.*

Also:
Buying it.
Buying into something.

By a hair **By a nose** **By a whisker** **By this much** **By that much**	By a very small amount.

He almost made it, but missed it by a hair. He came in third among two thousand contestants!

Remember:
Maxwell Smart missed it by that much!

By a long shot
Origin: Gambling, Sports

By a large margin.
By a large amount.

When you say: *Our team won the game by a long shot,* you mean something like: *When we won, our team was ahead by many points.*

When you say: *We're not out of trouble by a long shot,* you mean something like: *We're not out of trouble at all. We have a long way to go.*

Also:
It's a long shot, means: *It's unlikely.*

Q. *Do you think they can win?*
A. *No, it's a long shot.*

By all means

For sure.
Of course.

Q. *Will you cooperate with us?*
A. *Yes, by all means. You can be sure.*

By any means

By any means necessary

By any means possible

Any way possible, as in: (Positive.)
Q. *Are you sure we can get a ticket to the game?*
A. *Yes, I'm going to get it by any means possible.*

Not at all, as in: (Negative.)
That is not the whole story by any means!

By proxy *Legal*	Through a representative. *When the political prisoner married her husband, she did it by proxy because they wouldn't let him in the prison!*
By the book *Legal*	Correctly. According to the law, or according to the rules. *I want you to do everything by the book to make sure that we won't make a mistake again!*

A large-pot without cover does not hold water. *(Haitian.)*
People who talk too much can't keep a secret.

By the wayside	Wayside means the side of the road, but it is also used as follow: *Falling by the wayside,* means: *Giving up.* *Leaving something by the wayside,* means: *Leaving it behind.* *Going by the wayside,* means: *Being left alone, obsolete, etc.*
Call me!	Telephone me. Also: Give me a call (or a ring, or a buzz, or a jingle).
Calling for something	Asking for something, as in: *Q. What do these people want?* *A. Nothing unusual. They're calling for justice!* Requiring something, as in: *Q. What kind of an agreement do you have?* *A. Well, for one thing, it calls for the strike to end on Monday.* Being appropriate for something, as in: *A. I got my raise.* *B. Great, this calls for a celebration!*
Calling it a day	Stopping to work, usually for the day. *That's enough work for today. It's time for me to call it a day and go home, or to the movies, whichever is closer!*

Calling it like it is **Saying it like it is**	Telling the truth. Making an honest comment.

Q. *When you appraise a property, do you usually say it's worth more than it really is, or less?*
A. *I call it like it is, no more, no less.*

Also: Shooting from the hip.
Calling it like you see it.

Calling it quits	Stopping or ending something.

By now, we know that we're not going to succeed. We might as well call it quits, before we lose all of our savings.

Calling on	Making a request.

I'm calling on you to punish her.

I'm calling on all of you to participate in our fight against elderly abuse.

Calling out	Challenging.

I would like to have called him out on his claim, but I wasn't so sure myself.

Calling someone **on something**	Pointing out a mistake, an exaggeration, a deception, or a lie.

Q. *Why did you interrupt the principal in the middle of his report?*
A. *Well, he was obviously exaggerating. I had to call him on those numbers!*

One idiot throws a stone in the well, and it takes a hundred wise men to (try to) get it out. *(Armenian, Persian.)*

Calling the shots	Making the decisions. Telling people what to do.

Q. *Who's calling the shots around here?*
A. *I am.*
Q. *Well, then, can I borrow your step ladder for a few minutes?*
A. *I don't know. Let me ask my wife!*

Calling to mind	Reminding. Remembering. When someone says: *Julio's comments call to mind my younger days,* they mean something like: *They remind me of when I was young.* Also: Bringing back memories.
Calming the waters	Quieting things down.
Can do without.	Something that's not really needed. *A luxury car is a nice thing to have, but it's something that I can do without.*
Can it!	Get rid of it! Also: Shut up! Be quiet! Stop talking.
Can keep a large number of balls in the air and still smile.	Good at multi-tasking. Can juggle several things at one time. Can handle many difficult things and still keep cool.
Can't afford to do something.	Not being able, or willing, to do something for some reason. *I can't afford to miss this class. If I miss it, I won't graduate.* *You can't afford to stay home from the party, because you'll miss all the fun.* *She couldn't afford to argue with me. I'm her boss, and I might fire her!* *I cannot afford to go to the movies. Ticket prices are way too high now!* "Can afford" can also be used in the positive as shown below: *I can afford to stay a bit longer. It's only five o'clock.* *Why don't you have some more ice cream and cake? Come on, you can afford it. You're so thin!*

Can't bat in someone's league.	Not good enough to be in someone's team or group, or to be friends with someone.
Origin: Sports	*I can't bat in Dawn's league,* or *She's out of my league,* means something like: *I can't have her,* or: *Compared to me she's more educated, more wealthy, more glamorous, more powerful, more sophisticated, more prestigious, etc.*
Can't hear oneself think.	This is about one's surrounding area being very noisy.
	Q. Can we talk now? *A. Well, let's talk at the office. This place is so noisy, you can't hear yourself think!*
Can't let this get to you.	You can't let this affect you. You shouldn't let this ruin your plans, or our life, etc.
	A. Now that I've lost my job, I don't know what we can do! *B. Oh, we can't let this get to us. We'll think of something.*

Cast the iron whilst it is hot. *(Dutch.)*
Strike while the iron is hot. *(English.)*
Make hay while the sun shines. *(English.)*
Bake the bread while the oven is hot. *(Persian.)*
One should do the blacksmithing while the iron is hot. *(Dutch.)*
Do it while the opportunity is still there.

Can't wait (to do something).	Being so anxious and eager (to do something) that it's difficult to wait until the time comes.
	I can't wait to see you. *He can't wait to go home.* *She couldn't wait to finish college.*
Capitalizing on something	Using an idea to make money. Using an opportunity to one's advantage.
	Compare to: Cashing in on something.

Captive audience | People who are there specifically to hear you and no one else.

People who are completely engrossed in what is being said. Very interested in the message, captivated by it.

People who have no choice but to listen to or watch an entire presentation, as in a class, or traffic school, etc.

Care for | Care, as in: Liking someone or something.

When someone says: *I don't care for politics or politicians,* they mean: *I don't like them.*

When someone says: *Do you care for some coffee,* they mean: *Would you like to have some coffee?*

Caring, as in: Taking care of someone or something.

When someone says: *I'm caring for my mother,* they mean: *I'm taking care of my mother.*

I wasn't born yesterday. *(English.)*
I haven't swum here on the roux soup. *(German.)*
I haven't come from behind the mountains. *(Persian.)*

I am not stupid!

Carrot and stick
Carrot or stick | This is about rewarding someone for doing something good, or threatening to punish them if they don't. The carrot represents the reward, and the stick represents the threat.

She used the old carrot or stick trick with her son to get him to eat the spinach; Some ice cream tonight, or no ice cream for a week!

Compare to:
Carrot on a stick.

Background:
Some believe this has to do with mules: There are two ways to get a mule move forward. Dangle a carrot in front of it, or hit it in the back with a stick.

Carrot on a stick   This is about tempting, prodding, motivating, or luring someone into doing something. It is also referred to as: *Dangling a carrot in front of someone.*

She used the old carrot on a stick trick and promised her son some ice cream before she could get him to eat the spinach.

Compare to:
Carrot and stick.

Background:
Some believe this has to do with mules: A carrot would be tied to a stick and held in front of a mule that was pulling a cart. Since mules like to eat carrots, this helped to make the mule move forward and pull the cart along.

One hand has no sound. *(Persian.)*
One hand will not clap. *(Armenian.)*
One hand washes the other, and both wash the face. *(Greek.)*
Two hands make a sound. What does one hand have? *(Turkish.)*
Reference to the effectiveness of cooperation among people, to do good or evil.

Carrying on   Talking continuously without stopping, as in:
Quit carrying on about your car, and give me a ride.

Continuing, as in:
I'm carrying on my family's tradition of being musical.

Carrying someone   Helping someone along in life in a big way.

I've always carried him, financially or otherwise. He can never do anything on his own.

Carrying weight   Having influence, importance, or significance.

A. *I'm still looking for a job, but I haven't found one.*
B. *Ask your father to help you. He carries a lot of weight around here.*

Case closed
Origin: Legal

Done.
Finished.
Mystery solved.
No more discussion.

When someone says: *I'm not buying a new car, case closed,* they mean something like:

My decision on buying a new car is final.
I'm not buying a new car, and I don't want to talk about this subject any more; etc.

Compare to: I rest my case.

Cashing in

Profiting from something.
Making money on something.

Also see:
Capitalizing on something.

Cashing out

Getting all of one's money out of an account.

I'm not happy with this bank! I'd like to cash out and close my account.

In real estate:
A cash-out refinance is a type of refinance that will result in a new (larger) loan, but will let the borrower have some cash to use as he or she pleases.

To catch fish in each hand. *(Thai.)*
He who hunts two rats catches none. *(Parts of Africa.)*
Don't pick up two watermelons with one hand. *(Persian.)*
If you run after two hares, you'll catch none. *(Vietnamese.)*
One who drinks water with one hand remains thirsty. *(Swahili.)*
            Don't do too many things at the same time.

Caught flatfooted

Caught unprepared.
Caught or taken by surprise.

Bank executives were caught flatfooted by the public anger over their large year end bonuses.

Also:
Blindsided.
Caught off guard.

Caught red-handed	Caught doing something wrong. Caught while committing a crime. Q. *Why are they holding him? How do they know he's guilty?* A. *They caught him red handed. He couldn't deny it!* Also: Caught in the act. Caught with his pants down. Caught with his hands in the cookie jar.
Cautious to a fault	Too cautious or careful. *If he wasn't cautious to a fault, he could have opened his own business by now.* Similar combinations with other adjectives can be used also, as in: Nice to a fault. Beautiful to a fault. Considerate to a fault; etc.
Center stage	Important. Center of attention. Position of importance. *The oil prices have taken center stage again.*
Chain of command	Hierarchy. The order of importance, or authority, for people in an organization. *If you want to succeed in this company, you must follow the chain of command. For example, in order to file a complaint, you must first go to your immediate supervisor; you don't go to the president of the company, you fool!*
Chalking it up to something	Thinking of it as something. Considering it to be something. Q. *You lost a lot of money in that deal, didn't you?* A. *Well, I did, but I'll chalk it up to experience.*

Changing for the better	Things getting better. Conditions improving.
	The economy has been bad, but I can see things changing for the better.
	Also: Turning for the better.
	Opposite: Changing for the worse.
Changing hands	Exchanging. Changing ownership. Ownership of something going from one person to another.
Charity begins at home.	Take care of those who are close to you (your family, friends, community, hometown, etc.,) before you attend to others.

For fleeing enemies, a silver bridge. *(Spanish.)*
For the enemy that leaves, build a golden bridge. *(Greek.)*
If your enemies are trying to end hostilities, try to compromise.

Chasing rainbows	Going after something that's not achievable.
Chasing windmills	Going after imaginary enemies. Going after something that's not achievable.
Cheap shot	A lowly attack. An unfair attack. A non-chivalrous attack.
	A. *It wasn't nice what he said about your mother.* B. *What else did you expect? He always takes cheap shots!*
	Compare to: Below the belt.
Checks and balances	A control system. A quality control system.
	We have an elaborate system of checks and balances in place to make sure that we have a reliable quality-and-cost control in our company.

Chew out	This isn't a nice thing to say, but it means:
Chew someone's ass out	Shouting angrily at someone. Yelling at someone for doing something.
	Maisha is going to chew her boss's ass out if she ever finds out what he's done!
	Maisha's boss chewed her out for falsely accusing him of talking behind her back.
Chew someone up and spit them out	Destroy someone verbally. Verbally tear someone to shreds.

What will I eat with? is better than *What will I eat? (Swahili.)*

Chicken little	A pessimist. A person who always warns people about bad things happening when they're not.
	A. *I hear gas prices will be going up and then there will be rationing!*
	B. *You should stop listening to these chicken littles.*
	Background: From the story *Chicken Little,* about a small chicken who, when an acorn fell off a tree and hit him on the head, claimed *The sky is falling! The sky is falling!* This sent the town into a panic.
Chickens come home to roost.	Someday you'll have to explain your actions. What you do today will have consequences that you'll have to face. Bad or silly things said or done in the past are now beginning to cause problems
	A. *I've lost so much money in real estate. I was either too greedy or too optimistic!*
	B. *You didn't use good judgment, and now the chickens have come home to roost.*
Child prodigy	A person who, at an early age, shows signs of great talents or skills that are normally expected of talented adults.

- Give me a ring when you're done.
- I have a ring with me now, Mr. Clark. Do you want it?

For a definition, see:

- **Call me.**

Chinaman's chance (in hell)	Not a good chance. (Is used with a negative verb. This could be considered racist and highly offensive. Don't use it.)
	Q. *Do you think he has a chance to get admitted to the university at all?* A. *He hasn't got a Chinaman's chance!*
	Also: Chance in hell. Ghost of a chance. Snowball's chance in hell.
Chopped liver	Ignored. Unimportant.
	Everybody got a gift except me! What am I, chopped liver?
	Q. *You've seen your boss's wife. Do you think she's in charge at home?* A. *Of course! He's like chopped liver when she's around.*
City of Angels	This is a nickname for the City of Los Angeles.
City of Brotherly Love	This is a nickname for the City of Philadelphia.
Claim to fame	An accomplishment (or lack of it) that someone is famous for.
	Her claim to fame is that she's been nominated for an award eleven times without ever winning one!

Be a smart man, like drooping rice. *(Indonesian.)*
However much fruit a tree bears, it humbles its head that much more. *(Armenian.)*

> *The more wisdom one acquires, the more humble they become.*

Claiming lives	Taking lives.
	The accident claimed two lives, means: *Two people were killed in the accident.*

Classified information
Origin: Political, Military

Information that is available only to certain people with the appropriate permission or clearance.

Clay pigeon

An object used for target practice.
A person in a defenseless position.

Compare to:
Sitting duck.

Close call

An escape out of a bad situation by a very small margin.

Q. *How bad was your accident?*
A. *It was such a close call. I almost died!*

Also: Narrow escape.

Close to the vest

Guarded.
Closely held secret, often of a financial nature.

Q. *Can I trust you with a secret?*
A. *Sure, I'll keep it close to the vest.*

Also:
Playing cards close to the vest.

Closing in

Trapping someone.
Almost trapping someone.

He killed himself as authorities were closing in on him.

Closing ranks
Origin: Political

Uniting.
Joining forces to show solidarity.

After the earthquake, politicians closed ranks with the president and called for immediate help for the victims.

Closing the door before the horse gets out of the barn

Doing something before it's too late.

Cold call

An unexpected or unsolicited call (by phone or in person) by someone usually trying to sell an item or a service.

Cold case *Legal*	An unsolved (criminal) case from some time ago that has been set aside for lack of evidence or suspect.
Cold turkey	Quitting a habit abruptly instead of doing it gradually. Q. *How long did it take you to quit smoking?* A. *No time at all. I quit cold turkey!*

The mouse couldn't fit through the hole, and then it tied a broom to its tail. *(Armenian, Persian.)*

Refers to people who take on more responsibilities than they can handle.

Collective sense	All having the same kind of emotion, reaction, position, etc. When someone says: *There was a collective sense of anger,* they mean something like: *They all felt angry.*
Comb over **Comb-over**	Combing long pieces of hair over one's bald spots on the top of their head.
Come hell or high water	No matter what. It doesn't matter what happens.
Comes out in the wash.	Things will be okay. Things will even out. Truth will come out when tested.
Comfort food	Food that gives a sense of wellbeing. The kind of food easily prepared for informal gatherings and good times. Compare to: Soul food.
Coming a long way	Doing very well. Accomplishing a lot. Achieving a lot compared to where someone has started from. When someone says: *You've come a long way,* they mean something like: *You've been very successful.*

Coming across as
Appearing to have a certain characteristic or personality.

When someone says: *Sumaya is coming across as being truthful,* they mean something like: *She seems to be a person who tells the truth.*

Coming apart at the seams
Failing.
Falling apart.
Breaking down.

Q. *What's happening with your company? It doesn't look good.*
A. *Thanks to our incompetent management, it's coming apart at the seams.*

Compare to:
Bursting at the seams.

Coming clean
Telling the truth.

When someone says: *Bill came clean on Monica,* they mean something like: *He told the truth about the Monica incident.*

Coming from behind
Unexpected.
Coming forward from a weak position.

Q. *Were you surprised that our team won?*
A. *Of course, nobody thought they would win. It was a true come-from-behind victory!*

Coming into one's own
Getting to the point of having one's own style, identity, ideas, wealth, status, position, etc.

When someone says: *She's considered a gifted performer and is finally coming into her own,* they mean something like: *She has her own style and is not imitating anybody.*

Coming of age
Growing up, reaching adulthood, as in:
My son is coming of age.

Getting relatively or fully developed, as in:
The coming of age of the solar energy technology isn't too far off.

Coming on strong

Being confident.
Using strong words.
Being sure of oneself.

Note:
Coming on strong can have a negative effect.

Coming out (of the closet)

Telling the truth about oneself voluntarily.
Disclosing something about oneself that's been a secret, usually about being gay.

Q. *Are you finally coming out of the closet?*
A. *Yeah, I think it's better that way. I think I should have come out a long time ago!*

When the father's generation eats salt, the child's generation thirsts for water. *(Vietnamese.)*

Coming out of one's ears

Having a lot of something.
An overabundance of something.

When someone says: *He has cash coming out of his ears,* they mean something like: *He's very rich.*

Coming out of the woodwork

Appearing unexpectedly.
Coming from everywhere.

Crawling out of the woodwork

You've got people coming out of the woodwork, screaming for more bus service. Everybody's asking for more service.

Background:
This expression has to do with the fact that insects come out of an infested wooden structure in large numbers, especially if it's suddenly disturbed.

Coming to

Medical

Gaining consciousness.
Waking up after passing out.
Waking up after being drugged.

Q. *Is he still unconscious?*
A. *Yes, but be quiet. He's coming to!*

Compare to:
Bringing to.

Coming to a head
Ending in a crisis.
Climaxing, building up to something, and then having it end.

The health care issue is coming to a head. We really have to come to an agreement soon.

Coming to blows
Fighting.
Beginning to heatedly disagree.
Starting to hotly argue over something.

We were about to come to blows when he suddenly apologized.

Coming to fruition
Seeing the final results of an action.

Q. When are you going to retire?
A. Soon I hope, but I'd like to see the library project come to fruition before I leave.

Coming to pass
Something happening.

We were supposed to have a reunion last month, but it didn't come to pass.

Coming to terms
Accepting.
Facing, understanding, and accepting an unpleasant or difficult situation.

It's not easy, but I've been trying to come to terms with my father's death.

Also: Coming to grips.

Coming to the conclusion
Making a decision.
Reaching a conclusion.

Q. Why are you smiling?
A. I've come to the conclusion that we're both idiots!

Common ground
Origin: Political

Something all parties can agree to.
Something the different parties have in common.

We have found some common ground. We're both single parents, in our thirties, enjoy going to the movies, and we both think I'm cute!

Common sense   Something that makes sense to, and is easy to understand by, an average person.

When someone says: *It's common sense,* they mean something like:

You should know that;
Everybody knows that;
You should have expected it; etc.

Common thread   A common factor.

The police are looking for a common thread to tie the recent robberies together.

Comparing apples and oranges   Comparing different things.
Things of a completely different nature.

A. *Comparing Republicans and Democrats is like comparing apples and oranges.*
B. *Definitely not. If you ask me, Republicans and Democrats are very similar!*

It's not a shame to ask. It's a shame not to know. *(Persian.)*
Shameful is not the one who doesn't know, but the one who doesn't ask. *(Azerbaijani.)*
He who asks is a fool for five minutes. But he who does not ask remains a fool forever. *(Chinese.)*

Comparing notes   Exchanging notes.
Learning from each other.
Sharing information for a more complete picture or assessment of something.

Okay class, you've all been to the lecture. Now I want you to compare notes, and get ready for our discussion tomorrow.

Con artist   A cheat.
A charlatan.
An untrustworthy person who can easily convince other people to trust him and believe his lies.

Similar:
A snake oil salesman.

Conduct unbecoming
Origin: Military

Unacceptable behavior.

You're a professor! You're not supposed to be dancing on tables! Your conduct is unbecoming for a professor.

Connecting the dots

Putting the facts together in order to understand something.

Q. *There were many indications that he was planning to run away. How did you miss them?*
A. *Sorry. We screwed up. Nobody connected the dots.*

Also:
Drawing conclusions.
Seeing the big picture.

Your future does not depend on the lines of your hands because people who do not have hands also have a future. *(Indian.)*

Consumed by something

Only thinking about one thing, as in:
My mother-in-law is consumed by greed.

Contract killing
Legal

A planned killing, by a hired killer, paid for by someone.

Q. *Was there a contract out on the victim?*
A. *Yes, we've arrested the hired killer.*

Conventional wisdom

The traditional or existing way of thinking.
What is accepted by people as being correct.

Conventional wisdom tells us not to drive if we've been drinking.

Cornering the market

Having a monopoly on something.
Having a controlling share of the market on something.
Having so much of something that you can manipulate the prices.

Q. *I've done some stupid things, but do YOU think I'm stupid?*
A. *You, my dear, have cornered the market on stupidity! You are a complete moron!*

Coughing something up

Surrendering something, usually money, unwillingly.

It's the first of the month, and time to pay your dues. Come on, cough it up. It's for your own protection!

Counting on something

Believing something, or depending on it, as in:

Q. *Do you think she hates me?*
A. *Yes! Count on it!*

Relying on someone or something, as in:

Listen guys. I'm going to start campaigning for better wages, but I can't do it alone. Can I count on your help?

Fishing behind the net. *(Dutch.)*
Coat after the rain. *(Hungarian.)*
Finding the dog in the jar. *(Dutch.)*
The old lady with cakes has already passed by. *(Croatian.)*
Clothes after the New Year are good for the top of the minaret. *(Persian.)*

A reference to being too late to do something.

Courtesy of someone or something

From someone, as a way of saying thanks, as in:

Q. *What are the boxes of chocolate doing here?*
A. *They are Christmas gifts, courtesy of the boss.*

Because of someone or something, as in:

I'm sorry to announce that, courtesy of the new tax laws, we'll be paying higher taxes this year!

Covering all the bases

Origin: Sports

Considering everything.

When someone says: *We covered all the bases,* they mean something like: *We talked about every possibility.*

Also:
We covered everything.
We addressed all issues.
We didn't leave any stones unturned.

Covering someone or something *Origin: Military, Political*	In the military: When someone says: *Cover me while I'm crossing the bridge,* they mean something like: *Keep them busy so I can cross the bridge safely, without getting shot at.* In journalism: When someone says: *Cover these candidates,* they mean something like: *Follow them around and report on their activities.* At the restaurant: When someone says: *I'll cover the bill,* they mean: *I'll pay it.* At the workplace, with "for": When someone says: *Please cover for me while I'm at the hospital,* they mean: *Perform my duties in my absence. Answer my calls, meet with my clients, etc., until I come back.*

From children and drunks will you hear the truth. *(Danish.)*
From a child and a crazy person you learn the truth. *(Greek.)*

Crack of dawn	Very early morning. The very beginning of a new day. *I've been working since the crack of dawn.*
Cracker barrel **Cracker-barrel**	Typical of country life. Suggestive of casual discussions, about any subject, by persons (typically gathered around a barrel containing crackers!) at a general store. Related: Cracker barrel philosophy. Cracker barrel discussions.
Cracking down *Origin: Legal, Political*	Regulating. Investigating. Enforcing the existing regulations. *The police should really crack down on violence, and arrest some of these drug dealers before things get even worse.*

Crashing a party   Showing up at a party uninvited.
Going somewhere without an invitation.

Q. *We're going to crash the party at Bobby's house. Do you want to come with us?*
A. *No, and you shouldn't go either! He was really upset the last time we did it.*

Related: Gatecrasher. Party crasher.

He who cannot dance will say: The drum is bad. *(Parts of Africa.)*

Crazy like a fox   Very smart.

Q. *I think your friend is crazy; otherwise, why is he doing all of these stupid things?*
A. *Yeah, he's crazy like a fox! He knows exactly what he's doing.*

Cream of the crop   Best of the best.

Background::
This has to do with the cream (or sweet cream), the part of milk that rises to the top, generally considered to be the best part by a lot of people.

Creating a buzz   Getting people to talk about you or your product.
Making yourself or your product interesting so that everyone's talking about you or it.

Related:
Buzzword.
Buzz-phrase.
Catch phrase.

Creating a monster   You cause or help someone to flourish in some respect. Later, however, they get out of control (or carried away or conceited) and turn around and hurt you.

When I encouraged my ex-wife to become a lawyer, I didn't know I was creating a monster. Now she's using her legal mind to drive me out of business!

Crediting someone	Giving credit to someone.
	In her books, she credits her family members and thanks them.

Crocodile tears	Fake tears. False sadness or sympathy.
	The killer cried in court, but those were just crocodile tears. He wasn't really sorry.
	Note: *Alligator tears* is used, but it is incorrect.

Cross my heart.	Creating trust. Assuring the listener that the statement is true.
	Q. *Can I be sure you'll be there?* A. *I'll be there. I promise. Cross my heart!*
	Background:: The complete idiom is: *Cross my heart and hope to die.* It makes a reference to the sign of the cross. It was, and still is, believed that by crossing your heart you will keep the devil away.

It's a transition, said the fox who was skinned. *(Norwegian.)*

Crossing the line Origin: Sports	Disrespecting; Doing or saying the wrong thing; Going too far in what was said or done; as in:
	I don't care who he is. He crossed the line and needs to apologize.
	Joining the other side, as in:
	If this infighting goes on, some of the voters will cross party lines and vote for the other party's candidate.

Crying one's eyes out	Deep, heavy sobbing. Crying a lot or for a long time.
	Q. *What's the matter? Was it a very sad movie?* A. *Yeah, I think I'll go home and cry my eyes out.*

Crying uncle Giving up.

They're trying to make her cry uncle, but I know her better. She'll never give up.

Crying wolf Delivering a false alarm.
Lying or exaggerating about being in danger.

Background:
From *The Boy Who Cried Wolf,* the story of a young shepherd who used to cry and make villagers believe that a wolf was attacking his sheep so that they would all come running to help him. After he did this a few times, the villagers stopped believing him. When one day the wolf actually attacked his herd, and he cried out for help, no one came to help him.

The love from a child is as long as a stick; the love from a mother is as long as a road. *(Indonesian.)*

Curiosity killed the cat! If you don't mind your own business, or if you ask too many questions, you'll get in trouble!

Also:
Don't stick your nose where it doesn't belong.

Curve ball
Sports

A tricky situation.
A deceptive action.
Something that takes you completely by surprise.

Q. *How can you blame her? She was thrown a curve ball!*
A. *I know but, in her position as the chairwoman, she should have been more prepared.*

Background:
The term comes from baseball. A curve ball is thrown in such a way that it follows a curved path in the air. This, combined with the high speed at which the ball is going, makes it difficult or tricky for the opponent player to handle. Curve balls are also thrown when the batter is not expecting it, to throw them off.

- Sir, do you want your drink on the rocks?
- No, you moron. I want it on the couch!

For a definition, see:

- **On the rocks**

Cut and dry **Cut-and-dry**	Clear. Obvious. Ordinary. Prepared. Easy to follow. Already decided. Nothing special about it.

Q. *You think you can do this?*
A. *Oh yes, it's pretty cut-and-dry.*

Also:
Cut and dried.

Cut out for   Made for.

When someone says: *This job was cut out for you,* they mean something like: *It was made for you. It is perfect for you.*

Water finds the pothole. *(Persian.)*
The kettle rolled down and found the lid. *(Greek.)*
          People with similar characteristics find each other.

Cut to the chase!   Let's get started.
What's on your mind?
Stop wasting my time.
What is the real problem?
What are you trying to say?
What is really bothering you?
Let's talk about the things you really want to talk about.

Also: Get to the point.
Compare to: Beating around the bush.

Cute as a button   Very cute.
(Often used for young children or infants.)

Cutting both ways   Maybe, maybe not.
Having advantages, but also disadvantages.

Q. *What do you think of the loan?*
A. *It cuts both ways. It adds to your monthly payments, but it also helps your business.*

Cutting corners	Doing things cheaply. Not following all of the rules. Lowering the quality to save money.
	A. I know for a fact that some of the contractors are cutting corners to save money. *B. If that's true, it may be unsafe, and may even be illegal. I think we should fire them.*
Cutting one's losses	Stopping one's losses. Getting out of a losing situation.
	When someone says: *Let's sell this business and cut our losses,* they mean something like: *We've lost a lot so far. It's time to stop losing.*
	Also: Stop the bleeding.
Cutting the legs *Legal*	Striking a decisive blow that will cripple an idea, a person, a competing business, a case, etc.
	The new evidence has really cut the legs out of the defense. Actually, they don't even have a defense any more.

Don't stretch your legs beyond your quilt. *(Persian.)*
Stretch your legs as far as your quilt allows. *(Arabic.)*
While the blanket is short, learn to curl up to fit. *(Filipino.)*
You stretch you legs according to your blanket size. *(Romanian.)*
Know your limits and adapt to the situation.

Dancing around the issue	Avoiding the issue. Not addressing the issue.
Dancing around something	*I asked you a question, and I would appreciate it if you would stop dancing around it! Do you want to get married or not?*
	Also see: Cut to the chase. Beating around the bush.
Dancing in the end-zone *Sports*	Celebrating a victory, especially in a sporting event

Dark horse *Political*	Underdog. A promising, but previously unknown, political candidate. Someone you don't expect to win, but who ends up winning.
Date back **Dating back**	A date in the past. Determining a date in the past. When someone says: *These pictures date back many years,* they mean something like: *The pictures were taken many years ago.*
Day in and day out **Day-in and day-out**	Constantly, all of the time. Every day for a long time. (Usually denoting a boring activity.) *I really need a vacation. I've been stuffing envelopes day-in and day-out for five months. It's killing me!*
Day of reckoning	Judgment day. Day of judgment. The day when you have to answer for your actions.

Time goes and does not come back. *(Chinese, Haitian.)*

Dead in the water	A situation where nothing can be done. When someone says: *We're dead in the water,* they mean something like: *There's nothing we can do.*
Dead man walking	A man on death row walking to his execution. A person who will most certainly be in trouble soon. Someone who will definitely be losing their job. An announcement that a man on death row is walking to his execution. A person given the death penalty, waiting for the execution to take place. A person who has a mob hit on them; someone hires someone to kill someone else, and they're considered to be a dead man walking.

Dead meat	In serious trouble.
	Q. Are you going to tell your wife what happened?
	A. No! If she finds out I'll be dead meat.
Dead or alive	This is used when:
Wanted dead or alive	Someone is wanted, no matter what. The police want to capture a suspect no matter what! The goal is to put someone out of commission, regardless of guilt or innocence.

A house not seen by the sun is seen by the doctor. *(Greek.)*
In a house where the sun gets in, the doctor doesn't. *(Portuguese.)*

Dead presidents	Cash.
	Monetary bills.
	Dollar bills, paper money, in general, because they mostly have portraits of the late U.S. presidents on them.
	A "Hot one" is a $1 bill.
	An "Abe" is a $5 bill.
	A "Jackson" is a $20 bill.
	A "Grant" is a $50 bill.
	A "Benjamin" or a "C-note" is a $100 bill.
Dead ringer	Exact duplicate.
Origin: Sports	Exact look alike.
	I couldn't believe my eyes. She's a dead ringer for your mother!
Deal breaker	Something that makes going through with a deal impossible.
	Q. By the way, I smoke. Is that okay?
	A. Well, smoking is not allowed. You know I would like to rent a room to you, but this is a deal breaker!
Deal with it!	Handle it!
	Accept it!
	Look. I don't like it any more than you do, but we have to get rid of our cat. Deal with it!

Deal! **It's a deal!**	Okay. I agree. Let's do it. A. *I'll do my homework regularly if you buy me a drum set.* B. *It's a deal!*
Dealing from the bottom of the deck *Origin: Gambling*	Cheating people. Cheating when playing cards. Dealing with people in an unfair way.
Deck the halls.	Decorating (mainly) for Christmas, but also for other special occasions.
Dedicated someone or something	An item or person assigned for a specific purpose. *We have a dedicated computer for the kids,* means something like: *Grown-ups should use another computer.* *We have hired a dedicated weight and balance engineer,* means something like: *He only does weight and balance calculations. For design purposes we go to our design engineer.*
Deep pockets	Rich people, or large companies, with lots of financial backing.
Deep sixing **Deep-sixing**	Destroying. Getting rid of or throwing away. Rejecting beyond resurrecting. *I'm not deep-sixing my chances, am I?* *I made a proposal to the Board of Directors, but they deep-sixed it.* **Background:** Probably comes from burial procedures, referring to bodies being buried six feet under the ground. It could also be a nautical term relating to ships and submarines sinking so deep that they could not be resurrected.

Departure from the norm	Not normal. Not the usual. *What you're proposing sounds okay to me. For him, however, it's a departure from the norm and doesn't make sense.*
Devil is in the details.	Details are important. Overlooking the little things can get you into trouble. Details can ruin something by making it too confusing. *Q. This looked so simple! How did we get in trouble?* *A. The devil's in the details! We simply should have been more careful.* Also: It's the little foxes that spoil the vine!
Devil's advocate	One who argues against a policy, cause, plan, position, etc., not because they're against it, but because they want to find its weaknesses or to refine it. *Listen. I like what you're trying to do, but let me play the devil's advocate for a minute. How are you going to pay for it?*
Different strokes for different folks	People are different and have different tastes. Also see: Beauty is in the eye of the beholder.
Digging in one's heels	Getting ready. Getting established in a place or position. Taking a position and sticking to it, even if there is a lot of opposition.
Digging oneself into a hole	Getting oneself into trouble. Getting into a position that may be challenging to get out of. *We dug ourselves into this hole, and we have to get out of it ourselves.* *When you're in a hole, stop digging further and find a way out!*

Digging up bones
Looking into the past and uncovering old secrets.

Don't you have anything better to do than to dig up bones? Come on, don't waste your time. Get on with your life!

Dime a dozen
Dime-a-dozen
Very cheap or inexpensive, as in:
I can find cheap polyester shirts everywhere. They're a dime-a-dozen these days!

Also see:
Dirt cheap.

Dirt cheap
Very cheap or inexpensive, as in:
You can build your own computer at home. The parts are dirt cheap.

Also see:
Dime-a-dozen.

Dirty old man
An older man who thinks a lot about having sex with younger women, or actually does or says things about it.

Also a humorous way of saying that an older man is thinking too much about sex and sexual themes.

Don't worry about him. He's just a dirty old man!

Dissin' someone
Dissing someone
Disrespecting someone.
Ignoring or avoiding them.

Hey man, stop dissin' me!
Joe and Moe haven't talked to each other ever since Joe dissed Moe's wife.

Dittohead
Ditto head
Someone who agrees with another person mindlessly.
Someone who always agrees with a person who is in a powerful position.

Also:
A sheep.
A suck-up.
A brown-noser.
A kiss ass. (Same thing, but not very polite!)

Do it, and die!	Don't do it.
	If you do it, I'll kill you.
	If you do it, you'll be sorry.
	Similar: Don't you dare do it!
Do over	A second chance.
Do-over	*I wish there was a do-over for life.*
Dodging the bullet	Avoiding trouble.
Dog and pony show	A publicity event, not a true representation of facts, often to impress and gain the approval of a (potential) client.
Dog-and-pony show	
	Q. *What are all the decorations for? Is the chairman coming for a visit again?*
	A. *Yes, along with several potential clients, so we're having another dog-and-pony show.*
Dog eat dog	Dangerous.
Dog-eat-dog	Characterized by mean behavior; people fighting like dogs to get what they want. A world where people only look after themselves and won't hesitate to hurt you.
	When someone says: *It's a dog-eat-dog world out there,* they mean something like: *Be careful, it's very dangerous!*
Doggone it!	This phrase is a nicer way of saying:
	Darn it!
	Dang it!
	Dammit!
	Goddammit!
Doing a double-take	Looking again. Looking at something, or thinking about it, again. Having to look more than once because you don't believe what you just saw.
	When I saw Susie, I had to do a double-take because her appearance had changed so radically!

Doing a number on someone or something	Hurting someone or damaging something. Causing a person to hurt or suffer emotionally, mentally, physically, financially, etc

Q. *Why are you still upset with your brother? Is it for borrowing your car without telling you?*
A. *He did a number on me AND my car. I missed my class, and my car is damaged!*

Monday morning quarterback. *(English.)*
After a battle, everyone is a general. *(Czech.)*
Graves are filled with after-the-fact wisdom. *(Italian.)*

It's easy to say why something went wrong after it has happened.

Doing justice	Telling or showing the true extent of someone's character or accomplishments, etc.

When someone says: *This picture doesn't do her justice,* they mean something like: *It doesn't show the full extent of her beauty.*

Doing someone in Legal	Murdering someone.

The street gang members were afraid one of their younger members would betray them, so they did him in.

Doing someone's bidding	Doing someone's work. Doing something that someone else tells you to do.

She can easily trick him into doing her bidding by pretending to be helpless.

Doing something 'til the sun shines	Doing something for a long time. Doing something until the sun comes up.

Doing something like there's no tomorrow	Doing a lot of something. Doing too much of something. Doing something as if there will be no consequence for it tomorrow.

He was drinking like there was no tomorrow.

She's spending money like there's no tomorrow.

Don't be a stranger!	Keep in touch. Call, or come and see us, from time to time.
Don't be long.	Do it quickly. Come back soon. Don't take too much time.

A friend in need is a friend indeed. *(English.)*
When in need, you shall know a friend. *(Czech.)*
In time of need, a thousand friends shrink to a few grams. *(German.)*
In times of trouble, when you need help, you will see your real friends. *(Filipino.)*

Don't bet on it! *Gambling*	Don't be so sure. A. *I think this time they will come to an agreement about the global warming issue.* B. *Don't bet on it!* Also: Don't hold your breath!
Don't bite the hand that feeds you.	Don't insult (hurt, criticize, attack, etc.) those who are helping you.
Don't get mad, get even!	Get revenge. Don't react out of anger. Use your head before you retaliate. Instead of wasting time being angry when someone has upset you, do something to upset them!
Don't get me wrong.	Don't misunderstand me. Oh no, that's not what I meant!
Don't go there. **Don't even go there.**	Don't talk about it. Don't you dare talk about it! Don't bring it up, I'm serious! Q. *Do you want me to tell your wife?* A. *Oh, don't even go there, or you'll be sorry.*
Don't know from Adam.	When someone says: *She doesn't know him from Adam,* they mean: *She doesn't know him at all. She doesn't know what he looks like.*

Don't leave me hanging.	Tell me now. Don't keep me waiting and wondering.
Don't spit where you eat.	Be nice to people who are nice to you. Be good to the people you depend on or they may not help you anymore. Compare to: Don't bite the hand that feeds you.
Don't you dare!	This expression by itself is a serious warning and means: *I'm warning you, don't.* *I'm warning you, don't do it.* It is also used with other verbs to make more specific warnings: *Don't you dare talk to her. (I'm warning you, don't talk to her.)* *Don't you dare smoke in here. (I'm warning you, don't smoke in here.)*
Done for	Ruined. Destroyed with no chance for recovery.

Buying a pig in a poke. *(English.)*
You don't buy a cat in a bag. *(Haitian.)*
Buying a cat in a bag. *(Dutch, German.)*
Buying a water buffalo in the marsh. *(Thai.)*

A reference to risky purchases.

Done in	Tired. Finished. Exhausted. *A. What a busy day!* *B. I agree. I can't go on any more, at least not today. I'm really done in.* Similar: Used up. Worn out. Washed-out. Ready to drop. On my last leg.

Dot your i's and cross your t's.	Make sure every detail is attended to. Take care of all of the details before you submit your work.
	Background: A paper or an essay is not complete if the letters are not written correctly. Hence the reference to crossing every letter "t" at the top, and making sure that every letter "i" has a dot.
Doting on one's kids	Spoiling one's kids. Being very attentive to one's kids.

Amongst calves a handicapped cow is wise. *(Indian.)*
Where there are no sheep, they call goats Abdur Rahim Chelebi. *(Turkish.)*
In the land of the blind, the one-eyed man is king! *(Dutch, English, Greek, Italian, parts of Africa, Persian, etc.)*

Double backing **Double-backing**	Changing tactics. Doing something the other side isn't expecting. *We double backed on the board of directors and caught everyone by surprise.*
Double entendre	A word or phrase having a double meaning, especially when the second meaning is a little on the "dirty" side!
Double talk **Double-talk** **Double-speak**	Talk that is different from action. Saying something but intending something else, in a misleading way. *Q. Why are you so upset with me?* *A. Well, I don't like your double-talk. You always say one thing but do something else.*
Double whammy **Double-whammy**	Twice as bad. When two bad things happen at once or almost at once. Also: Triple-whammy.
Double-edged sword	A dangerous situation. When no matter what you do, you can't win. An action intended to hurt someone else, which could actually backfire and hurt you.

Down and out **Down-and-out**	Miserable, mostly in the financial sense. Also: Down on (one's) luck.
Down the hatch	Has to do with: Drinking or having a drink.
	If you give someone a drink, and say: *Down the hatch,* it means: *Drink it! Gulp it down!*
	However: If you raise your drink and say: *Down the hatch,* it means you're going to gulp it down yourself, similar to saying: *Cheers!*
Down the rabbit hole	Following someone into the unknown. Getting into a difficult or confusing situation. Also: Into the matrix.

Don't look where you fell, but where you slipped.
The Earth moves at different speeds for different people.
If the bush is on fire, the antelope will not fear the hunter's bullet.
You don't need a light to see someone you know intimately at night.
If you try to cleanse others, you will waste away in the process, like soap.
What an old man will see sitting, a child cannot see standing on a mountain!
(Parts of Africa.)

Down the toilet **Down the drain**	Ruined. Wasted.
	When someone says: *It's money down the drain,* they mean: *It's a waste of money.*
	When someone says: *This scandal is going to send my future down the toilet,* they mean: *It will ruin my life.*
Down to earth **Down-to-earth**	Realistic. A practical person. An easy person to get along with.

Down to the wire **Going down to the wire.** **Coming down to the wire.** *Origin: Sports*	Getting very close. Until the last moment. *We're coming down to the wire on turning our report in.* **Background:** The origin of this expression has to do with horseracing, where a wire used to be stretched across the track at the finish line.
Downplaying something	Saying or implying that a bad situation isn't as serious as it seems. *He's down-playing the effect of the economy on his business.*
Dragging on	Taking too long.
Dragging one's feet	Doing things too slowly. Taking too much time to do something because the person doesn't really want to do it. *He's dragging his feet. I don't think he wants to give me a refund.*

Son of old age won't know his father. *(Greek.)*
It's not good to have children when you're old.

Dragging through the mud	Bad-mouthing someone. Destroying someone's reputation. *I won't run for public office again. The last time I did it, the media dragged me and my family through the mud like never before.* Similar: Dragging someone's name through the mud.
Drawing a line in the sand	Setting limits. Establishing a limit or a boundary to show which things (or actions) are considered acceptable, and which ones are not. *My dear sir, when are you going to draw a line in the sand, and say, Enough is enough?*

Continued on the next page.

Drawing a line in the sand

Continued from the previous page.

Also:
Drawing a line.
Drawing the line.

When someone says: *Fernando wants to have fun, but he draws the line at going to wild parties,* they mean something like:

He won't go to wild parties.

He who eats the pastry is not crazy. Crazy is the one who gave it to him. *(Bulgarian.)*

Drawing someone a picture

Making things more clear.

Q. *Do you understand what I'm saying?*
A. *Yes, you don't have to draw me a picture, but it would help!*

Drawing to a close

Ending.
Coming to an end.

His political life has now drawn to a close. He won't be active as a politician anymore.

Also: Drawing to an end.

Drawn-out

Lengthy.

When someone says: *It was a drawn-out process,* they mean: *It took a long time.*

Drifting apart

Gradually becoming separated, emotionally or otherwise.

Drinking oneself to death

Drinking so much that one dies, or could die.

If you say: *She drank herself to death,* you mean something like:

She drank so much she died;
She drank so much it ruined her life;
She was an alcoholic for a long time and her drinking habits killed her; etc.

Can also be used with other verbs, such as:
Working oneself to death.

Driving a point home	Making a point understood.
	I want to drive my point home about abortion and make them understand it.
Dropping a dime	Snitching on someone (maybe to one's own advantage).
	Calling the police (to turn someone in, or to betray them).
	Q. I wonder who let the cops know about the drug deal!?
	A. I did! I dropped the dime on them. I don't want any drugs in my neighborhood!
Dropping it like a bad habit	Not doing it.
	Stopping it quickly.
	Stopping to do it right away.
Dropping names	Mentioning important people during conversation to impress others.
	Q. Have you talked to this new guy at work? He knows a lot of famous movie stars!
	A. No, he doesn't. He's just dropping names to make everybody think he's special.

He who leans against a good tree gets good shade. *(Venezuelan.)*
If you lean on a good tree, you will be protected by a good shadow. *(Spanish.)*

You can trust a good friend.

Dropping the ball	Failing.
Origin: Sports	Screwing up.
	Missing an opportunity.
	Making a mistake, especially a simple or stupid mistake.
	You really dropped the ball when you wrecked my car and didn't even tell me about it.

Background::
This expression comes from sports, especially football, but it's used very often and for all kinds of mistakes.

Drug of choice	When someone says: *My drug of choice is music,* they mean something like:
	Music is what I like; *Music is the drug for me;* *Music is what puts me in a good mood; etc.*

The night is a good counselor. *(Portuguese.)*
The night brings advice. Take advice of your pillow. *(French.)*
Sleep on it. Think about it. Don't rush.

Due diligence *Legal*	Necessary work and effort used in research. (Mainly used in legal or investment context.)
	A. *Here's the contract to sign, sir.* B. *Have you done your due diligence? Do we know what we're getting into?*
Dummy up!	Keep quiet. Pretend you don't know anything!
Dumping on someone	Criticizing someone.
	Also: Unloading one's problems on someone else.
	I'm not trying to dump on you guys, really!
Dust in the wind	Dead. Gone. Helpless. Meaningless. We are here on earth but for a moment. We've come from dust, and we'll return to dust.
	Q. *Have you heard from Martin lately?* A. *My ex husband? Oh, he's dust in the wind. Forget about him!*

Background:
This is a line from a very famous song written by Kerry Livgren when he was with the band *Kansas.* It has philosophical and religious significance, but has also been used to convey less philosophical meanings such as suggested in the example above.

- Your honor, I rest my case.
- Not so fast. Not on *that* table!

For a definition, see:

- **I rest my case!**

Early bird gets the worm.	If you start early, you're more likely to succeed. The sooner you prepare yourself, or get started, the better your chances.
	Also: Early bird catches the worm.
Eastern seaboard	The area along the eastern coastline (mostly of the U.S.)
Easy to look at	Beautiful. Attractive. Pleasant looking.
	Also: Easy on the eyes.
	Q. *So, what do you think of her?* A. *Well, I must admit, she's really easy on the eyes!*

Near the dry, the damp will burn. *(Turkish.)*
Bugs infesting the wheat get ground along with it. *(Indian.)*
Once the fire starts burning, the damp and the dry will burn together. *(Persian.)*
Be careful who you choose to be your friends.

Eat your heart out!	When someone says: *I'm going on a trip, eat your heart out,* they mean something like:
	I'm going on a trip but you're not. I hope that makes you jealous!
	When someone says: *I just got a promotion, eat your heart out,* they mean something like:
	I got a promotion but you didn't, and I know that's killing you!
	Depending on who says it and how it is said, this could be a mean or a humorous statement.
Eating out	Eating at a restaurant, or somewhere else, instead of at home.
Edge of possibility	Almost impossible.
	Akira's claim is at the edge of possibility. What he says is possible, but highly unlikely.

Editor at large **Editor-at-large**	A writer who has more leeway than a hands-on, day-to-day worker but less control than an executive editor. Someone who contributes what they want on a freelance basis but are not involved in the nuts-and-bolts operations of a magazine. Similar: Buyer at large. Reporter at large.
Egg on one's face	This is about: Looking foolish. Being embarrassed. *I was trying to bring peace to the community, but things went wrong and I ended up with egg on my face. Now nobody wants to work with me.* **Background:** One explanation for the origin of this expression makes reference to the fact that people in the audience used to throw eggs at actors with whose performance they weren't happy, or at politicians with whom they didn't agree.
Eighty-sixing	Saying no. Eliminating. Turning down. Denying service. Taking off the list. Getting rid of something or someone. Banning someone from an establishment. Also see: Good riddance to bad rubbish.
Element of surprise	If you use the element of surprise in doing something, it means you'll be surprising people. *I was going to surprise him with the new evidence and get him to confess, but that was before you told him about it. Now I've lost the element of surprise.*

Eleventh hour	Last minute.
	When someone says: *We came up with a decision at the eleventh hour,* they mean: *A decision was made at the last minute.*

It's all Greek to me. *(English.)*
This is Chinese to me. *(Hungarian.)*
I only understand "train station." *(German.)*
I don't understand any of this.

Emotional roller coaster	This has to do with being moody.
	Q. *Why did you break up with your girlfriend?*
	A. *She was on a constant emotional roller coaster! I couldn't take it any more.*
	Also: Having mood swings.
Emotionally raw	Feeling extremely vulnerable. Having been through a lot emotionally.
Empty nest	A household where the kids have all grown up and left.
	Side note: The sadness felt by the parents after the kids have grown up and left is called the: *Empty Nest Syndrome.*
End justifies the means.	This means: It's okay to do anything necessary to achieve your goal. It doesn't matter what you do, or how you do it, as long as you achieve your goal.
	Q. *Do you believe that the end justifies the means?*
	A. *No.*
	Q. *Then why did you beat the hell out of the suspect to get information?*
	A. *Because a little girl's life was in danger.*
	Q. *Then you do believe it?*
	A. *Well, I guess I do, sometimes!*

Ending up Becoming someone (or something) at the end, sometimes with a touch of disappointment.

We were planning to go to the game, but the game was canceled and we ended up going to the movies!

She was everyone's hero. Because of a mistake, however, she's going to end up in court for committing fraud.

Also see:
Turning out to be.

Enough already! Stop.
Stop it, I mean it.
That's enough, I'm serious.

Equal footing Equal treatment.
Equal opportunity.

When someone says: *I welcome a three way meeting if we're on equal footing,* they mean something like:

I'll meet with them if we're all treated equally and with mutual respect.

Keeping up with the Joneses. *(English.)*
If you see that your neighbor has shaved his beard, you'd do best to start lathering yours. *(Spanish.)*

Error in judgment A mistake.
A wrong or mistaken decision.

Q. *You say you're against corruption, but you admit that you accepted a bribe. Why?*
A. *That was a one-time error in judgment, not my policy!*

Et al And others.
And all others.

When someone says: *Send a memo to Roger, et al,* they mean something like: *Send a memo to Roger, and all of the others (related to him, or related to his case, or in his department).*

ETA	This is an abbreviation for: **E**stimated **T**ime of **A**rrival. *What is the ETA on your flight?*
Even keel **On an even keel**	Steady. In a balanced way. A condition of equal opportunity. No particular advantage in any direction.

If a toad jumps around in the daytime, it is either chasing something, or something is chasing it. *(Parts of Africa.)*

Evening the score	Retaliating. Taking revenge. Getting even, in a bad way. Q. *Do you know that Mike took over my project while I was on vacation?* A. *Well, no, but how are you going to even the score?*
Ever the ...	Always a ... *Ever the lady,* means: *Always a lady.* *Ever the gentleman,* means: *Always a gentleman.* *Ever the good listener,* means: *Always a good listener.*
Every other	Alternating. Every second one. Every second item in a series. *Every other day,* means: *One day, skip a day, then the next day, etc.* *Every other Monday, means: One Monday, skip a Monday, then the next Monday, etc.* Q. *You want me to read every book on the list?* A. *No, just every other book, okay?*
Every rose has a thorn.	Nobody is perfect. Everybody has problems. Even something that's beautiful and looks perfect has something wrong with it.

Exploding onto the scene	Appearing suddenly in a big way. *She exploded onto the scene,* means: *Suddenly everybody was talking about her.*
Extending an olive branch	Symbol of peace. A sign of wanting to have peace.
Giving an olive branch **Waving an olive branch**	A. *I think you should compromise with your partners. You should at least try.* B. *I extended an olive branch by agreeing to meet with them! Isn't that enough?* Compare to: Waving the white flag.

An absent person has his excuse. *(Arabic.)*
Gone to the judge alone, and is back happy. *(Persian.)*
There are two sides to every story.

Eyeing something	Looking at something you may want. Wanting something, or thinking about it. *I have my eye on the supervisor's job. I'm eyeing the job.*
Face the music.	You have to face life. You can't run away from life. You can't hide from the truth. You brought this upon yourself, now you have to face the consequence.
Facing headwind	Facing, seeing, or experiencing resistance. *He campaigned while facing a lot of headwind. As you know, there was a lot of resistance against him at the time.* Compare to: Having a tailwind.
Failing to do something	Not doing something. When someone says: *Meshkin failed to go on a fishing trip,* they mean: *He didn't go on the trip.*

Fair game

The object of an attack, especially when certain restrictions do not apply.

Celebrities' personal lives seem to be fair game for criticism these days.

The candidates' financial activities are fair game and open to questions and criticism.

Compare to: Open season.

Fair shot

A chance.
An opportunity.

They deserve the opportunity to prove themselves. Give them a fair shot.

Falling for someone

Falling in love with someone.

Q. *You seem very happy! What's going on?*
A. *I'm falling for Latisha, and I'm falling deep!*

Falling for something

Believing a lie, maybe due to optimism.

A. *I want to give Mitch some money. He has a good idea for a windmill project.*
B. *You're not going to fall for that, are you?!*

Fallen from the elephant's nose. *(Armenian, Persian.)*
Said about a person who acts like a snob.

Falling in line
Origin: Military

Doing as expected.
Agreeing on something.

Q. *Will they fall in line and come out of the meeting united?*
A. *I sure hope so!*

Also see:
Playing by the rules.

Falling on deaf ears

Being ignored.
Going unnoticed.
Nobody listening or paying attention.

The fire department warned them repeatedly, but the warnings fell on deaf ears and, when the wildfires came, no one was prepared.

Falling on one's sword	Resigning from one's post under pressure. Accepting responsibility or blame for a bad situation.
Falling out	Having had an argument. Going through a separation.
Falling victim	Becoming a victim. *Hundreds have fallen victim to the recent fires.*

Follow the custom or flee the country. *(Danish.)*
The countries you visit, the customs you find. *(Italian.)*
One must howl with the wolves one is among. *(Danish.)*
If you don't want to be found out, take the appearance of the people around you. *(Persian.)*
If one goes to a land where they cut off ears, one should cut off one's ears and offer them. *(Nigerian.)*
When in Rome, do as the Romans do.

Far cry	Very different. *Watching a movie at home is a far cry from going to the movies.*
Fat chance	No way. Not a chance. *A. They want you to apologize.* *B. They want ME to apologize? Fat chance. There's no way I'll apologize to them.* Also see: Chinaman's chance.
Feather in the cap	A symbol of accomplishment. *Her becoming a supervisor is another feather in her cap.*
Feeding one's habit	Enabling someone's habit. Spending money on one's addiction: Drinking, smoking, skiing, drugs, reading, traveling, etc.
Feeling free	Being comfortable. Doing what one wants to do. *I won't be going to work tomorrow. Feel free to come over and watch the game with me.*

Feeling for someone	Feeling or sharing someone's pain. Having feelings and compassion for someone.

Q. *Have you heard about the earthquake?*
A. *Yes, it's very sad! I feel for those people, and I'm gonna help them.*

Fever pitch	Out of control. Almost out of control.

Her anxiety reached fever pitch on Friday.

Related:
Beyond containment.

Fifteen minutes of fame	Easily forgotten fame. Short lived fame and celebrity, worthy of being forgettable.

Q. *Why did she subject herself to such public humiliation?*
A. *I guess she wanted to have her 15 minutes of fame.*

Background:
This expression is attributed to artist Andy Warhol, who said, "In the future, everyone will be world-famous for 15 minutes." It became a famous saying and widely used, so much so that it is commonly used, in one form or another, to refer to publicity seekers of today.

For those who can read, a dot is a letter. *(Portuguese.)*

Fig leaf	A cover for concealing an unpleasant thing.

The police chief used the story as a fig leaf for addiction issues in the city.

Fighting chance	A slight chance. A chance to win, but with difficulty.

A. *Are you going to try for the team?*
B. *No, we don't have a fighting chance.*
A. *Then I won't either.*
B. *No, you should. You can still do it, but you really have to work at it.*

Figment of one's imagination	Something imagined. Something that's not real. A. *I think I saw Elvis at the mall today.* B. *I think it was a figment of your imagination!*
Figure of speech	Using words where they don't have their usual (literal) meaning, to stress a point. Q. *Are you really going to break your brother's neck if he eats your ice cream?!* A. *Of course not. That was just a figure of speech. I love my brother!* Compare to: Rhetorical question.
Figuring something out	Finding a solution. Understanding something. Understanding how something works.
Fine print **Small print**	Details. Details in a contract. *You should always read the small print before you sign something; otherwise, you might get in trouble.*

The patient who made his doctor his heir will never get better. *(Greek.)*

Fine-tooth comb **Fine-toothed comb**	Used with *"go over"* or *"go through"* this is about being very thorough. When someone says: *I'll go over this report with a fine-toothed comb,* they mean something like: *I'll investigate it very thoroughly.* Compare to: Under scrutiny.
Finger pointing **Finger-pointing**	Blaming others. Drawing attention, mainly for blaming purposes. *There's a lot of finger-pointing going on here, and nobody is willing to take the blame.* Note: Pointing a finger at someone during an argument or while speaking is an insult.

Fire away

Begin doing something (especially talking, asking questions, shooting).

If you say: *Explain away,* you mean: *Start explaining.*

If you say: *Do you want to fire us? Then fire away,* you mean: *Start firing us.*

If you say: *It's time for questions and answers, so fire away,* you mean: *Start asking questions.*

Similar:
If he wants to appeal the case, let him appeal away.

Even monkeys may fall from trees. *(Japanese, Korean.)*
Even experts make mistakes.

Fire in the belly

Drive.
Motivation.
Excitement.

Related: Fire shut up in my bones.

Fire line

When faced with a raging fire, firefighters occasionally remove vegetation (sometimes by actually starting a controlled fire) from areas where the fire is heading. Thus, when the fire gets to these areas, there's nothing left to burn and the fire stops. These are called fire lines.

Firing on all four cylinders

Working or performing at full power.

First dibs

First choice.

When someone says: *We got our first dibs on the equipment,* they mean something like:

We get to choose first.

Also: Calling shotgun.

Also see: Having dibs on something.

First order of business

The first thing we need to do.
The first thing on the agenda.
The first thing that needs to be done.

Firsthand **First hand**	Directly. Eyewitness. Without a middleman. Q. *Do you know this firsthand?* A. *Of course! I saw it with my own two eyes.*

Paradise without people is not worth living in. *(Arabic.)*

Fishing **Fishing expedition**	Looking for something, aimlessly. Looking for information, when one isn't even sure there is any. An attempt to garnish information, sometimes by pretending just to chat in a friendly way but really having an ulterior motive to find things out. *They are hoping to find something, but they don't really know what they're looking for.* *They're just fishing. It's a fishing expedition.*
Fishing in the **wrong pond**	Doing the wrong thing. Going in the wrong direction. Doing the wrong thing in the wrong place. Q. *Do you think it's dangerous to question these guys?* A. *All I can say is, be careful. I think you're fishing in the wrong pond!* Also: Barking up the wrong tree. Tilting at the wrong windmill. Pissing in the wrong pool. (Not polite.)
Fists were flying.	They were all fighting. Fighting was going on.
Fit to be tied	Frustrated. Very angry. Not acting logically. Q. *Did you see him this morning? Wasn't he fit to be tied?* A. *You're right. I actually thought about tying him down to something!*

Fitting a mold	Having similar characteristics. Having certain common features.
	We don't all fit a mold because we're not all alike, or similar, or the same, or identical.
Flattering oneself	Giving oneself too much credit. Speaking highly of one's own achievement.
	A. I'm glad I gave a good speech! Now it's your turn.
	B. Don't flatter yourself! Who says you gave a good speech?
Floodgates opening	Going into panic. One thing causing a series of things to happen.
	I told my friend the gossip about Ann. Now the floodgates are open and she wants to know all of the gossip about everyone.
	The flood gates of anxiety opened as soon as the investors heard the announcement on the stock market problems.
	Similar: All hell breaking loose. Everything going to hell in a hand basket.

He who buys what he does not need will eventually have to sell what he needs. *(Croatian.)*

Fly by night **Fly-by-night**	Unreliable, especially with respect to businesses.
	Q. Hey boss, why don't you want to deal with these guys?
	A. Oh, I don't feel comfortable around them. They're running a fly-by-night operation.
Fly in the ointment	Something bad ruining things. An item that ruins the whole thing.
	Q. How was the interview?
	A. It went smoothly. The fly in the ointment was that, as I was leaving, I accidentally burped!

- I'm hearing complaints about you around the office. I want you to start playing ball with everyone.
- Right here?

For a definition, see:

- **Play ball.**

Fly on the wall

An insider.
A person on the inside, with inside information.
(Much like a fly on the wall that can see and hear what's going on inside the room.)

Q. *What do you think they were talking about?*
A. *Oh, I don't know! But I sure wish I was a fly on the wall when they had the meeting.*

Flying by the seat of one's pants

Not having a plan.
Getting into something using one's own judgment and not knowing quite how it will be carried out.
Spontaneously dealing with a situation without guidance or strategy or foresight.

Also see: Winging it.

He who thinks does not marry; he who marries does not think.
(Portuguese.)

Flying off the handle

Going crazy.
Losing self-control.
Becoming very angry.

He flies off the handle every time his wife says: Are you really going to wear that?

Food for thought

Something to think about.
Something worth thinking about.
Something that stimulates the mind.

Hey Ricky, here's some food for thought: Teen obesity is on the rise!

Footing the bill

Paying the bill.
Taking care of the payment.

Q. *Who's footing the bill today?*
A. *It's on me. I just got a new job. Next time, however, you'll be picking up the bill!*

Also:
Picking up the bill.
Picking up the tab.
Picking up the check.

For better or for worse	No matter what. Under good or bad conditions. *I'll stay with you for better or for worse. Whether things are good or bad. Whether we're rich or poor. Whether — Do you want me to go on?!*
For crying out loud	An expression of exasperation, as in: When someone says: *For crying out loud, don't do it,* they mean: *Please don't do it.* It can also mean any of these: *I can't understand;* *You've got to be kidding me;* *What you're doing or saying is unbelievable,* *etc.* Also: For God's sake. For Pete's sake. For heaven's sake. For goodness sake. Example: *For crying out loud, why did you do this?*

When an old man sees a snake and refuses to run, he is prepared to die. *(Parts of Africa.)*

For good	Forever.
For good measure	Additional amount to make sure. In addition to what's needed, or what's already being provided. Q. *How many pizzas did you order?* A. *We really only need five, but I ordered six for good measure.*
For one's part	As far as one is concerned. So far as one is concerned. Q. *I'll be making the reservations for the trip to Japan this summer. What about you?* A. *For my part, I'll be learning Japanese.*

For that matter	Too. Also. As far as that matter is concerned. *You're always welcome to use my car, or my boat, for that matter.*
For the life of me	An expression of exasperation. *For the life of me, I don't understand* why she's leaving*!* Also see: For crying out loud.
For the time being	For now. At this time. *I don't know about next week but, for the time being, you are grounded. Got that?*
For weeks on end	For a long time. For many weeks. Week after week. Similar: For days on end. For hours on end. For months on end.
For your eyes only	Don't tell anybody about it. No one else is allowed to see this. Also: A security term for classified information.
Forced moment	An uncomfortable or unfriendly encounter. *Of course, we said hello and had a little conversation when we ran into each other on the street. But we weren't friends! These were forced moments, really.*
Foregone conclusion	Certain. Definite. *They're laying off a lot of people, and we're not getting any contracts. I think it's a foregone conclusion that our company will go bankrupt soon.*

Four-one-one **411**	Details. Information. Telephone number for directory assistance. *What's the 411 on the nightclubs in this town?*
Freaking out	Going crazy. Getting scared. Also: Buggin', or Buggin' out. Wiggin', or Wiggin' out.
Free fall **Free-fall**	The part of the fall during a parachute jump before the parachute is opened. Also a very fast drop, as in: *The economy was in a free-fall for a while.*
Free pass	Permission to do anything, or go anywhere. *Q. What's that boy doing, skating in the hallway?* *A. He's the boss's son. He has a free pass around here.*

Fear the goat from the front, the horse from the rear, and man from all sides. *(Assyrian.)*

Free range **Free-range** **(chicken)**	A chicken or other farm animal that's raised on a farm, not in a cage, and is free to roam around. Similar: Free-range livestock.
Fringe benefit	Additional benefit. Additional advantage. Benefit in addition to regular pay. *I don't like the pay at my new job, but the fringe benefits are amazing!* *I go to this deli for the food, which is great. The view is a fringe benefit.* Also: Frosting on the cake.

From day one	From the start. From the beginning Also: From early on.

Old age does not come alone. (Greek.)

From here on in	Starting now. Starting now and forever in the future. Also: From now on. From here on out. From this moment on.
From scratch	From zero. From the get-go. From the beginning. Q. *This vacuum cleaner we'll be working on, is it an improved version of Model F3?* A. *No, it's a whole new machine. We're designing this one from scratch.* Also used when cooking with real (not partially prepared) ingredients.
Front man	An unofficial leader. A lead singer or spokesman for a musical band.
Full throated **Full-throated**	Complete and unconditional. Producing a full, loud, or rich sound. Using all of the power of one's voice. A. *The senator's wife offered full-throated support of her husband.* B. *He must be very happy to have gotten away with it again!*
FYI	This is an abbreviation for: <u>F</u>or <u>Y</u>our <u>I</u>nformation. *FYI, I'll be home late tonight.*
G **Grand**	One thousand dollars. *I paid five Gs for the antique piano. Then I had to spend another six grand to restore it!*

Gag order
Legal

An order by a judge that tells certain people not to talk about certain things.

When someone says: *I'm under a gag order,* they mean:

I can't (I'm not allowed to) talk about it.

Game of chicken

Finding out who is more of a coward in a group. A game to determine who gets scared more easily.

Get a load of this!

Look at this.
Listen to this.

Get lost!

Go.
Go away.

This is used when you don't want to talk to someone, or see them, and you're not trying to be nice about it either! The following are also used:

Beat it.
Scram.
Get out.
Piss off.
Hit the road.
Hit the road, Jack.
Get the hell out of here.
Get the f—k out of here. (Not a nice thing to say at all!)
Don't let the door hit you on the way out. (Which means: Get out, and do it fast!)

Get moving!

Start.
Move.
Hurry up.

Also:
Move it.
Get going.
Get started.
Move your butt. (Not so nice.)
Move it or lose it. (Not so nice.)
Get your rear in gear. (Not so nice.)

Get one's goat **Get someone's** **goat**	Annoying people. Making people angry. *If that's an attempt to get my goat, well, you've succeeded!* Compare to: Pushing someone's buttons. **Background:** The most likely explanation has to do with horse racing. It was a common practice to put a companion animal, mostly a goat, in the stall with a restless racehorse to help calm the horse. If someone managed to steal the goat before the race, it irritated the owner because it could result in the horse losing the race.

A word before is better than two after. *(Portuguese.)*
A fight in the beginning is better than peace in the end. *(Persian.)*
Go over the details before you agree to something.

Get outta here! **Get out of here!**	Are you joking? You must be joking! You cannot be serious! Come on, you must be kidding! Also, of course, see: Get lost!
Get to the point!	Let's get started. What is really bothering you? What is the heart of the matter? Stop giving me all these details and tell me the main idea. Let's talk about the things you really want to talk about. Also see: Cut to the chase. Compare to: Beating around the bush.
Get your mind off it.	Don't think about it.
Get your mind out of the gutter.	Stop thinking about dirty (pornographic) things.

Get-go	The very beginning.
	I knew there was something weird about her from the get-go.
	Also: From zero.
Getting (our) stories crossed	This is when different people's explanations of the same event don't match. Somebody must be mistaken, or lying!
	Also: Getting (our) stories mixed-up.
Getting (our) stories straight	This is when people, who are involved in an activity or incident, work on an alibi or story to tell the authorities. This way, if they are questioned about the incident, they won't get their stories crossed!
Getting a lump of coal	About being bad or deserving punishment. Also: Coal in one's stocking.
	Our political leaders deserve coal in their stocking this Christmas!
	Background: This goes back to a Christmas story about Santa Claus and somebody not being a good boy or girl during the year. So, instead of getting gifts and toys in their stocking, they got a stocking filled with coal.
Getting a read on something	Understanding something. Learning more about something.
	Q. *What do you think of that new guy at work?* A. *I don't know. I can't get a read on him.*
Getting a shot	Having an injection.
	Q. *Have you got your shot yet?* A. *I'm not going to. I don't believe in getting flu shots.*

Getting a shot at   Having a chance or an opportunity.

Q. *Why are you directing such a small budget movie?*
A. *This is my first shot at directing any kind of movie, and I'm not going to miss it!*

Getting a ticket   Receiving a traffic ticket.
Receiving an order to pay a penalty, or otherwise get punished.

Also:
Being cited.
Getting ticketed.
Getting a citation.

Getting a word in edgewise   Getting a chance to say something.

Q. *Why didn't you deny his accusations?*
A. *I couldn't get a word in edgewise. He wouldn't stop talking long enough to even take a breath!*

The devil knows more from being old than from being the devil. *(Spanish.)*

About the importance of age.

Getting around (doing) something   Not doing it.

Q. *Let's go hiking tomorrow, okay?*
A. *My wife wants us to visit her parents. I'll see if I can find a way to get around that. If I do, then I can go with you!*

Getting away with something   Doing something wrong and not getting caught or, if caught, not getting punished for it.

Q. *Did they catch the guy who stole your car?*
A. *No, he got away with it.*
Q. *But they caught the guy who stole your bike, right?*
A. *Yes, but he got away with it, too. I guess he was good at explaining things!*

Related: Getting away with murder!

Also see: Beating a rap.

Getting canned	Getting fired.
	When someone says: *I got canned,* they mean to say: *I got fired.*
Getting even with someone	Getting revenge on someone.
	Compare to:
	Don't get mad, get even!
	Being even with someone.
Getting in the groove	Learning the tricks.
	Getting into the flow of things.

Where there are no eagles, I am one, said the grasshopper. *(Indonesian.)*

Getting in the way	Being an obstacle.
	Slowing things down.
	Causing a slowdown by getting in the way of things.
	My dear sir, please step aside. You're getting in my way.
	Also:
	Being in the way.
	Obstructing the flow of traffic.
Getting it	Understanding it.
	Understanding the situation.
	A. *I've been telling you about my problems, but you don't get it.*
	B. *Of course I get it. You want to borrow money!*
	Also:
	Getting the idea.
	Getting the picture.
	Getting the gist of it.
Getting knocked over with a feather **Getting bowled over with a feather**	This has to do with being extremely surprised!
	He was so surprised you could have knocked him over with a feather!
	Similar: Knocked for a loop.

Getting off on the wrong foot	Having a bad start. Starting something the wrong way. Q. *How are things with you and your new assistant?* A. *We got off on the wrong foot, but I think it'll be okay.*

She tells the sun, "Don't rise. I've come out!" *(Armenian, Persian.)*
She's so beautiful!

Getting one's ears lowered	Getting a haircut.
Getting one's feathers up **Getting one's feathers ruffled**	Getting upset. When someone says: *Don't get your feathers up,* or: *Don't let it ruffle your feathers,* they mean: *Take it easy.* *Don't be upset.* *Don't let it bother you.*
Getting one's foot in the door	Finding an opportunity. Using or creating an opportunity. Getting into a company at entry level. Q. *Are you having any luck getting your book published?* A. *I don't know anyone in the business. If I could only get my foot in the door!* **Background:** This obviously has to do with door to door salesmen. Getting a foot in the door to keep it open allows you to continue your sales pitch. If the door is closed, you might as well leave.
Getting one's hopes up	Being hopeful. Having high expectations. *Don't get your hopes up. You'll be disappointed.* Compare to: Getting someone's hopes up.

Getting one's panties in a bunch	Getting nervous, upset, uptight, etc. *Don't get your panties in a bunch before you hear what I have to say!* Also see: Getting one's feathers up.
Getting one's walking papers	Getting fired. Being dismissed from a job. Getting a dishonorable discharge from the military. Being on the receiving end of a relationship breaking up. *Q. Why do you look so upset? Have you gotten your walking papers?* *A. Yes, they gave me my walking papers this morning!*
Getting out of hand	Getting out of control. *Q. Did you tell the kids to go out in the backyard?* *A. Yeah, they were running around in the house, and things were getting out of hand.*

The dead do not know the value of white sheets. *(Haitian.)*
Funerals are for those still living.

Getting over something	Overcoming something. Forgetting about it, or recovering from it. *Q. Why are you still so upset?* *A. I can't get over the fact that she cheated on me. It's still bothering me.*
Getting someone's hopes up	Giving someone hope, maybe false hope. *Q. When I finalize my next deal, I'm going to help everyone here to buy a new house.* *A. Please don't get our hopes up unless you're sure you can deliver.* Compare to: Getting one's hopes up.

Getting the best of someone	Taking over.
	My emotions got the best of me, means any of the following:
	I lost control; I wasn't logical; I wasn't thinking; I became emotional; I didn't use my head; I lost control of my emotions; etc.
	Also, in a fight, if someone says: *He got the best of me,* it means: *He did more damage to me than I did to him!*
Getting the boot	Getting fired. Being dismissed from a job.
	Also: Getting booted out of a job.
Getting the groundwork in	Doing the preliminary steps.
	I'm getting all my groundwork in for my meeting with my future father-in-law!
	Also: Planting the seeds. Laying the groundwork.
Getting the pink slip	Getting fired. Being dismissed from a job.
	Due to a bad economy, a lot of our employees are going to get pink slips this year. We're sorry to do this, but there's nothing else that we can do.
	"Pink slip" also refers to the paperwork that establishes the ownership of a vehicle.
Getting the show on the road	Starting. Getting started.
	Okay, let's get the show on the road and start the meeting. We've been waiting long enough for those two guys.
	Also: Get it on. Get the ball rolling.

At the job interview:

- Well, it looks like my friend has recommended you for a job here. He says that he has confidence in you, and he says that you can hold your own.
- My own what, sir?!

For a definition, see:

- **Holding one's own**

Getting to it	Doing it. Getting started on it.
Getting to the bottom of something	Finding out the truth about it. *We should have been more careful. If she really wants to, she can easily get to the bottom of this situation and find out everything about our plan!*
Getting under one's skin	Being irritated, as in: *Seeing him snooping around gets under my skin. I hate it!* Being obsessed (can't stop thinking of someone or something), as in: Q. *You really love her, don't you?* A. *Oh, yes, she's gotten under my skin, and there's nothing I can do about it!*
Give me a break!	Are you joking? You can't be serious! A. *They want us to work this weekend.* B. *Give me a break! We've been working weekends for three weeks straight!*
Give-and-take	Compromise. *We definitely need a little give-and-take here.* Also see: Meeting halfway.
Given	Considering, as in: *Given the present economic situation, I won't be buying a new car at this time.* Obvious, for sure, as in: *Well, we know the murderer is a man! That's a given.* When someone says: *It's a given,* they mean: *Of course.* *That's a part of it.* *Well, everybody knows that.*

Giving a black eye *Origin: Sports*	Bringing shame. Ruining a reputation. Disgracing someone or something. Q. *Do you know that some of our drivers are rude to the passengers?* A. *If that's true, it's going to give our business a black eye. We should stop it.*

When the cat is missing, the mice dance. *(Italian.)*
When the cat is not home, the mice dance on the table. *(Dutch.)*
The mountains are high, and the emperor is far away. *(Chinese.)*
When the boss is out, there's a holiday at the shop. *(Portuguese.)*
About abusing the opportunity in the absence of authority.

Giving a helping hand **Lending a helping hand**	Helping. Helping out. *The earthquake victims need a helping hand. Please help them before it's too late.*
Giving a leg up **Getting a leg up**	Giving or getting help. Giving or getting a head start. Q. *You think he can do the report on his own?* A. *Yes, but if you give him a leg up, I would really appreciate it.*
Giving a once-over	Giving someone a thorough beating, as in: *Give him a once-over, and maybe he'll talk!* Cleaning a place quickly, but not necessarily thoroughly, as in: *Please give the dining room a once-over before the guests arrive.* Giving a situation a quick, but thorough, examination, as in: *Let's give this proposal a once-over before the meeting tomorrow.* Looking at someone to see if you could notice or learn something about them, as in: *We gave him a once-over, and decided he wasn't the burglar.*

Giving chase	Chasing. Pursuing. Running after.
Giving one's all	Doing something the best way that one can. Q. *Do you think she will make a good effort?* A. *She's doing this for her daughter. I know that she's going to give it her all.* Also: Giving it one's all. Giving (it) one's best.
Giving someone a run for their money	Making one earn one's money. Making one work for one's money or position. When someone says: *They gave me a run for my money,* they mean something like: *They didn't just give it to me. They made me work hard for it.* *If two people are in a close competition for something, we can say that the one who lost gave the winner a run for his money.*
Giving someone a rundown.	Giving someone the details. Telling someone (in detail) what happened.
Giving someone some room	Leaving someone alone. Moving away from someone and letting them think in peace. *Let's give him some room. He needs to think (decide, travel, etc.) by himself for a while.* Also: Giving someone space.
Giving someone the slip	Losing someone in a crowd. Slipping away from someone deliberately. Getting away from someone in a way so as not to let them notice you doing it. *We were following her up close, but somehow she managed to give us the slip. We can't see her any more.*

Giving the finger
Raising the middle finger

This expression, which is very rude, has to do with making an insulting gesture by showing the middle finger. It's usually done when a verbal insult cannot be heard because you are in a moving vehicle, or you are far away from the other person, or the place is too noisy.

When someone says: *Ana gave him the finger,* they mean something like:
She raised her middle finger at him.

Also:
Flipping the bird.

High trees catch lots of wind. *(Dutch.)*
The tallest blade of grass is the first to be cut. *(Assyrian.)*
The nail that sticks out gets hammered down. *(Japanese.)*
The head of the rooster that crows out of time will be cut off. *(Turkish.)*

Important persons, or those who stand out from the rest, are in more danger than others.

Giving the fish eye

Staring in surprise.
Turning your head and giving a startled look, with usually only one eye being visible.

We were walking and talking when I made a comment about her father. She turned around and gave me the fish eye, obviously surprised and not knowing why I had said that.

Giving the third degree

Interrogating someone.
Asking too many questions.
Asking someone many questions all at once.

Why are you giving me the third degree? Don't you trust me?

Giving two winks

Paying attention.
Giving importance.

She doesn't seem to give two winks about what I think.

I don't really give two winks to whether you are on time or not.

Glass ceiling	An unwritten obstacle or restriction, especially affecting minorities. A limit as to how much someone can make financially, or how high in the corporate world one can reach.
	She surprised everyone by breaking the glass ceiling and becoming the company's first female president.
Gloves coming off *Sports*	Getting ready to fight. Situation getting worse. Expecting fighting to begin.
	Q. *It's a nasty campaign. Do you think gloves will be coming off?* A. *As far as I'm concerned, the gloves are off already!*
Go figure!	I can't understand it! Can you believe that? See if it makes sense! See if you can understand it. Who would have expected that? See if you can figure that one out!
	Q. *He was working under you, now he's your boss! How did that happen?* A. *Yeah, I don't know. Go figure!*

One will take someone to the spring and bring them back thirsty. (Armenian, Persian.)

A very cunning person.

Go off half-cocked *Origin: Military*	Act without thinking, or too quickly.
	I understand you're angry and you want to do something, but please don't go off half-cocked.
	Note: When used alone, *half-cocked* means *very drunk*.
Go with it **Run with it**	Do it! It's a good idea. Okay, do it that way.

God bless someone's soul This expression is used as a sign of respect, or a small prayer, when talking about someone who is not alive anymore.

My mother, God bless her soul, was a nice lady.

It is also used after you insult someone with the hope of reducing the rudeness of the insult.

You're such an idiot, God bless your soul!
Sue is a lousy painter, God bless her soul!

Only mountains never meet. *(French.)*
Mountain won't meet mountain, but man will meet man. *(Turkish.)*
A mountain won't catch up to a mountain, but a person will catch up to a person. *(Persian.)*

Be nice to people on your way up because you might meet them on your way down.

Going someone
Going something Doing things in line, or associated, with someone or something.

When someone says: *A famous soul singer plans to go country,* they mean something like: *She wants to do country music.*

When someone says: *Voters are going Republican,* they mean something like: *Voters are starting to vote for Republican candidates.*

When someone says: *Companies are going green,* they mean something like: *They are doing things in line with saving natural resources.*

Going a long way Having a big impact.
Making a big difference.

A little humor goes a long way.
Showing some kindness goes a long way.
A bit of patience goes a long way with her.
Pretending you're human can go a long way.
Your dollar goes a long way in this store, which means: *You can buy more with your money.*

Going all the way	Finishing the job. Doing the whole thing.
Going at something	Doing something. Doing something persistently.

> Q. *Where's everyone? I told them to start working on the new project.*
> A. *They're going at it, sir!*

Going into a tailspin	Losing control. Failing in a big way.

> *Skyrocketing prices have sent the economy into a tailspin.*

> *My wife's sudden decision to leave me is the reason I am in this emotional tailspin.*

Going into overdrive	Becoming very active suddenly. Working hard, then working very hard suddenly.

> *Lately it feels like my desire to sleep has gone into overdrive.*

When pigs fly. *(English.)*
If the crow turns white. *(Filipino.)*
When hell freezes over. *(English.)*
If you see behind your ear. *(Persian.)*
When willows bear grapes. *(Croatian.)*
When chickens will have teeth. *(French.)*
When sabots begin to flower. *(Bulgarian.)*
Human out of a mullah, almond out of an oak tree. *(Azerbaijani.)*
 A reference to something that will never happen.

Going off the deep end **Jumping off the deep end**	Losing one's mind. Becoming irrational. Losing touch with reality. Acting in an angry manner.

> A. *I know I haven't known her long, but I love her. We want to get married and go traveling.*
> B. *Well, I'm happy for you, but use your head! Don't be going off the deep end!*

Going off without a hitch	Taking place without a problem. Happening without anything going wrong.

> Q. *How was your interview?*
> A. *Great! It went off without a hitch.*

One swallow doesn't make a spring. *(Czech.)*
Spring will not come with one flower. *(Armenian.)*
One cuckoo bird does not bring the spring. *(Greek.)*
With a single flower, there won't be spring. *(Persian.)*
One swallow does not a summer make. *(English, Norwegian, Slovak.)*
   One needs more than one indication to draw conclusions.

Going out of one's way	Doing more than expected. Doing something for somebody else even if it's inconvenient or takes extra effort.

She's a nice lady. She goes out of her way to help others.

Similar:
Going the extra mile.
Bending over backwards.
Going beyond the call of duty.

Going out on a limb	Taking a risk. Putting oneself at risk. Getting into a dangerous situation.

I'm going out on a limb for you. Are you sure we won't get in trouble?

Going postal	Suddenly becoming angry or violent.

> Q. *Did you want to see me about my performance review, boss?*
> A. *Yes. But first I want you to promise me that you won't go postal when we go over it!*

Background:
This term became popular after a number of incidents in which postal service employees, for a variety of reasons, became violent and started shooting and killing their co-workers and others.

Going public **Becoming public**	Not being a secret any more. Everybody knowing about the issue. *Her money problems have gone public and now everybody knows that she was in jail for stealing.* Also: Out in the open. Public knowledge.
Going south **Going downhill**	Going badly. Not on a positive note. On the road to destruction. Q. *How's the market doing?* A. *Not very well. Actually, stocks have been going south for a while.* **Background:** Graphically speaking, "going down," as opposed to "going up," is one way of saying whether things look "bad" or "good." Using "south" and "north" is another way of referring to the same thing.

The blacksmith's mare walks without horseshoes. *(Czech.)*
In a blacksmith's house, all knives are wooden. *(Spanish.)*
About those who take care of other people's problems but neglect their own family.

Going through **with something**	Completing an action. Doing something after some reluctance or hesitation. Q. *Did you know that your sister was going to drive the car into the pool?* A. *Well, she had talked about it, but I didn't know she would actually go through with it!*
Going to bat for someone *Origin: Sports*	Giving assistance. Coming to someone's defense. *After the campaign was over, Hillary started going to bat for Obama.* Also: Sticking up for someone.

Going to the dogs	Getting ruined. Breaking down. Q. *Have you been to the downtown area recently? It's in bad shape.* A. *Forget about downtown. It's gone to the dogs. The whole place is falling apart!* Also: In ruins. Going downhill.

The shroud has no pockets. *(Turkish.)*
The last shirt has no pockets. *(German.)*
The safe does not follow the hearse. *(Haitian.)*
  You can't take material possessions with you when you die.

Going to town	Doing something vigorously, as in: *She really went to town on the competition preparation, didn't she?* Spending a lot of money, as in: *I'm cashing my paycheck and going to town. Watch me!*
Going under	Failing. Sinking. Losing everything. Q. *Is it true that your company is going under?* A. *Yes, it is! We're going bankrupt and laying everyone off.*
Gold-digger **Gold digger**	A person who gets romantically involved with someone for their wealth and/or status, regardless of age. Compare to: Trophy wife. Starter wife.
Golden years	The time of life usually after retirement. The time of life approximately between 60 and 80 years old.

Gone awry!	When you say: *Something has gone awry,* you mean:
	There's something wrong. *Something has gone wrong.* *Something bad has happened.*
Gonna	This is a slang abbreviation for: Going to.
	When someone says: *He's gonna study today,* they mean: *He's going to study today.*
Good riddance (to bad rubbish)	Being happy to be rid of something or someone.
	I was about to throw him out but, fortunately, he left on his own. Good riddance!
	Compare to: Eighty-sixing.

If marriage were a good thing, it wouldn't need witnesses.
(Portuguese.)

Goody two-shoes	A person who thinks of himself or herself as being better than others. A female who is too proper in every respect, to the point of making everybody sick and tired.
	Note: Calling someone a *goody two-shoes* can be used as an insult.
	Similar: Goody-goody.
Goose is cooked!	There's no hope.
	When someone says: *Your goose is cooked,* they mean something like:
	You're in big trouble. *You've been caught doing something wrong and you are going to pay the consequences.*
	Harry wasn't supposed to stop to bet at the racetrack on the way home, but he did, and his wife found out about it. When he gets home, his goose is going to be cooked!

- Is he trying to make ends meet, Dad?
- I guess you could say that!

For a definition, see:

- **Making ends meet**

GOP	This is an abbreviation for:
G.O.P.	The **G**rand **O**ld **P**arty.
	It refers to the Republican Party in the U.S.
Grace period	A time after a deadline during which one will not be charged a penalty for being late.
	When someone says: *The grace period for paying your electric bill is five days,* they mean something like: *If you pay your electric bill within five days after it is due, you will not have to pay a penalty.*
Grace under fire	Always being cool. Being calm, even under pressure. Being graceful even under enemy fire.
Graveyard shift	Late night or after-midnight work shift.
	Compare to: Swing shift.
Gravy train	A source of easy money. An unearned supply of money.
	A. *Lately, there hasn't been any money coming in from my stock dividends because the market has been so bad.* B. *So, the gravy train stopped then. I'm sorry!*
Gray area	An area or concept that's not clearly defined. A subject that's not easy to make a decision on, one way or another.
	Q. *What's your position on stem cell research?* A. *I don't really know which way to go. It's one of those gray areas.*
	Opposite: Cut-and-dry. Black-and-white.
Grease monkey	A mechanic. An auto mechanic. Anybody whose job requires them to get their hands dirty, particularly with grease or oil.

Green light   Permission to go or to start something.

We've gotten the green light from the city engineer. We can now go ahead and get started on the office building project.

Green with envy   Very jealous.

You should have seen her looking at my dress. She turned green with envy, maybe even greener than my dress!

If you enter the Turkish bath, you will sweat! (Turkish.)
If you can't take the heat, stay out of the kitchen. (English.)
If you work in the slaughterhouse, you'll get blood on you. (Haitian.)
If you can't handle the stress, then don't take on a tough job.

Grinding halt   A complete stop due to a major failure. A work stoppage due to a major failure, mechanical or otherwise.

Production at our manufacturing company came to a grinding halt when we couldn't receive additional orders.

Ground zero   The place where things begin. The place where things are occurring.

Q. Where are we right now?
A. We're at ground zero of civilization. This is where it all began, I guess!

Grounded   Not allowed to do fun things, as in:

My son's grounded. He can't go to the movies for a while as a punishment.

Not allowed to be used, as in:

The airplanes are grounded. They're not allowed to fly until the landing gear problem is corrected.

A regular person, as in:

Our boss seems to be grounded. He seems to be a level-headed person who hasn't forgotten his humble beginnings.

Growing pains

The pains kids feel in their bones as they are growing.
Problems and difficulties associated with children growing up.
Typical problems that any organization, place, etc., experiences while growing or expanding.

Our start-up business is experiencing growing pains, as we attempt to meet increased customer demand.

Guilt by association

The assumption that, because you know somebody, or spend time with them, you are alike in every respect. It typically has a negative connotation.

A. *Everyone thinks I'm an artist because I'm helping you with your art show!*
B. *Yes, my friend. You are guilty by association!*

Hair trigger
Hair-trigger

A very sensitive or easily started thing.

A *hair-trigger apparatus* sets itself off easily.

A person with *hair-trigger temper* gets angry very easily.

A *hair-trigger political situation* refers to an explosive political atmosphere.

Hairpin turn

A very sharp turn.
A 180-degree turn.
A complete change.

Starting in 2005, life took a hairpin turn for me and my situation changed completely.

Coming back with Hunain's shoes. *(Arabic.)*
Coming back with arms longer than legs. *(Persian.)*
Coming back without success.

Half a chance

A chance.
An opportunity.
Time for something to work.

Give him half a chance. Take it easy on him.

Half-assed	This phrase is not a polite thing to say, but it means:
	Sloppy.
	Incomplete.
	Incompetent.
	Not done with professionalism.
	A *half-assed job* is an incomplete or poorly done job, especially by someone lazy, or if they are not taking time to do things properly.

Habit is the body's skin. *(Swahili.)*
The belly dancer dies, and her waist is still moving. *(Arabic.)*
First leaves the soul of a person and then his quirks. *(Greek.)*
The trumpet player dies, and his finger is still playing. *(Arabic.)*

Habits are difficult to break.

Hand holding	Lacking objectivity, as in:
Hand-holding	*There's been a lot of hand holding around here. They're letting their friendship affect their decisions.*
	Providing support, as in:
	This is her first time away from home. She may need some hand holding.
Hand me down	Used items, especially clothing.
Hand-me-down	Q. *Hey, that's a nice jacket. Is it new?*
	A. *No. It's a hand-me-down from my brother.*
	Also:
	Second-hand.
Hand over fist	Fast.
Hand-over-fist	Quickly.
Hand-over-foot	*Before the recession, everybody was making money hand over foot.*
Handing it to someone	When someone says: *I've got to hand it to you,* they mean something like:
	I really have to give you credit.
	You did a good job, and I admire you for it.
	I appreciate the great job that you've done.

Handing over	Delivering or surrendering someone or something to someone else.
	Q. What did you do with the shoplifter? *A. We handed him over to the police.*
	Q. Are we going to do the bridge project now that we're done with the research? *A. No. They used us to do the calculations, but then they handed the project over to our competitor!*
Handling with kid gloves **Treating with kid gloves**	Handling carefully. Treating with respect. Handling in a gentle manner. Trying not to disturb the original idea.
	Listen. A lady will be coming here today. She represents the board of directors and should be handled with kid gloves!
	Sometimes the term *white gloves* is used, which is a reference to performing a white-glove inspection of equipment in sensitive areas, or any inspection where dust would show on a white glove.
	Girls and boys, these machines are optical equipment. Give them the white-glove treatment.
Hands on experience	Actual experience.
	He's a good manager. He has had plenty of hands-on experience.
Hanged for a sheep as a lamb	This is short for *Might as well be hanged for a sheep as for a lamb,* which means:
	If you're going to get in trouble for stealing a small amount anyway, you might as well risk it and steal bigger things because the punishment is the same.
	If you're going to do something, do it fully. Don't hold back. Go for the best.

Continued on the next page.

Hanged for a sheep as a lamb	*Continued from the previous page.* Compare to: In for a penny, in for a pound. **Background:** This expression has its roots in theft, and the penalty for it, in the old days. It basically says, if you're going to be hanged for stealing a lamb, you might as well risk it and steal a sheep, for which you'll also be hanged!
Hanged, drawn, and quartered	Gone through a lot of tough times and hardship. Compare to: Through the wringer. **Background:** This refers to a method of execution that was practiced in England and some other European countries. Mainly it was carried out against men convicted of treason, and consisted of hanging the convicted person until nearly dead, then dragging him to another place, and then cutting him into pieces while he was still alive.
Hanging (up) one's hat	Settling down. Residing somewhere. *I decided to hang up my hat in San Diego a long time ago.*
Hanging by a thread **Hanging on by a thread**	Not being in a strong (or stable) position. When something is barely holding together. Being in a situation where you rely on uncertain circumstances. *The union bosses are hanging (on) by a thread and could lose (or fail, or get destroyed, etc.) very easily at any moment.*
Hanging in there	Not giving up or losing hope. Continuing to do what one is doing. *Q. Hi, how are you? How is life treating you?* *A. Well, I'm hanging in there.* When someone says: *Hang in there, Eduardo,* they mean: *Eduardo, keep it up. Don't give up.*

Hanging on someone's coattail **Riding (on) someone's coattail**	Getting a free ride to success. Trying to benefit from associating with someone else who is at the top, or rising quickly to the top.

> Q. *Have you noticed how the new manager's coattail is getting longer?*
> A. *Sure. Ever since he married the chairman's daughter, everybody's trying to hang on to it!*

At a deaf man's door, get in through the window. *(Greek.)*
At a deaf man's door, knock as much as you can. *(Greek.)*

> *Some people ignore any advice or guidance.*
> *Use any means to get through to them.*

Hanging on someone's every word	Listening with intensity. Listening to, or watching, someone carefully.

When you say *They're hanging on his every word,* you mean: *They're taking his words and actions very seriously,* or: *They're intently thinking about everything he says, or does.*

Similar: Hanging on someone's every move.

Hanging out to dry	Letting someone take the blame. Leaving someone on his (or her) own. Abandoning someone who is in need of help.

Note:
As this is done by people who know each other, the person who's left behind feels betrayed.

> Q. *Why are you so upset with me?*
> A. *You left me hanging out to dry. You didn't even TRY to help.*

Also: Leaving someone behind.

Hanging up one's gloves *Origin: Sports*	Retiring. Quitting. Giving up.

Also:
Hanging up one's fiddle (or one's sword).

Happy as a pig in mud	Very happy.
Happy camper	A happy person. A person who is fun to be with. A person who is in a joyful state of mind.
Hard dog to keep on the porch	Difficult to control. Someone who has his (or her) own agenda. *A. I hear you're having difficulty with Mike.* *B. Yes! He's a hard dog to keep on the porch.*
Hard to swallow **Hard pill to swallow**	Unbelievable. Difficult to accept. *You're telling me a fantastic story! It's a hard pill to swallow. I can't believe your explanation.* *They've lost their jobs, and now taxes are being raised, too. This is hard for them to swallow.*
Hat in hand	Hoping for (or expecting) a favor, sympathy, charity, etc. *I turned him down at first, but when I realized that nobody else wanted to buy my house, I went back to him, hat in hand, hoping that he would still be interested.* **Background:** The origin has to do with the fact that people begging for money usually collect the donations using their hat.

Where they pluck turkeys, chickens don't laugh. *(Haitian.)*

Have another thing coming	This is about: Being mistaken. Finding out very soon how wrong one is. Also: Have got another thing coming. When someone says: *If you think this is it, then you've got another thing coming,* they mean something like: *You're quite mistaken if you think that this is the end!*

Have it coming
Deserving something.
(This has a negative connotation.)

When someone says: *She had it coming,* they mean something like:

She deserved it, or
It was her own fault, or
She should have expected it, or
She shouldn't be complaining, etc.

Compare to:
Serves one right!

Have one's cake and eat it, too
When you say: *You can't have your cake and eat it, too,* you mean something like:

You can't do both;
It's either this or that;
You can't have it both ways;
You can't always have everything; etc.

Out of the frying pan into the fire. *(English.)*
Came out of the pothole, fell into the well. *(Persian.)*
Out from the tiger's mouth, into the crocodile's mouth. *(Indonesian.)*
You may get out of one problem but
then find yourself facing a bigger problem.

Having a ball
Having a good time.
Being in a joyful mood.

Q. Did you go to the company party last night?
A. Oh, yes. It was great. We had a ball.

Having a beef with someone
Having a problem, disagreement, or argument with someone.

Q. Do you have a beef with me? (Or: Have you got some beef with me?)
A. No, sir. I just have a question!

Beef also means something of value, or substance, as in:
Hey, Joe! I've been going over your proposal, but I don't see anything of value in it. Where's the beef?

Having a bone to pick	Wanting to clarify something. Having an issue or wanting to raise an issue with someone over something they did or said that is upsetting to you or confusing to you.

Q. *Why did you start arguing with him? He was just standing there.*
A. *I had a bone to pick with him. He owed me money from before.*

A deceased person, much prayed for, goes straight to hell. *(Portuguese.)*   *Evil men have big funerals.*

Having a chip on one's shoulder	Being in a fighting mood. Looking for a fight, or wanting to be challenged.

When someone says: *He has a chip on his shoulder,* they mean something like:

He thinks he's better than anybody;
He'd love to be challenged and get into a fight.

Having a cow	Being very upset, angry, agitated, etc., about something.

Having a lot on one's plate	Having a lot to do. Having a lot of things to deal with.

Q. *Sergio, do you think you can also handle the hotel reservations for us?*
A. *I have a lot on my plate right now. I don't think I can take on any new responsibilities!*

Having a mouth	Being vulgar. Talking to people in a rude way.

She has a mouth on her, means: *She talks to people in a rude way.*

Similar: Back-talking.
          Talking back.

Having a nose for something	Being good at something. Understanding something, or knowing a lot about it.

I'm going to ask my brother to help me to buy a painting. He has a good nose for these things.

Having a problem with	Not liking (or accepting) someone or something.
	When someone says: *Do you have a problem with that?* they mean: *Don't you like it?*
	Note: Depending on the way it is said, this simple question may sound like a threat!
Having a say (in something)	Being involved (in something). Being in a position of authority (about it). Being allowed to say something (about it).
	Opposite: Having no say (in something).
Having a sense of humor	Being funny. Appreciating something humorous. Understanding comical words or situations.
	When someone says: *Olga has a sense of humor,* they mean:
	She's funny, or She understands my jokes, or She appreciates the comical things in life.
	When someone says: *Katrina doesn't have a sense of humor,* they mean:
	Katrina takes things too seriously.
Having a smooth ride	Nothing going wrong. Everything going as planned.
	Q. How was the meeting? *A. Oh, we had a smooth ride. (Or: It was a smooth ride.)*
Having a tailwind	Having help. Having assistance.
	When someone says: *He arrived with a tailwind,* they mean something like:
	He had some help getting here, or He had help before he even got here.
	Compare to: Facing headwind.

At the manager's office:

- John, I don't want to keep hearing complaints about your attitude, and I hope this is the last time. Are we going to be on the same page from now on?
- I don't know, sir. Do you think we'll fit?

For a definition, see:

- **On the same page**
- **On the same wavelength.**

Having a take on something	Having an opinion. Having a different perspective.

> Q. *Our new principal is really good! What do you think?*
> A. *I have a different take on her decisions than you do.*

Having a voice Not having a voice	Having a way of communicating with others. Having a way of telling others about one's activities or ideas.

I don't have a voice, means something like:

I have no weight.
It's like I'm invisible.
When I talk, people ignore what I say.
People don't know about me or my ideas.
I have no way of telling people how I feel.

I'm dead and buried in the countryside. *(Hungarian.)*
I'm busy. Don't disturb me.

Having a way with things	Having a special talent to do certain things. Having a unique way of dealing with certain things.

> A. *Kids love your wife and they always behave around her!*
> B. *I know. She has a way with kids.*

Having all (of) one's ducks in a row	Being very organized. Having one's facts, paperwork, etc., in order.

I have all (of) my ducks in a row, finally, and can proceed with the case.

Having an agenda	Having something other than the obvious in mind. Doing things for reasons other than what is announced.

> A. *I don't know why Fred is suddenly interested in helping the poor!*
> B. *He has a personal agenda. It's not as if he is suddenly a caring man!*

Having an axe to grind	Having a grudge. Being unhappy or upset with someone or about something. *He has an axe to grind with his ex wife.* Also see: Holding a grudge.
Having an earful **Getting an earful**	Having a lot to hear. (Positive.) Getting lectured about something. (Negative.) Used in a positive way: *There were great speakers at the meeting today! We sure got an earful.* Used in a negative way: A. *Bob, you marked up the papers wrong! You were supposed to use a red pen!* B. *I know! I know! I've already gotten an earful about it from three other people!*
Having an edge	Having an advantage. *You should be more careful because she has an important edge over you.*
Having baggage **Coming with baggage**	Having emotional problems. Having kids or other dependents. Having some negative characteristics. Having a lot of problems in the past that you don't want to deal with. Having been in a lot of troublesome relationships with the opposite sex Q. *So, are you going to marry this guy you've been dating?* A. *I'd love to, but it's not simple and I have to think about it. He has a lot of baggage!*
Having catching up to do	When you say: *They have a lot of catching up to do,* you mean something like: *They're behind in their work.* *They haven't seen each other for a long time and will have a lot to talk about.*

Having company   Not being alone.

When you say: *We have company,* you could mean something like:

We're not alone.
Someone's here.
We have guests.
The police are listening!

I have an aunt who plays the guitar. *(Spanish.)*
What is the connection with Alexander's mustache? *(Armenian.)*
What does that have to do with the price of tea in China? *(English.)*
I'm coming from town, and you are talking about the peak of Salamina Island. (Greek.).
What does fire in Rameshwar have to do with firefighting in Someshwar? *(Indian.)*

About lack of communication or when the problem and solution don't match.

Having currency   Being effective.
Having monetary value.
Having value or importance.

Q. Do you think we should bring Soraya with us?
A. Yes. Having her presence is like having currency.

Also see:
Carrying weight.

Having dibs on something   Having an option on something.

I have dibs on that, means something like:

It's mine.
I get to use it.
I have an option on that.
I will have first choice because I told everybody that I wanted it.

Also see:
First dibs.

Having empathy   Having understanding.
Feeling and understanding other people's pain.

Having guts	Having courage. Not being afraid. When someone says: *Toshiro has guts*, they mean something like: *He's brave.* *He takes risks.* *He speaks out.* *He's not afraid.* *He says what's on his mind.* Also: Being gutsy.
Having in store	Having in possession. Having something planned or prepared for the future. (Could be negative or positive.) A. *I wonder what the economy has in store for us this year, raises or lay offs!* B. *I'll tell you in a few months.* Related: What's in store for us?

The grass is greener on the other side. *(Danish, English, French.)*
The neighbor's pan smells better then the pan at home. *(Maltese.)*
The jasmine flowers in the backyard don't have any fragrance. *(Indian.)*
                    People are never satisfied with what they have.

Having issues	Having problems with something or someone. Q. *Is there something going on between your teams?* A. *They have some issues with us, but we're working to resolve everything soon.*
Having legs	Having credibility to stand on its own. *If a story has legs, it means that it's supported by facts and will probably be talked about for a long time.* Q. *So, do you think the Madoff story has legs?* A. *Well, it sure looks like it. Too many people have been affected.*

Having long teeth	When someone says: *This (discussion) has got long teeth,* they mean: *The discussion has gone on for a long time, much longer than it should have.*

Compare to :
Having teeth.

He who laughs last laughs the loudest. *(English.)*
He who laughs last laughs best. *(English, Dutch.)*
Don't skin the bear before it's been shot. *(Danish.)*
They count the chickens at the end of autumn. *(Persian.)*
Don't sell the hide until you've shot the bear. *(Norwegian.)*
Don't count your chickens before they hatch. *(English, Danish.)*
Don't sell the bear's skin before you've killed it. *(French, Spanish.)*
Don't act as if you have something until you really do.

Having no idea   Having NO knowledge (on the subject of conversation).

Q. *What will you do now?*
A. *I have no idea. I really don't know.*

Q. *How does this work?*
A. *I have no idea. I don't know anything about it. I don't understand it.*

Also:
Beats me.
Search me.
You got me.
I don't know.
That's beyond me.
I don't have a clue.
I'm drawing a blank.
It's beyond comprehension.
Your guess is as good as mine.

Having none of it   Not taking it or accepting it.

A. *Simon says if you apologize, she'll talk to you again.*
B. *Apologize to Simon? I'll have none of that. I refuse to apologize to him.*

Having one's fingers crossed **Keeping one's fingers crossed**	Warding off evil. (A superstitious belief.) Hoping for something to happen or not to happen. (Wishful thinking.) *I just had an interview. I had my fingers crossed most of the time throughout the interview.* Note: Some school kids believe crossing their fingers behind their back while making a verbal promise means that they don't have to honor their promise! Also: Crossed fingers. Crossing one's fingers.
Having one's work cut out	Someone having plenty of difficult work to do. A. *The director has his work cut out for him.* B. *He sure has. He has all of these different and complex problems to address.*
Having second thoughts	Having doubts, as in: *I know that I said I would go on the trip with you guys, but now I'm having second thoughts about it. Sorry, I won't be going!* Compare to: Second thought. On second thought.
Having someone do something	Making, telling, ordering, arranging for, or asking someone to do something. *I'll have my secretary call you.* *Please have your brother come to my office.*
Having someone's back	Watching someone's back for support. Protecting the area where one cannot see. Supporting or protecting someone in any way. Defending someone if someone else says something negative about them, especially if they're not there to defend themselves. A. *Hey, Joe, I don't know if I should do this?!* B. *Go ahead. I have your back. I will help you, if necessary.*

Having something to say for oneself	Offering an excuse or explanation.
	When you say: *What do you have to say for yourself?* you mean:
	What's your explanation? *What do you have to say in your own defense?*
Having teeth	Having power and authority.
	The new civilian government has a lot of good ideas but, without the support of the military, it has no teeth to actually be able to do anything.
	Compare to : Lacking teeth. Having long teeth.
Having the last word	Making the final decision, as in:
	Q. *Are you going to buy that dream car of yours?* A. *I can dream as much as I want but, as you know, my wife will have the last word!*
	Saying the last statement that is uttered in an argument, as in:
	Whenever we argue, Suzie always has to have the last word!
	Compare to: Last word.

Out of the rain and into the eaves. *(German.)*
Fell from the sky, got stuck in a date palm. *(Indian.)*
> *You may get out of one problem but then find yourself facing a bigger problem.*

Head butting **Butting heads**	Power struggle. Hitting someone's head with one's forehead. Disagreeing with someone intensely about how something should be done or how things should be run.
	Q. *Why is there blood all over your shirt?* A. *I head-butted Abraham. It turns out that his head is a lot harder than mine!*

Head on a platter   When someone says: *I want Larry's head on a platter,* they mean something like:
I hate Larry;
I want him to fail;
I wish someone would hurt him, etc.

This saying could also be used jokingly!

Background:
This is a reference to John the Baptist being beheaded. His head was then brought to the king on a platter!

He is two spoons in all liquids. *(Hungarian.)*
He sticks his nose in everything.

Head over heels
Head-over-heels   Crazy or wild about something, usually in reference to being in love.

I'm head-over-heels in love with you, baby!

Head start
Head-start   An advantage (over others) at the beginning of a task.

We're so confident in our team that we'll give you a five-minute head-start. Go ahead. We'll wait five minute before we get going.

Heads will roll.
Heads are going to roll.   People will get in trouble.
Someone will pay for this.
Employees will lose their job.
Players will get cut from the team.
Someone will take responsibility for this.

If the team keeps losing, heads will roll.

If we don't get a new contract, heads are going to roll.

Hearing someone out   Listening to someone's side of the story.
Listening to ALL of what someone has to say.

When someone says: *Hear me out,* they could mean any of the following:
Let me finish.
Listen to what I have to say.
Let me tell you my side of the story.

Heart being in the right place

Being a good person.
Having good intentions.

Q. *What do you think of your noisy neighbor?*
A. *I don't know him well, but I think his heart is in the right place. I don't think he realizes how much the sound escapes from his walls.*

Heart-to-heart

Frank.
Private.
Honest.
Intimate.
A conversation that has the above characteristics.

Q. *Can we talk about something personal but very important?*
A. *Sure. Let's have a heart-to-heart!*

Heavens to Betsy!

This is an exclamation of shock or surprise.

Oh my god!
Good heavens!
Oh, my goodness!

Also: Heavens to Murgatroyd!

It's darkest under the lamp stand. *(Korean.)*
Men are blind in their own case. *(Vietnamese.)*
The camel does not see her own hump. *(Greek.)*
No one sees his own hunchback. *Jewish/Yiddish*
The darkest place is under the candlestick. *(Czech.)*
It's easier to see the straw in someone else than the beam in oneself. *(Spanish.)*
   We see other people's faults but fail to see our own.

Heavy handed

Heavy-handed

Tough.
Someone who uses more force than necessary to persuade others.

Also:
Strong-armed.

He'd sooner talk to them than fight.

He prefers to talk to them first, not fight.

Heebie-jeebies A creepy, strange feeling.

Thinking about it gives me the heebie-jeebies.

Also:
The creeps.
Creepy crawlies.

I'm speaking to you, but listen, oh neighbor. *(Arabic.)*
Door, I'm speaking to you. Wall, you listen. *(Persian.)*
I speak to you, my daughter, and let you hear, my daughter-in-law.
(Arabic.)

Hell bent Determined.

Hell-bent *She's hell-bent on firing me. Her mind is made up. I'm telling you, she's very serious about it.*

Hell breaking loose Nothing working.

All hell breaking Complete state of confusion happening.

loose
Q. *Do you think the government is doing okay?*
A. *I guess so. But if something goes wrong, all hell's going to break loose!*

Hell, no! No! (With emphasis, but impolite.)

Also:
No chance.
Not in your life.
Not a chance in hell.

Here's the thing! Let me explain.
Here's the story.
Here's something you should know.

Hill of beans Not worth much.
Of little or no value.

Q. *How much is it? Is it valuable?*
A. *No, it doesn't amount to a hill of beans!*

Also:
It won't amount to anything.
It isn't worth sh-t. (Not very polite.)
It isn't worth a rat's ass. (Not very polite.)

Hindsight is 20-20.	It's easy to complain after the fact. If you knew then what you know now, your choice would be clear. It's easy to make the right decision AFTER things have happened.

A. *If I hadn't sold my ocean-view house last year, I'd be a millionaire today!*
B. *Yes, hindsight is twenty-twenty!*

Hit and run *Sports*	A play in baseball. Compare to: Hit-and-run.

Hit it! **Hit me!**	When someone says: *Hit me, or hit it,* they could mean any of the following:

Do it.
Start it.
I'm ready.
Tell me about it.
Pour me a drink.
Deal me another card.

Also:
Bring it on.
Sock it to me.
Let me have it.

Hit the ground running	This is about being ready, especially for a new task.

We need the new management team to hit the ground running if we want to reach our financial goals.

Hit-and-run *Legal*	A hit-and-run is when you hit someone in a vehicle (have a car accident with them), but you don't stop to help them, to identify yourself, or to exchange insurance information. A hit-and-run accident results in a more serious punishment than if you stop, because it is actually a crime.

Compare to: Hit and run.

- It looks like a civilized party, don't you agree?
- Yeah, but it's only eight o'clock. It ain't over 'til the fat lady sings.
- Why? Is your wife performing tonight?

For a definition, see:

- **It ain't over 'til the fat lady sings!**

Hitting a brick wall	Running into resistance.
	When someone says: *I'm hitting a brick wall here,* they mean something like:
	I can't go forward with this plan. My progress is being blocked.
Hitting rock bottom	Reaching the lowest point possible.
	The economy is bad, but we haven't hit rock bottom yet. It will get even worse than this.
	Some people don't come to their senses about alcohol until they hit rock bottom. I was one of them!
Hitting the nail on the head	Being correct about something. Doing or saying the right thing about something. Perfectly understanding a situation and expressing it in words to someone else.
	Q. So, am I right or not? *A. You're right. You hit the nail on the head.*
Hitting the right note	Talking about the right issue. Doing or saying the thing that gets the right response.
	A. The president's approval ratings went up when he concentrated on creating new jobs. *B. I know. He hit the right note with that one.*
	Also: Strike a chord.
Hitting the skids	Losing control. Getting in trouble. Losing value or dignity.
	They were in Spain before their marriage hit the skids.
	Our company hit the skids when we lost our biggest client.
	Similar: On the skids. On the way down.

Hold that thought!	Just a minute. Don't forget what you were saying. *Hold that thought while I order some food.*
Holding a grudge	Not being able to forgive someone for something they've said or done. Staying angry with someone, maybe even with the thought of taking revenge, long after an incident has passed. Also see: Having an axe to grind.
Holding at bay **Keeping at bay**	Keeping something negative away. Keeping something volatile under control. Keeping something harmful at a safe distance. *Pesticides are keeping the mosquito infestation at bay for now, but we need to find a long-term, permanent solution for this problem.*
Holding down a job	Keeping a job. Being successful at having and keeping a job.
Holding (down) the fort	Taking care of things in the absence of someone, and making sure everything's okay. Q. *What did the prisoner tell you, detective?* A. *He said not to worry, that he asked his son to hold down the fort while he was in jail!*
Holding one's breath	Stopping everything. Waiting in anticipation. *I know there's going to be tax benefits for first-time home buyers, but I'm not holding my breath. I'm buying now because the government often goes back on its word.*
Holding one's cards close *Gambling*	Keeping one's ideas, plans, feelings, etc., a secret. Q. *Why is Dimitri acting so secretive these days?* A. *He likes to hold his cards close. I guess he doesn't trust us any more.* Also see: Close to the vest.

Holding one's nose	Trying to ignore the fact that one is doing something unpleasant or wrong.
	When someone says: *Hold your nose, but do it,* they mean something like:
	Do it even if you don't like it. Force yourself to do it even if you don't like the smell.
Holding one's own	Being able to handle things by oneself.
	Q. *Are you going with your kid brother to the meeting?* A. *There's no need. He can hold his own.*
Holding someone's feet to the fire **Keeping someone's feet to the fire** **Putting someone's feet to the fire**	Putting someone under pressure. Forcing, or trying to force, someone to do something. Holding someone accountable for what they've done, or what they need to do to rectify a bad situation. A. *He's not coming to my wedding.* B. *I know him. You'll have to hold his feet to the fire before he changes his mind.*

A corpse isn't asked about the choice of shroud. *(Swahili.)*

A person in trouble doesn't get to choose the kind of help they are offered.

Holding the bag	Being tricked.
	When someone says: *I was left holding the bag,* they mean something like:
	They tricked me and left me to take the blame for something I didn't do.
	Compare to: Taking the blame. Hanging out to dry.
Hole in one *Origin: Sports*	A major success. A success that's achieved on the first attempt.
Holier-than-thou attitude	Thinking of oneself as being (morally) better than others.

Home advantage *Sports*	The advantage of being, or playing, at one's home, or home town, or home state, where you are familiar with the surroundings. Also: Home-field advantage. Home-court advantage. Home-game advantage. Home-diamond advantage.
Home schooling	Children being taught at home instead of going to a public school.
Home stretch *Origin: Sports*	Last part of something. Final stage in a series of stages. Final leg of a racetrack before the finish line. *On home stretch,* could mean: *Going home;* *Almost finished;* *Getting close to your destination; etc.* *Q. Are we on home stretch yet?* *A. No, we still have a few things to do.*
Hook, line, and sinker *Origin: Sports*	Completely. The whole thing. When someone says: *We bought it hook, line, and sinker,* they mean something like: *We believed the whole (false) story.* This expression is used with such verbs as buy, accept, fall for, etc. It has to do with being deceived.
Hope floats.	Hope doesn't go away. Something good will happen Having hope gets you through a tough situation.
Horse trader	A smart dealer. A dishonest person. A crook or con artist. *There's always a lot of horse trading going on in there.*

Horsing around	Joking around. Fooling around. Playing around in a rough way.
Hot button (issue)	A touchy, sensitive, or controversial issue or subject. *Oil has become as much of a hot-button political issue as health care.*
Hot headed	Crazy, irrational, headstrong, easily angered.
Hot off the press **Fresh off the press**	Just printed. Just reported. Just announced. *Q. Is that an old story?* *A. No, it's hot-off-the-press! I just heard it on the radio.*
Hot potato	Too hot to handle. A controversial issue. A risky thing to handle. Something nobody wants to touch, handle, or get involved with. Something you want to pass off quickly to someone else. *Q. Why do they call it a "hot potato"?* *A. Try holding a hot potato in your hands, and then you'll know!*
Hot-dogging	Showing off. Showing a lot of excitement. *Q. Why are they dancing in the end zone?* *A. They're hot-dogging it after the touch down. I guess they're happy.*
House of cards	Something that looks solid but is flimsy. An unstable situation, or structure, or company that may look to be stable. *Q. Will you invest in this company?* *A. No, it's not very stable. It's a house of cards and can fail very easily.*

How are things on your end?	How are things with you? How are things in your area?
How come?	Why?
How do you like them apples?	A humorous or sarcastic way of saying: *How do you like that?* *How do you feel about that?* Also see: How does that grab you?
How do you plead? *Origin: Legal*	A legal term, which can mean any of these: Did you do it? Well, what do you say? Are you guilty or innocent?

God loves the thief but loves the master of the house more.
Once for the thief, twice for the thief, three, and it's his bad day.
(Greek.)

The thief will be caught eventually.

How does that grab you?	This is a humorous or sarcastic way of saying: How do you like that? How do you feel about that? Also see: How do you like them apples?
How will that play out?	How will it work? What will happen? How will it unfold?
Humoring someone	Making someone happy. Agreeing with someone to make up for something you did wrong. Doing something for someone just because they asked, even if you think it's silly. *A. He was absolutely wrong, but he wants ME to apologize!* *B. Never mind if you're right. Just humor him. He's our guest.* *You say you have a good reason for being late? Well, humor me! Tell me your reason.*

I already have a mother!	Leave me alone. Don't tell me what to do.
I appreciate it.	Thank you for what you did. I understand what you did, and I thank you. I can understand what you went through to do it, and I thank you for it.
I beg to differ!	I disagree. I'm sorry, but you're wrong. A. *I think health insurance should be provided by the government.* B. *Oh, I beg to differ!* Compare to: On the contrary.
I can't overemphasize this.	It's very important. I can't emphasize it enough. I can't emphasize it any more than this.
I can't stand it any more.	I can't do it any more. I can't handle it any more. I can't tolerate it any more. I can't put up with it any more.

Don't trouble trouble till trouble troubles you. *(Vietnamese.)*

I can't thank you enough.	Thank you very much! No amount of thanks would be enough.
I could eat a horse.	I'm very hungry.
I could use some help here.	I need some help. Similar: The food could use some salt. They could use some guidance.
I couldn't agree with you more!	I agree with you completely. I could not agree with you more than I do. However: When someone says: *I can't agree with you ANY more*, it means they DON'T agree with you! They've stopped agreeing with you.

| **I couldn't be happier.** | I'm very happy.
I'm as happy as possible.

Similar:
Couldn't be colder;
Couldn't be less helpful;
Couldn't be more helpful; etc. |

Measure seven times; cut once. *(Armenian.)*
Measure a hundred times; cut once. *(Maltese.)*
Someone cut before they measured! *(Persian.)*
Turn the tongue seven times before you speak. *(French.)*

Think thoroughly before you act.

I couldn't care less.	I don't care. I don't care at all. I'm not interested. Compare to: Who cares?
I couldn't have said it better myself!	I agree with you completely. I would have said the same thing. Also: I couldn't agree with you more. I couldn't have said it any better.
I couldn't help laughing.	I laughed. I kept laughing. I couldn't stop myself from laughing. Similar usage: *I can't help crying,* means: *I'm crying.* *I couldn't help talking,* means: *I kept talking.* Another usage: When someone says: *I can't help but think about the situation,* they mean: *I keep thinking about it.*
I digress.	Sorry, I went off course. I got distracted and started talking about something else.
I have my own share of problems.	I have problems, too, you know!

I have your number.	You can't fool me. I know all about you. I know how you think. I know what you want. I know what you're after. I know what you're thinking about.
I rest my case. *Legal*	I'm finished arguing. I'm not arguing any more. I've said all I'm going to say about it. I have nothing more to add. Also it is sometimes used to conclude that the speaker is right. A. *Where were you when the robbery took place?* B. *I don't remember.* A. *You don't remember? Well, I rest my case. (Which means something like: As you can see, I was right.)* Compare to: Case closed.
I wasn't born yesterday.	I'm not naive. I know how it is. You can't fool me. I know what's going on.

Don't speak of the noose in the hanged man's house.   *(Spanish.)*

I won't touch that.	I won't get involved with that. I won't talk about that subject. Q. *Do you want to work on this case?* A. *No, it's about a very controversial issue. I won't touch it.* Q. *How about this other case from yesterday?* A. *That's even worse. I wouldn't touch it with a ten-foot pole.*
I wouldn't change it for the world.	I'm not sorry about it. I would do the same again. I'm glad it happened the way it did. I wouldn't change it, no matter what.

I wouldn't do it for all the tea in China.	I won't do it. I will never do it. No matter what is offered to me, I won't do it. Also: I wouldn't do it for anything. I wouldn't do it for the world.
I wouldn't do it.	Don't do it. You shouldn't do it. If I were you, I wouldn't do it. I don't recommend that you do it. If you're asking me, then don't do it.

She will put both of his feet into one shoe. *(Greek.)*

On discipline.

I'd kill him with a dull axe!	I really hate him. I want him to suffer.
I'll be damned if ...	The following examples show when someone wants to strongly, and rudely, object to doing (or having done) something: *I'll be damned if I go there,* means something like: *I definitely won't go there!* *I'll be damned if I knew,* means something like: *I really didn't know!* Similar: Hell if I do it! Damned if I do it! A semi-humorous response would be something like: *You may very well be damned, but you still have to do it!*
I'll shake the dust from this town fast.	I'll forget about it quickly.
I'll take that as a No.	I'll understand that your answer is No. Then your answer is No. Is that right?

I'm afraid ...	An expression of concern.
	When someone says: *I'm afraid so,* they mean something like:
	I'm sorry, but that's true; *I'm sorry to say that what you're saying is true.*
	I'm afraid it's going to explode, means something like:
	I'm sorry to say that it's going to explode. *I have a bad feeling that it's going to explode.*
I'm done.	I give up. I'm leaving. I'm finished.
	Also, related and humorous: *Stick a fork in me! I'm done.*

In trying to put make-up around the eye, they blinded it. *(Arabic.)* They tried to fix the eyebrow and ended up blinding the eye, too. *(Armenian, Persian.)*

> *Instead of fixing the problem, they made it worse.*

I've had it up to here!	This is used (usually while motioning to one's eyes or over their head) to show one's frustration with someone or something.
	When someone says: *I've had it up to here with them,* they mean something like:
	I'm sick of them; *I'm tired of them;* *I'm fed up with them;* *I don't want to deal (or work) with them anymore; etc.*
	Also: I've had it up to my eyeballs. I'm up to my eyeballs in this mess.
I've stepped on better things than him!	He's a low-life. He's a scumbag. He has a very low personality.

- Why don't you order something, Mom?
- I can't stay. I have to leave. I have a lot on my plate!
- Where on your plate?!

For a definition, see:

- **Having a lot on one's plate**

Ice water in one's veins	This has to do with: Being cool. Having no emotions. Being very coldhearted. *Q. If you need money that much, why don't you ask for an advance?* *A. You don't know my boss. He has ice water in his veins!*
Identifying oneself	Introducing oneself. Making one's identity known to others.
Identifying with someone	Being similar to them and/or understanding them or their situation. *The reason our candidate lost is that most people could not identify with him.*
If I had a dollar for every pen I've lost, I'd be a rich man!	I've lost a lot of pens in my life! Similar: *If I had a dollar for every idea I've had, ...* *If I had a penny for every song I've written, ...* *If I had a nickel for every time I've been rejected by an ugly woman, etc.*
If I may say so	This is a nice way of expressing your opinion, even if no one is asking for it. It sounds as if you're asking someone's permission to do so (although you're not, because you're doing it anyway) and it makes your unsolicited advice or opinion sound less offensive. When someone says: *If I may say so, it's getting late,* they mean something like: *May I say something? It's getting late.* *Forgive me for saying this, but it's getting late.* *I know you don't care how I feel about it, but I think it's getting late!*
If I told you once, I told you twice!	I've told you many times! *If I told you once, I told you twice. I don't want you to drive my car!*

If you can't take the heat, stay out of the kitchen!	If you can't handle it, then don't do it. If you can't handle the stress, then don't take on a tough job.
If you will	If you are willing. If you feel that way. If that's how you want to look at it. This expression can be used to allow the listener to play a role in accepting the speaker's choice of words or to imagine what the speaker is trying to convey. *Think of her as your friend, if you will.* *I was feeling very sick, afraid of dying if you will, so I stayed home.*
Ill will	Bad feelings. Feelings of hostility. Privately wishing someone misfortune. *The initial secrecy by her husband toward her created some of the ill will between them.*
In a blink **In the blink of an eye**	Quickly. Very fast. *In this dry weather you can lose your house to a fire in the blink of an eye.*
In the hole	Financially in trouble, or in debt, as in: *I'm always in the hole, which is why I can't go on a vacation.* Loss of money, as in: *Because of this deal I'm $500 in the hole.*
In a nutshell	Summing things up. Summarizing something. A. *I'm in a hurry. Please put it in a nutshell for me.* B. *In a nutshell, I'm late because my car broke down!* Related: *Tell me (or give it to me) in a nutshell.*

In a pickle
In a mess.
In extremely bad shape.
In a tough situation that may not be easy to get out of.

Do a good thing, and throw it in the sea. *(Arabic.)*
A drop of water shall be returned with a burst of spring. *(Chinese.)*
Do good things, and forget them. Do bad things, and remember them. *(Maltese.)*
Do a good thing and throw it in Dejleh (river). God will reward you in the desert. *(Persian.)*

In a roundabout way
In an indirect way.

Q. *Did Lalainia tell you how she will vote?*
A. *Well, she said it in a roundabout way. So, I'm not really sure what she'll do!*

In chief
The top person.
The top person in each field.

Editor-in-chief;
Financier-in-chief;
Commander-in-chief; etc.

In deep sh-t
This expression (which is not polite) means:

In trouble.
Under pressure.
In a messy situation that's not easy to get out of.

Q. *Have you seen the test results?*
A. *Yes. We're in deep sh-t!*

Also see:
In hot water.

In effect
Effectively, or for all practical purposes, as in:
She is my wife. In effect, she is my boss!

Enforced, or observed, as in:
The cell phone law is in effect in San Diego. So, they'd better not catch you using your cell phone while driving!

In for a penny, in for a pound	This is about making investment decisions. It basically says: *If you're taking a risk, you might as well go all the way; don't stop halfway.* Compare to: Hanged for a sheep as a lamb. **Background:** The original English saying is: *If you owe a penny, you might as well owe a pound.* (Because the punishment for both is the same.)
In for the long haul **In it for the long haul**	Will not back out. Deeply committed and involved. Will stay with the project until it's completed. Involved in something that will take a long time to finalize.
In hindsight	When one looks back. When someone says: *In hindsight, we didn't do it right,* they mean something like: *Now that I think about it, I realize we really screwed up!* *If I knew then what I know now, I would have done it differently!*

He's eating the brush. *(Hungarian.)*
   He's dealing with the consequences of his bad decisions.

In hot water	In trouble. Under pressure. *Political scandals have landed several public figures in hot water.* Also see: In deep sh-t. (Not a polite thing to say.)
In its entirety	In its complete form. *If you just wait a minute, I'll tell you the story in its entirety.*
In knots (over something)	Confused, twisted, worried, troubled, etc., because of something.

In light of	Considering.
	In light of your numerous mistakes, I'm reconsidering the extent of your future participation in our activities!
In one piece	Alive. Okay.
	Q. We just want to know if our son is in one piece. Will you let us know? *A. Yes, Mr. and Mrs. Jefferson. We'll let you know as soon as we hear anything new.*
In one's element	In an enjoyable environment. In an area someone has expertise in. In familiar or comfortable surroundings.
	Q. Are you a comedian first, or an actor? *A. I'm really a comedian. Of course, I can act, but I'm not in my element when I do so.*
In one's hair	Annoying one. Not leaving one alone.
	Q. Why are you always mad at my brother? *A. He's constantly in my hair. (Or: He constantly gets in my hair.) He doesn't leave me alone!*
In one's heart of hearts	Deep down in one's heart. Something you know in your heart, but you don't necessarily talk about.
In one's own right	Because of one's own ability, skills, accomplishments, etc.
	When someone says: *Zoobinshid deserves praise in his own right*, they mean: *We must give him credit for what he's accomplished himself, and on his own.*
	Similar: *I know that Jane Fonda is Henry Fonda's daughter, but she's a great actor in her own right.*

In one's shell	Quiet.
	Not open.
	Keeping to oneself.
	He's a powerful speaker but, as soon as someone wants him to talk about his feelings, he goes into his shell. Can you believe that?
	Also:
	Clamming up.
	Staying in one's shell.
In police custody	In jail.
Legal	Under arrest.

If a blind man says that he will throw a stone at you, he probably has his foot on one. *(Parts of Africa.)*

In short	Briefly.
	Without going into details.
	Q. So, how was your trip?
	A. In short, I'm lucky to be alive!
	Similar:
	Long story short.
	To make a long story short.
In someone's corner	Protective of someone.
	Supportive of someone.
Origin: Sports	In agreement with someone.
	Defending someone or their ideas.
	Willing to fight for someone else or their honor, beliefs, ideas, etc.
	Q. Is Masako in our corner?
	A. Yes. She said that she agrees with us!
In the hot seat	Being faced with questions that one doesn't want to answer.
On the hot seat	Being held accountable for something that one has said or done.
	Faced with questions about his personal indiscretions, the senator is finding himself in the hot seat.

In the interest of justice *Legal*	For justice. If justice is to be served. When someone says: *In the interest of justice, he should be imprisoned,* it means: *If you want justice, he should go to jail;* *If justice is to be done, he should go to jail.* *Based on the new DNA evidence, we must put him in jail in the interest of justice.* Similar: For the sake of justice.

One is nineteen, the other is one less than twenty. *(Hungarian.)*
Both of them are troublemakers.

In the long run **In the short run**	Considering the distant, or near, future. *Providing education for our children will benefit us in the long run. In the short run, however, it will obviously hurt us because of its cost.* Also see: Long term. Short term.
In the moment	Under the influence of what's happening at the moment. When someone says: *I'm in the moment,* they mean something like: *I'm focusing on what's going on right now; no past regrets, or future worries.* When someone says: *I was caught up in the moment,* or: *I was acting in the heat of the moment,* they mean something like: *I did what I don't usually do; I didn't know what I was doing; I was affected by what was happening at the time; etc.*
In the public eye	In public. In public view. In front of every body. Where it will be public knowledge.

In the red	Being in debt. Owing money. Losing money. *Our company has been operating in the red for the last five years.* Opposite: In the black.
In the tank	Ruined. In bad shape. *The economy as a whole is in the tank and commercial real estate is, of course, no exception.* Also: Tanked. Tanking.
In the tank for someone	On someone's side. *The news media were accused of being in the tank for the new candidate from Michigan.*
In the toilet	In very bad shape, physically, mentally, financially, or otherwise. *Our company is in the toilet, which is why we're filing for bankruptcy.* Also: In the basement.
In touch	Involved in communication. Maintaining contact with someone. Having an understanding of the situation. When someone says: *I'm in touch with Freddy,* they mean: *We call each other, we sometimes meet, etc.* When someone says: *I'm in touch with our community,* they mean something like: *I know how people feel, what their problems are, etc.* When someone says: *Keep (or stay) in touch,* they mean: *Don't stop communicating with me!*

Continued on the next page.

In touch

Continued from the previous page.
Compare to:
Up-to-date.
Up-to-speed.

In tow

Together.
Pulled behind.
Under protection.

My sister came here with her kids in tow.

In tune with

In agreement with.

I'm definitely in tune with my wife's feelings. I can tell when she's had a bad day before she even says anything.

Also: In harmony.

In witness protection

In the Witness Protection Program

Legal

Hiding or living in an undisclosed location, with the help of the government, and with a new identity.

Similar:
In protective custody.
Under police protection.

Inflated ego

Feeling of self-importance.
Having too much self confidence, excessively bragging about one's accomplishments, being conceited.

Ins and outs

Details.
Specifics.
Characteristics.

Q. *Are you new here?*
A. *Yes. I've just started working, and I don't know the ins and outs of the system yet.*

Inside the box

Inside-the-box

This has to do with:

Old ways.
Traditional ways.
Doing things, or thinking, within the usual and commonly accepted ways.

Continued on the next page.

Inside-the-box

Continued from the previous page.

When someone says: *I want you to stop thinking inside-the-box,* they mean something like: *I want you to become more creative, and think of new alternatives.*

Compare to:
Outside-the-box.

In-your-face (attitude)

When someone says: *She has an in-your-face attitude,* they mean something like:

She is uncompromising.
She always wants to fight.
She doesn't want to give up anything.
She's unafraid of what you might say or do.

Also: All-up-in-your-face attitude.

Don't insult the crocodile until after you cross the water. *(Parts of Africa.)*

IOU

This is an abbreviation for:

I Owe yo**U**.

A note promising to pay someone something.

Hey, Joe, all you have to do is give him an IOU, and you'll owe him for the rest of your life!

It ain't over 'til the fat lady sings.

It ain't over till the fat lady sings.

It ain't over until the fat lady sings.

Wait until it's finished.
It's not finished until I tell you.
It's not finished until it's completely finished.

A. *The game is almost over. I guess we've lost again.*
B. *No! Let's wait. It ain't over 'til the fat lady sings.*

It didn't cross my mind.

It never crossed my mind.

I didn't think of it.

Q. *Didn't you think about calling her and telling her that she was in danger?*
A. *No, sir, that thought didn't cross my mind!*

Also see: It never occurred to me.

It goes without saying.	It is accepted. It is understood. Everyone knows it. There's no need to say it. Also: It is needless to say. A. *It goes without saying that college graduates make more money than us.* B. *Why do you say it then?*
It got me thinking.	It made me think. It made me start to think. Similar: *It got me working* means: *It made me work.* *It got me running* means: *It made me run.*

Beware of the anger of a patient man. *(Irish.)*

It has its blessings.	There are certain good things about it. A. *One thing good about smoking is that people don't get too close to you during breaks.* B. *Sure. Smoking has its blessings!* Similarly: It has its problems. It has its disadvantages. It has its ups and downs.
It jives.	It makes sense. Q. *You don't believe me?* A. *There's something wrong with your story. It just doesn't jive!* Also: It (all) adds up.
It leaves much to be desired.	It's very bad. It's very unsatisfactory. *Your son's behavior leaves much to be desired. Actually, it reminds me of yours!*

- Boss, there's no connection between these two cases. I went over everything with a fine-toothed comb.
- Oh, really? Whose comb did you use?

For a definition, see:

- **Fine-toothed comb**

It never occurred to me.	I never thought of that. *It never occurred to me that my own friends would desert me!* Also see: It didn't cross my mind.
It pays to do something.	It's worth doing it. *Q. Do I really have to follow these rules?* *A. Yes, it pays to follow them if you want to get ahead in this company.* *Q. Does it pay to go to college?* *A. Of course it does. If you don't, you might end up like me!*
It spells something.	It signals something. It's a sign of something. *A. Our teenage sons are home by themselves this weekend while we're here on a trip.* *B. Two teenagers, an empty house, and parents on a trip. That spells trouble!*
It sucks.	It's bad. I hate it. *Q. Don't you hate it when you have a flat tire on a rainy day?* *A. Yes! It sucks!*
It takes two to tango.	It takes two people to do it. Two people are needed to do this task.
It won't do. **That won't do.**	It won't work. It isn't enough. It isn't the right one. It isn't good enough. It isn't good for this job. *A. I'm sorry I didn't call you, but I'll come in tomorrow and work overtime.* *B. No, that won't do. You're fired!* Also: It won't cut it. It will never do.

It's a lot of dough.   It's a lot of money, or it costs a lot of money.

Similarly:
It's a lot of glue, ice cream, coffee, etc.

It's a mouthful.   It's difficult to say.
It's difficult to pronounce.

Also, the word *mouthful* used with *say* means "a profound statement" as in:

For his age, he said a mouthful.

It's a tie.

It's a draw.   *Sports*   In a sporting event, when someone says: *It's a tie, or it's a draw,* they mean: *The two sides have equal scores.*

It's a wash.

Call it a wash.   When someone says: *It's a wash, or Call it a wash,* they mean something like:

You're even.
You're back where you started.
You've gained as much as you've lost.
You didn't really gain anything, and you didn't really lose anything.

It's all Greek to me.   It's unfamiliar to me.
I don't understand it.

It's the "X" that counts.   The answer is "X."
"X" is the important thing.
It's the "X" that makes a difference.

Examples:
It's the "spirit" that counts.
It's the "money" that counts.
It's the "winning" that counts.
It's the "end result" that counts.

It's a wrap.
Origin: Movie industry   We're done,
It is finished.

It's a wrap, we can go home now.

Also:
Wrap it up, means something like: *Stop what you're working on, put everything away, and get ready to go home.*

Jack slapping	Slapping hard and unexpectedly. Slapping hard after some rough play. Compare to: Bitch slapping.
Jacked-up	Messed up. Screwed up. Not in good shape. Under the influence of drugs.

In one ear and out the other. *(English.)*
In through the left ear, out through the right ear. *(Thai.)*
Hears it from this ear, throws it out through the other. *(Armenian.)*

Said about those who won't listen to good advice.

Jaw-dropping	Stunning. Very surprising. Really amazing.

Q. Was he surprised to see you?
A. Oh, yes. His jaw dropped when he saw me.
Q. Are you serious?
A. Yes! It almost hit the floor!

Jerking someone around	Wasting their time. Not being straight forward with them.

Hey, stop jerking me around. If you're not going to give me the loan, just say so.

Joe Six-Pack	An average, ordinary person. A lower class or lower middle class person. A blue-collar worker who does not pay much attention to politics and is often undecided until the last few weeks before an election.

Also:
Average Joe. Average Jane.
Ordinary Joe. Ordinary Jane.

Jogging someone's memory	Trying to make someone remember something.

Q. I can't find the bankruptcy files you wanted. Where do you think they are?
A. Try jogging my secretary's memory. She might remember something.

John Hancock   Signature.

Please put your John Hancock here!

Note:
In Canada, John Henry is used (in place of
John Hancock) for the same purpose.

Background:
This is so, apparently, because of John
Hancock's unique signature which is famous
because he signed his name very largely and
prominently on the Declaration of
Independence. He said that this was to allow
the British to read his name without their
glasses. (Signing the Declaration was an act of
treason, punishable by death, and Hancock's
emphatic signature was a statement of
courage, telling everyone that the colonists
were ready to stand up for their independence.)

Joined at the hip   Not so different.
Origin: Medical   Never leaving each other's side.
Exactly the same or very similar.
Doing everything or going everywhere together.

*The two politicians are practically joined at the
hip. They are seen together morning, noon, and
night.*

Coming words will be beautiful if gone words were beautiful.
(Korean.)
                    What you say is what you will hear.

Judgment call   A decision based on one's experience or based
Origin: Legal   on what the facts appear to be in that moment.
It is usually a decision that needs to be made
immediately.

Q. *Why didn't you wait for the test results
before you operated on her?*
A. *It was a judgment call. I didn't think there
was enough time.*

Also see:
Using one's judgment.

Jumping bail *Legal*	Running away after being bailed out of jail and before the trial.
Jumping off a sinking ship	Saving oneself. Knowing something bad is coming and trying to avoid the situation before it gets worse.

Q. *Why did he leave the company to work somewhere else?*
A. *Well, I can't blame him for jumping off a sinking ship. He has a family to support.*

Compare to: Jumping ship.

Side note:
Rats desert a sinking ship, implies that deserting a sinking ship (or a troubled company) is not an honorable thing to do. You should try to stay and help the situation.

Jumping on something	Doing something right away. Getting started on something quickly before an opportunity is missed.

Q. *Do you want to think about the trip some more?*
A. *No! Jump on it before they sell all the tickets or raise the prices!*

Jumping on the bandwagon	Being opportunistic. Joining a popular movement without necessarily believing in it.

He's not really interested in saving energy. He has simply jumped on the "green" bandwagon (because that's the cool thing to do these days).

Jumping out (at)	*If something jumps out at you, you'd notice it right away.*

When someone says: *Is anything jumping out at you,* they mean something like:

Can you think of a reason?
Do you know what's going on?
Do you notice anything unusual?
Can you see anything wrong or different?

Jumping ship	Abandoning.
	Leaving one's post, ship, job, etc.
	Q. *Where's your old buddy, James?*
	A. *I don't really know. I guess he's jumped ship, and he shouldn't have!*
Jumping the gun	Acting too quickly or without thinking.
Origin: Military	Starting something before you're supposed to.
	Q. *Detective, the man you're holding has only one ear. Is it true that he's the One-Eared Burglar?*
	A. *Sorry, we won't jump the gun on his identity before conducting a full investigation.*
Jury is still out.	We don't know yet.
Origin: Legal	It hasn't been decided yet.
	A decision hasn't been made yet.
	When someone says: *The jury's still out on the trip,* they mean something like:
	We still haven't decided if we'll go on the trip.
Just like that	(Usually said while snapping the fingers:)
	Quickly.
	Very fast.
	My wife is very strong. She could break your neck just like that!
	Q. *Did it take them long to change your tire?*
	A. *No, they did it just like that!*
Just the same	See: All the same.
Keep in mind!	Remember.
Bear in mind!	Also: Keep it in the back of your mind!
Keep it up!	Be good.
	Continue.
	Keep the spirit up.
	You're doing a good job.
	Related:
	Keep up the good work.

Keep your shirt on!	Wait. Don't rush. Wait for a while. Don't get too excited just yet. Also: Hold it. Hold on. Hold your horses. Keep your pants on.
Keeping a low profile	Not attracting attention. Trying not to be noticed.
Keeping an eye on	Watching someone or something carefully. *I'm not sure about this guy. Keep an eye on him for a while, until we know more.*
Keeping in line *Origin: Military*	Staying in one's place. Keeping someone (or something) under control. When someone says: *I want you to keep the kids in line,* they mean: *I want you to keep the kids under control, and make them behave.*
Keeping it on the down-low	Keeping something a secret. Q. *When are you getting your promotion?* A. *It's not a sure thing yet. Let's keep it on the down-low for now.*

When your seven years are over, you go for good. *(Haitian.)*
When your time (life) is done you must go.

Keeping one on one's toes	Staying alert. Keeping one busy. Being ready to respond. *I don't have time to go anywhere. The kids are constantly keeping me on my toes.*
Keeping one's eyes open	Being careful, watchful, observant, etc. *There's some broken glass on the floor. Keep your eyes open while I'm vacuuming the floor.*

Keeping one's feet on the ground **Keeping both feet on the ground**	Having a solid foundation. Being sensible and reasonable. Not forgetting one's humble beginnings. Not losing one's balance while reaching for higher goals.

Q. Keep your feet on the ground and keep reaching for the stars. Who said that?
A. Who else? Casey Kasem!

Cattle in faraway lands have long horns. *(Irish.)*
The back of the neighbor's bride is red. *(Armenian.)*
The neighbor's hen is a goose to a neighbor. *(Persian.)*
People are never satisfied with what they have.

Keeping one's head above water	Surviving. Trying to stay in business. Trying not to fail in difficult times. Saving, or trying to save, oneself. Saving, or trying to save, one's business.
Keeping one's head down	Not attracting attention. Trying not to be noticed.
Keeping one's head in the game *Origin: Sports*	Staying focused. Paying attention to what one is doing, or needs to be doing.
Keeping one's head up	Being or feeling proud. Continue to stand tall, even if you've just experienced a disappointment.

Keep your head up, son. We're all proud of you!
Also:
Keep your chin up!

Keeping one's nose to the grindstone	Working extremely hard. Not taking any breaks from work.

A. We're going to the movies. Do you want to come with us?
B. Here I am, busy, with my nose to the grindstone, and you're going to the movies?!

Keeping pace *Origin: Military*	Not being too far behind. Staying close, as in a race. When someone says: *The world's oil supply is not keeping pace with demand,* they mean something like: *Not enough oil is being produced to meet the demand.*
Keeping someone company	Staying with them. *Please keep him (his) company. He's been very lonely since his dog left him for his neighbor!*

A face only a mother could love. *(English.)*
A beetle saw her children on the wall, and she said "They look like a string of pearls." *(Arabic.)*
     A mother loves her children no matter what they look like.

Keeping tabs on **Keeping an eye on**	Watching someone or something carefully. Q. *Do you really trust our new security guard?* A. *No. As a matter of fact, I've started keeping tabs on him!* Related: Keeping close tabs.
Kept man **Kept woman** **Kept person**	A person whose expenses are paid by someone else in return for companionship and often in return for sexual favors. This is not looked upon favorably and is considered a form of prostitution, if sex is involved. Compare to: Sugar daddy. Sugar mommy.
Kick in the pants	Inspiration. Encouragement. *The coach knows his team needs a kick in the pants, he just doesn't know how to inspire them.* *Tommy is an undisciplined, rebellious brat. He needs a good, swift kick in the pants to help him to straighten out.*

Kick in the teeth	Bad news.
	A humiliating thing.
	Humiliating bad news.
	Something bad happening, especially if it's on top of another bad thing.
	I knew my wife wanted to leave me, but taking the kids, too? Boy, that was a kick in the teeth!
	Compare to: Adding insult to injury.
Kick the bucket	To die.
	Before I kick the bucket, I like to see the world.
	Compare to:
	Bucket list.
Kick the habit	To quit an addiction.
	To stop doing something that's difficult to stop doing.
	Isn't it time you kicked the habit and stopped smoking, you moron?

Give me bread, and call me stupid. *(Spanish.)*

Kicked up one side and down the other	Attacked, hit, bothered, called upon, etc., from all sides.
	Also: Bashed up one side and down the other.
Kicking the tires	Testing.
	Making sure.
	Q. *What's taking you so long to read it? It's a simple contract.*
	A. *I'm kicking the tires. I want to make sure that everything is okay before I sign it.*
Kicking to the curb	Firing (from a job).
	Ending (a relationship).
	First my boss threw a party for me, then he kicked me to the curb.
	I had a messy fight with my girlfriend. I'll be kicking her to the curb one of these days soon.

Kicking up one's heels	Enjoying oneself. Having a good time.
	No more work for me tomorrow. I'm going to kick up my heels and watch football all day!
Killing time	Wasting time. Waiting around.
	This killing time is killing me!
	Also see: Whiling away the time.

We were many, and grandma gave birth! *(Venezuelan.)*
Things were bad, and now they are even worse.

Killing two birds with one stone	Doing two things at the same time. Solving two problems using the same solution.
Kissing something good-bye	Accepting the loss of something, as in:
	When someone says: *If you left your wallet at the casino you can kiss it good-bye,* they mean something like: *Forget about it because you won't see it anymore!*
	Not doing something anymore, as in:
	When someone says: *I've kissed college good-bye,* they mean something like: *I won't be going to college anymore.*
Kitchen table issues	Everyday family issues. Issues families talk about at home.
	A. *We need to address the tensions in the Middle East.*
	B. *Maybe so, but we have kitchen table issues that we need to worry about, too!*
Knocking someone's socks off	*It will knock your socks off,* means:
	It's great. *You'll love It.* *It's unbelievable.* *You'll be so surprised.*
	Also see: Blowing someone's mind.

See, you told him he had a chip on his shoulder, and now you've gotten him all confused!

For a definition, see:

- **Having a chip on one's shoulder**

Knocking the wind out of someone's sails *Origin: Sports*	Dashing their hopes. Abruptly stopping them. Destroying their hope or their chances. Bringing them down when they are excited.

Q. *You look terrible! What happened?*
A. *She left me! It has just knocked the wind out of my sails. I don't know what to do.*

Knowing how it is	Not being naive.

When someone says: *I know how it is,* they mean something like:

You can't fool me.
I know what's going on.
I wasn't born yesterday.

The dogs are barking, the caravan is moving on. *(Indonesian.)*
The dog barks, the caravan passes by. *(Azerbaijani, Portuguese.)*
If the cock crows on the dung heap, the weather may change or it may stay the way it is. *(German.)*
   Great achievements can't be prevented by insignificant people.

Knowing the ropes	Knowing all of the details. Knowing the tricks and rules about something.

Q. *When are you going to publish your book?*
A. *I don't know. I'm looking for someone who knows the ropes to help me with it.*

Knowing the score	Knowing the tricks. Being experienced.

I know the score, means something like:

I'm not naive.
You can't fool me.
I know what's going on.

Knowing where the bodies are buried	Knowing all of the secrets.

When someone says: *He knows where the bodies are buried,* they mean something like:

He knows how they operate;
He knows everything about them; etc.

Knowing which way the wind blows

Anticipating and using opportunities.
Being smart about using opportunities.
Knowing what lies ahead, and using it to one's advantage.

Keep an eye on Monica because she's going places. Somehow she always seems to know which way the wind will be blowing.

Background:
The origin most likely has to do with sailing and the corresponding benefits of knowing the direction of the wind.

Kumbaya

This word means *come by here* and is used to refer to *human and spiritual unity.*

Well, it looks like the kumbaya days are over!

Background:
Kumbaya is an old spiritual song that has its roots in African American culture. It became popular in the 1960s and is often sung in gatherings of spiritual and nature loving groups.

Lack thereof

Lack of.

When someone says: *It's all about money or the lack thereof,* they mean something like:
*It's all about money or the lack of money.
It's all about having money, or not having money.*

Lacking teeth

Being ineffective.
Not being forceful.

The new government lacks teeth mainly because it isn't even considered to be legitimate.

Compare to :
Having teeth.

Landing a job

Getting a job.

Q. *Have you found a job yet?*
A. *Yeah, I landed one last week.*

Landing on one's feet
The ability to survive a difficult situation satisfactorily.

A. *Alicia is in trouble again. I wonder what she'll do!*
B. *Oh, don't worry about her. Somehow she always manages to land on her feet.*

Last but not least
The last one, but not the least important one. The last reason, but not the least important reason.

And last, but not least, I want to thank my parents, without whose support I wouldn't be standing here today.

It is coming out of my elbow. *(Hungarian.)*
It's happening very often.

Last chicken in the shop
A very unattractive person.
The most unattractive person in a group.

Last chicken on the shelf, or in the window
Q. *Why are you going out with him? He's the last chicken in the shop!*
A. *I know, but it's the best I can do!*

Last straw
Final straw
The final, very small problem that causes a failure, or an angry outburst, or a chaotic situation, after a series of other smaller problems have happened.

Q. *Did Michelle leave her husband just because he got drunk?*
A. *She had wanted to leave him for some time. His getting drunk was the last straw!*

Background:
This is the shortened version of: *The straw that broke the camel's back.* It refers to an old proverb about a camel that was overloaded with straw. When the load was just at the last level that the camel could handle, the addition of a single straw broke its back. It shows how, when you're at the breaking point, the slightest problem would have a catastrophic effect.

Last word	The end of something. Saying the last words in an argument. When someone says: *We haven't heard the last word on immigration,* they mean something like: *It's not finished yet.* *We haven't seen the end of it.* *There will be more discussions.* Compare to: Having the last word.
Late! **Later!**	Bye! See you later!
Late someone	A polite way of referring to a person who is not living. *"Sitting on the dock of the bay" was performed by the late, great Otis Redding.*
Latter, former	When someone says: *Jenny and Diana are both beautiful, but I prefer the latter to the former,* they mean: *Diana is more beautiful than Jenny!*
Laughed out of a location	When someone says: *You'll be laughed out of the county,* they mean something like: *They'll laugh at you.* *That's a bad idea you have.* *You won't be taken seriously.* Can be used with other subjects (I, she, he, etc.,) and other places (city, company, etc.)
Laughing all the way to the bank	If someone's laughing all the way to the bank, it could mean one of the following: *They're getting paid too much.* *I hey got a very good deal, maybe even unexpectedly.* *You didn't want to do a "boring" job, so now HE is laughing all the way to the bank instead!* *We didn't think our idea would work, but now we're laughing all the way to the bank on a daily basis because of its success!*

Lawyering up *Legal*	Seeking legal counsel. Hiring lawyers, probably excessively and unnecessarily. *The suspect is probably guilty because she's lawyering up on us.*
Lay of the land	The way things are. The way things are set up or arranged. Also: Lie of the land.
Laying eyes on something	Seeing something. *Ever since I laid eyes on that old Mercedes, I've wanted it.*
Laying hands on something	Obtaining. *I'm willing to pay a lot of money to lay my hands on an old Beatles album.* Also: Get hold of something. Get one's hands on something.
Leap of faith	Trust. Lots of trust. *I've seen your babysitter, and I don't think I can trust her! Leaving my child with her would require a huge leap of faith, which I don't have!*
Leave well enough alone.	Leave it alone. If something is working, leave it alone. Don't change something that's doing what it's supposed to do. Q. *Aren't you sorry you screwed up the hotel reservation system?* A. *I know, I should have left it well enough alone.* Also: If it isn't broken, don't fix it.
Leave your personal opinion at home.	Be objective. Give me your professional opinion. I don't want to hear your personal opinion.

Left hand doesn't know what the right hand is doing!	This expression refers to two different things: On the one hand, secrecy: This could be about keeping separate matters independent of each other (as in conducting a secret mission) to the extent that one department doesn't know what another department is doing. On the other hand, confusion: It could represent a state of confusion or lack of communication (for example, within an organization), where no one knows what's going on, leading to inefficient management.
Left to one's own devices	Left alone. Left alone to take care of oneself.
Lending oneself to something	Being available, appropriate, supportive, etc., for something. When someone says: *Our ballroom lends itself to holding lectures,* they mean something like: *You can give lectures in our ballroom, or Our ballroom is suitable for use as a lecture hall.* When someone says: *He lends himself to our cause,* they mean something like: *He supports our cause.*
Less than something	*Less than honest,* means: *Not honest, very dishonest.* Similar usage: *Less than happy.* *Less than agreeable.* *Less than memorable.*
Let alone	When someone says: *He can't swim, let alone dive,* they mean something like: *If he can't swim, then obviously he can't dive. He can't swim. How do you expect him to dive?* Also see: Much less.

Let bygones be bygones.	Move on. Forget about it. Forgive and forget. Forget about the bad things that happened between you guys.
Let it all hang out.	Talk about it. Be totally honest, and don't hold anything back. Say all that is on your mind, and don't miss anything.
Let it ride.	Wait, don't do anything. Let the situation continue. *Let's let it ride for a while, and see what happens.* Also: Let's ride it out. Let it ride for now. Let it blow over, or wait until it blows over.
Let me have it!	See: Hit it.
Let me put it this way!	Let me explain. This is what I mean. Let me say it this way.
Let's hear it.	Start talking. I am listening. Tell me about it. Let us know about it.
Let's cross that bridge when we come to it.	Let's not worry about it now. We'll worry about it when it's necessary. Q. *What if we don't get the money by tomorrow?* A. *Well, let's cross that bridge when we come to it.*
Letting go	Forgiving. Forgiving and forgetting. Q. *Are you still mad at your boss?* A. *No, I've forgiven him. You have to learn to let go, otherwise you'll just hurt yourself.*

Letting go of	Releasing, as in: *Let go of my arm. I have to leave.* Moving on, forgetting about it, as in: *Let go of the past. You have to move on with your life.*
Letting it slide	Letting it go. Not doing anything about it. Being flexible, or letting it go for now. Q. *I'm really sorry, but I didn't have time to do my homework. Will you let it slide this time?* A. *I know you're sincere, so I'm going to let it go, but don't do it again.* A. *You're two pounds over the limit. I can't let you through.* B. *Two pounds over 400 pounds? That's nothing. Come on, please let it slide!*

The guilty one runs unchased. (Bulgarian.)

Letting one's guard down *Origin: Sports*	Not being ready. Being unprepared. Being overly relaxed. N*ever let your guard down,* means: *Be careful.* *Always be prepared.* *Don't trust everybody.* *Always expect the unexpected.*
Letting someone down	Disappointing someone. Not supporting someone. Related: *Letting someone down easy,* means: *Being kind to them when you're letting them down.*
Letting someone have it	Hitting or attacking someone, verbally or physically. Q. *Why did you fight with your uncle?* A. *I didn't really want to but, when he started bad mouthing my dad, I let him have it!*

Letting someone in on something	Revealing some inside information to an outsider. When someone says: *Let me in on it,* they mean something like: *Tell me about it.* *Let me know about your little secret.*
Letting the chips fall where they may	Letting things happen without worrying about their consequences. *I know I may be taking a big risk, but I'm going to buy that car and let the chips fall where they may.*

It's a good thing that the roads in Kerry go out of Kerry. *(Irish.)*
If you live in Kerry, you're glad that there's a way out.

Liar, liar, pants on fire!	You're lying. (Used mainly by children when they think someone's lying to them.) Also: When someone says: *On the dance floor, he moved like his pants were on fire,* they mean: *He's a really good dancer.*
Licking one's wounds	Comforting oneself. Taking a break after a defeat. A. *I know you're embarrassed, but you should really come back to our meetings.* B. *I will. I'm just taking a couple of weeks off to lick my wounds.*
Light at the end of the tunnel	Sign of hope. When someone says: *I see the light at the end of the tunnel,* they mean something like: *I am optimistic, or I have a feeling that things will be getting better soon.*
Lighten up!	Smile! Take it easy. Don't be so serious. Don't take things so seriously.

Light-year	A very long time.
	When someone says: *The electric car technology is light-years away,* they mean:
	That technology won't be available for a very long time.
Like a fish out of water	Being in unfamiliar or uncomfortable surroundings.
	When someone says: *He's like a fish out of water,* they mean something like:
	He can't function. *He doesn't know what to do.* *He feels really uncomfortable in the situation.*
Like trying to sweep sand off the beach	It's no use. It's a waste of time and effort.
	Also: Like bringing a cup of water to a forest fire.
Lion's share	Major share. Largest part of something.
Lip service	Just words.
	Q. *The city people keep saying that they'll fix the roads. Why isn't it happening?* A. *They're not going to do anything. They're just giving us lip service.*
Lip-lock **Locking lips**	Kiss. Kissing.
	The last time I saw them, they were lip locked.
	Julie and Ben were locking lips behind the water cooler. They don't know that I saw them!
Lipstick on a pig	Superficial or cosmetic improvement.
	When someone says: *It's like putting lipstick on a pig,* they mean something like:
	If you put lipstick on a pig, it's still a pig; Changing the appearance won't change the facts, or what's on the inside.

Litmus test	A test to show the validity of an idea or a person.
	The debate today will be the litmus test we've been waiting for. We'll finally know something about our new candidate's strengths and weaknesses.
Little black book	A listing of one's (sexual) conquests. A listing of one's private phone numbers, addresses, etc.
Little did they know!	They didn't know.
	Little did they know that they were about to lose their house!
	Similar: Little did we know; Little did she know; etc.

The saint who works no miracles isn't glorified! *(Greek.)*

Living for the moment	Concentrating on what's happening now.
	I may be wrong, but I'm not going to worry about the future any more. Instead, I'll be living for the moment from now on.
Living high on the hog **Living high off the hog**	Living comfortably, or extravagantly, with lots of eating or drinking.
	A. *He's making a lot of money. He must be living high on the hog.* B. *No, not him. He's always been careful with his money!*
Living off someone	Being supported by someone.
	Q. *Is he still living off his mother?* A. *Yeah, she's still supporting him. She's paying for all of his expenses.*
	Also: Being a mooch. Living off something. Mooching off someone. Sponging off someone or something.

I know you have an axe to grind, but do you have to grind your shotgun, too?!

For a definition, see:

- **Having an axe to grind**

Living on borrowed time	Living beyond the time when one is supposed to have died.
	When someone survives a deadly accident, you can say: *They're living on borrowed time!*
Living paycheck-to-paycheck	Having no savings. Spending all of one's earnings. Totally depending on one's job.
	Q. *Are you financially okay these days?* A. *Not really. I'm living paycheck-to-paycheck.*
Living up to someone's expectation	Not disappointing someone. Accomplishing what they expected of you.
	I've always tried to live up to my parents' expectations. So far, they've been proud of me!
Lo and behold!	Look! Look here! (With an element of surprise.)
	When someone says: *Lo and behold, she's here,* they mean: *Oh, look, she's here!*
	When someone says: *I walked in, and lo and behold, she was there,* they mean: *I walked in, and to my surprise, she was there!*
Loaded question	A question that:
	Could lead to other questions. Doesn't have a yes-or-no answer. Can get you in trouble when you answer it.
Lock, stock, and barrel	All. All of it. The whole package (needed for the job).
	A. *I bought the pizzeria on the corner.* B. *The equipment, too? What about the delivery cars?* A. *I bought the whole thing, lock, stock, and barrel.*
	Also: The whole shebang.
	Compare to: Whole nine yards.

LOL	This is an abbreviation for:
	<u>L</u>aughing <u>O</u>ut <u>L</u>oud.
	It is used by the younger, Internet and texting generation.
Long and short of something	A summary.
	The main parts.
	Well, here's the long and short of it. What you do with It, is up to you.
Long face	Sad looks.
	Unhappy face.
	Serious looking.
	Q. Why the long face?
	A. I lost a lot of money in the stock market today.

Eat the spicy chili sauce only from one cup. *(Thai.)*

Stay faithful to your wife!

Long running	Being around for a long time.
Long-running	*Q. What are your favorite long-running TV shows?*
	A. "Cheers!" and "Seinfeld!" They had long runs on television.
Long term, Short term	*Long term:*
	These are plans, policies, expenses, etc., for the distant future, such as building more schools to provide education for more children.
Long-term, Short-term	*Short term:*
	These are plans for the near future, such as purchasing more school buses.
	Also see:
	In the long run.
	In the short run.
Long time coming	Expected for a long time.
	Well, we're finally going to have some new health care policies, changes that were a long-time coming.

Long time in the making	In progress for a long time. *The conflict in the region has been a long time in the making. It didn't just happen, you know!* Also: Many years in the making.
Long-windedness	Talking too much. Using more words than really necessary. *Q. Are you coming to the lecture?* *A. No! I know the professor, and I know he's long-winded. You go, and tell me about it!*
Looking inward	Examining one's thoughts and beliefs. *I've been looking inward, wanting to know what I really want to do, or who I really am.* Also: Soul-searching.
Looking over one's shoulder	Not feeling safe or secure. Having worries about being followed, identified, attacked, etc. *A. She knows her ex-husband is in prison, but she's still worried.* *B. I know. She's constantly looking over her shoulder!*
Looking the other way	When you say: *He's looking the other way,* you could mean any of the following: *He can't see us.* *He doesn't want to talk to us.* *He doesn't want to get involved.* *He's helping us by pretending that he doesn't see us. That way we can do whatever we want to do, and he won't get in trouble for helping us.*
Looking up to someone	Admiring someone. Being proud of someone. *I look up to my father. I'm so proud of him.* Opposite: Looking down on someone.

Loose cannon

Out of control.
An irresponsible and reckless (therefore potentially dangerous) person.

I like him and I really wish I could nominate him for the job but, let's face it, he's a loose cannon!

Background:
The term refers to the days when cannons on battle ships could break loose on rough seas, and would then roll about and cause serious damage.

Loose ends
Origin: Legal

Unfinished business.
Unanswered questions.
Potentially harmful evidence left behind.
Something that, if not taken care of now, may harm you in the future.

Loosey-goosey

Very relaxed.
Having no plans, just having fun.
A person with few, or no, inhibitions.

Lose-lose (situation)

A situation where everybody loses.
Compare to:
Win-win and win-lose.

Losing one's footing

Losing one's balance.

I'm sorry I touched your wife's arm, sir. I lost my footing and had to grab something!

Losing one's shirt

Losing everything, especially money.

I lost my shirt (or the shirt off my back) when my landscaping business failed. It was bad!

Loud and clear

Getting the idea.
Understanding clearly.

When someone says: *I can hear you, loud and clear,* they mean something like:

I understand.
I know exactly what you mean.
You don't have to explain anything.

Continued on the next page.

Loud and clear   *Continued from the previous page.*

When you say: *She told me, loud and clear, not to bother her,* you mean something like:

I understood clearly that she didn't want me around.

Also: I read you, loud and clear!

Lovey-dovey   An overly done show of affection between people.
Very romantic public displays of affection without regard for others noticing.

I don't really care for movies that have a lot of lovey-dovey scenes.

Low-balling   Underestimating the value of something on purpose, usually in order to purchase it at a lower price than it is worth.

Low-down   Wrong, bad, as in:
The way he treated her, he was a low-down, rotten person.

Details, as in:
I want to know all the details. Give me the low-down on the situation.

Better a sparrow in the hand than a pigeon on the roof. *(Czech, German.)*
Better to have one bird in your hand than ten in the sky (or on the roof). *(Danish, Dutch, Norwegian.)*

Don't risk losing what you have for things that you're hoping to have.

Main Street   The general public.
Ordinary, everyday people and their businesses.

The effects of higher gas prices are felt on Main Street, means something like:

Higher gas prices are hurting ordinary people.

Compare to:
Wall Street.

Make believe	Something that isn't true or real.
Make-believe	Pretending, in a playful way, as kids do.
	Are you feeling sorry for the characters in the movie? Don't. It's only make-believe!
Make it so.	Do it.
	Also: Make it happen. Make it a reality.

A woman who cries, a man who swears to God, and a horse that sweats, are all impostors. *(Italian.)*

Make my day!	Make me happy! Make my day a good one! Make today worthwhile for me!
Make yourself at home.	Feel welcome. Make yourself comfortable.
Making a case *Legal*	Proving a point. Proving that the case is valid.
	When you say: *Tanya made her case through dozens of old letters,* you mean something like: *She used the letters to prove her point.*
Making a case for something *Legal*	Providing a convincing proof or argument for something.
	For many people, I'm sorry to say, the case for global warming has not been made yet.
Making a difference	Having an effect. Doing something (usually good) for others.
	When someone says: *It makes a big difference,* they mean something like: *It is very important.*
	A. Name two people who have made a difference. B. *Mahatma Gandhi* and *Louis Pasteur.*
	Also: Leaving a mark.

Making a habit of	Doing something regularly or on a regular basis.
	If you say: *Tomiko has made a habit of coming to work late everyday,* you mean: *Tomiko's coming to work late on a regular basis.*
Making a monkey out of someone	Making someone look bad, clumsy, stupid, etc.
	I'm relying on your serious input for writing this letter. I hope that you won't joke around and try to make a monkey out of me!
	Also: Making a fool out of someone.
Making a point	Stressing a point. Emphasizing something.
	Q. *Why does my father keep talking about my grades?*
	A. *He's trying to make a point.*
Making a point of doing something	Putting priority on doing something. Giving importance to doing something.
	A. *I saw Le Beau's daughter taking drugs.*
	B. *I think you should make a point of talking to her father. If you don't, I will.*
Making a splash	Making a noticeable appearance.
	She made a big splash at the party. Everybody noticed her there.

A bird in the hand is worth two in the bush. *(English.)*
An egg today is better than a chicken tomorrow. *(Italian.)*
A slap in the face now is better than promised candy later. *(Persian.)*

Making do	Managing things when there's little money. Working with what you have or what you've been given. Managing to make things happen in financially difficult situations.
	Times are tough, and I'm trying to make do with what's available.

Making ends meet   Earning just enough money to live and pay the bills.

Q. *How's life treating you?*
A. *Well, not very good. I'm trying to make ends meet.*

Also:
Making a living.

Making headlines   Being on the news.
Being mentioned by the media (radio, TV, magazines, etc.,) in a big way.

When someone says: *We'll be making headlines,* they mean: *We'll be on the news, and everybody will be talking about us.*

Heaven is under the mother's foot. *(Indonesian, Persian.)*
If you respect your mother, you'll go to heaven, that's how high a mother's place is.

Making it   Succeeding.
Reaching one's goal, maybe even with some difficulty.

Q. *How are you feeling?*
A. *I've made it, what else can I ask for? I'm telling you, I feel good!*

Q. *You left home late. Did you make it to the party?*
A. *Yes, we did. We almost missed it, but we did get there.*

Making landfall   Reaching the coastline.
Reaching land by sea or air.

The hurricane (now in the ocean) will make landfall tonight.

Making light of the situation   Making the situation seem unimportant.
Treating something as if it was not serious.

She made an effort to make light of the altercation, but everyone there knew that it was serious.

Making no bones about something	Accepting it. Not objecting to, or making a big deal about, it. Q. *What did he say when you told him that we knew about his trip?* A. *He didn't make any bones about it. He admitted it.*
Making off	Leaving in a hurry. Stealing. (Used with "with.") *Mr. Madoff made off with billions of dollars!*
Making one's bones	To earn a reputation. To become established in one's profession. To kill in order to become a gang member, especially if it's the first time. *You have to make your bones in this profession before anyone respects you!*
Making one's mind jump	Making one think. Making one think quickly about different things.
Making the grade	Succeeding. Passing the test. *At the rate you're going, you will probably not make the grade.*
Making up one's mind	Making a decision. Q. *Have you decided what you want to do tonight?* A. *No, I haven't. I can't make up my mind.*
Managing to do something	Being able to do something, despite low expectations. *She managed to remember the speech.* *Do you think you can manage to do it alone?* *I think I can manage to get there ahead of time.*
Manna from heaven	Heaven sent. An unexpected gift or help. *Did you see this raise I got today? It's manna from heaven!*

Many a **Many an**	This term, followed by a singular noun, simply means "many."
	Many a boy. (Many boys.) Many a night. (Many nights.) Many an apple. (Many apples.)
	When someone says: *Many a smart and self-reliant girl has entered the law profession,* they mean something like: *A lot of smart and self-reliant girls have entered the law profession.*
Marching to the **beat of a different** **drummer** *Origin: Military*	Doing things differently. Believing in a different set of rules. Doing things in one's own way, regardless of what others may think.
	Also: March to a different beat. March to a different tune. March to a different drum. March to a different drummer.

Better to live with the devil than with a mean woman. *(Greek.)*

Mark my words	Listen to what I am saying. Remember what I'm saying. It will happen the way I've said it will happen.
	I know that you don't take me seriously but, mark my words, one of these days I'm going to become famous.
	Similar: Read my lips.
Marriage of **convenience**	A marriage where the partners don't love each other. A merging of two entities for political, social, or financial reasons.
Matching **something**	When someone says: *You can match that,* they mean something like:
	You can do as well. *You can achieve the same results.* *You can find something compatible with that.*

Mayday! Mayday! Mayday!	Help! Emergency! Also see: SOS. **Background:** This is an internationally known cry for help, repeated three times, and is used in emergencies, particularly by ships or airplanes that are in distress.
Meal ticket	A person who is used for his or her money. *Q. Hey, Lulu, did you break up with Sheik Ahmad? A. Hell, no. He's my meal ticket!*
Meaning well	Having good intentions. *He means well. He just doesn't know how to say things in a nice and diplomatic way.*
Meat on the bone	Enhancement. More value or meaning for the argument. *Introduce yourself, talk about your accomplishments, put some meat on the bone, and let people know more about you.*
Meeting halfway	Compromising. Reaching a compromise. *You say $100; I say $80. Let's meet halfway at $90, okay?* Also: Splitting the difference. Also see: Give and take.
Meeting one's Waterloo *Origin: Military*	Failing in a big way. Something being brought to an unsuccessful end. *A. This is where I met my Waterloo. B. What happened? A. I met my ex-wife!*

- That's it. I've had it with you and your attitude. Do you want to step outside?!
- Are you crazy?! It's raining.

For a definition, see:

- **Stepping outside**

Men are from Mars, women are from Venus

Men and women are different.

A related children's song:
What are little boys made of? Frogs and snails, and puppy dog tails!
What are little girls made of? Sugar and spice, and everything nice!

Background:
This is the title of a book by Author John Gray, about understanding the differences between men and women. The book has become so popular that the title is now an expression.

MIA
Military

This is an abbreviation for:

Missing **I**n **A**ction.

This is a military term but is used outside the military as well. It refers to someone who's missing or cannot be located.

A. *Let's go. The show's going to start.*
B. *Okay, but we'll have to leave without David. He's still MIA.*

Middle of nowhere

Not a known location.
Far from populated areas.

He lives in the middle of nowhere. The nearest store is 25 miles away.

When someone says: *We're in the middle of nowhere,* they mean something like: *We're lost. We don't know where we are.*

Middle-aged

Someone who is between the approximate ages of 40 and 60 years old.

Might as well

When someone says: *We might as well go home,* they mean something like:

Let's go home!
There's nothing else to do here. Let's go home!

Q. *It's almost noon. Do you want to have lunch?*
A. *Yeah, we might as well!*

Milking the situation	Taking advantage of a situation by trying to extend the process. Trying to get as much from a situation as you possibly can. *He always milks these lucrative government contracts for as much as he can.*
Mincing words	Holding back. Not saying things clearly. Opposite: *Not mincing words* is: Not holding back, saying exactly what you think or feel about something. *They didn't mince words in describing their true feelings.*

A dog with a bone in his mouth has no friends. *(Haitian.)*

Mind your Ps and Qs.	Don't be nosy. Don't be sarcastic. Mind your manners. Don't be a smart ass. Mind your own business. Be careful about what you're saying or doing. **Background:** This may have its roots in the early days of printing. As it was easy to mistake the letters "p" and "q" on a typeset, printers were routinely warned to be mindful of these two letters. It may also have to do with bartenders warning the customers in the old days to be mindful of how many *pints* or *quarts* they were drinking!
Missing a beat *Medical*	Stopping briefly. *In recent months, when I suddenly hear a loud noise, my heart misses a beat!* *Despite all of the noise in the background, he continued the lecture after missing a beat.* Also: Skipping a beat. Compare to: Without missing a beat.

Missing link

Something that needs explaining.

There's a missing link here. Something that we cannot see or cannot explain.

Also:
Referring to the origins of man, as it relates to a stupid person, calling someone dumb, like a caveman!

Also:
Something missing without which something else will be incomplete.

We have a missing link here without which these theories do not make any sense.

Missing the boat

Being too late.
Missing an opportunity.

Are you coming to the movies with us? Make a decision fast, or you're going to miss the boat.

Monday morning quarterback

Sports

A person who finds fault, and blames others, AFTER everything has already been done.

A. *I would have done the whole thing differently and avoided the present mess.*
B. *Yeah, it's easy to be a Monday morning quarterback!*

Background:
Most (American) football games are held on Sundays. This leads to a lot of Monday-morning conversations among football enthusiasts at their work place, during which everybody comments on how the games should have been played. Hence the term *Monday morning quarterback.* (In American football, the captain of the team is called the quarterback.)

Money burning a hole in one's pocket

The urge to spend one's money.

If you say: *This money is burning a hole in my pocket,* you mean *I've got to spend this money!*

Also:
I've got a hole in my pocket, means: *I'm broke!*

Money is no object.	This is used when the price of something is not an issue. *Please arrange to have a piano in there for Farimah to practice on. And, remember, money is no object!*
Money talks!	Money buys influence. Money helps to solve everything. If you have money, you can do anything. If you have money, people will listen to you.
Monkey on one's back	An addiction. A constant burden. A problem that won't go away. *My house is a monkey on my back now. I can't afford to keep it, and I can't sell it either!*

Hatred is as blind as love. *(Vietnamese.)*

More holes than Swiss cheese	Something with a lot of problems. When someone says: *Your proposal has more holes in it than Swiss cheese,* they mean something like: *It's a bad idea. There are a lot of things wrong with it.*
More pronounced	More obvious. More noticeable.
More than you can shake a stick at	A lot. When someone says: *There are more problems here than you can shake a stick at,* they mean something like: *This is a serious situation.* *We can't ignore these problems.* *We have a lot of problems on our hands.* *We have to take these problems seriously.*
Mother lode	Treasure. A huge package. A large supply of something.
Motor City	This is a nickname for the City of Detroit.

Move it, or lose it!	This expression-like sentence (which is not a nice thing to say) could mean any of the following:
	Move. Move it. You're in the way. Get out of my way. Get out of the way, or you'll get hurt.
	Similar expressions (also not nice things to say) are as follows:
	Move your ass. Move your butt. Move your booty. Move your fanny. Get your ass in gear.
Movers, shakers	Those with influence in their fields. Those who get things done (movers) and those who benefit from them (shakers).
	If you want to have any success in Hollywood, you need to know a few movers and shakers in the movie industry.
Moving in single digits	Moving very slowly.
	The traffic is moving in the single digits.
	Also: You see a lot of brake lights. The traffic is bumper to bumper.
Moving mountains	Doing difficult things.
	If you believe in yourself, you can accomplish anything. You can move mountains!
Moving on	Not dwelling in the past. Continuing with one's life.
	When you say: *The earthquake survivors are moving on with their lives,* you could mean
	They're rebuilding their homes. *They're not just talking or thinking about it anymore.* *They've put the incident behind them and are looking forward.*
	Also see: Picking up the pieces.

Moving target *Origin: Military*	A difficult target to hit. A difficult situation to figure out. A changing situation, where finding a solution is difficult. Compare to: Sitting duck.
Much ado about nothing	A lot of talk about nothing. It's not as bad as it sounds.

If your wife wants to throw you off the roof, make sure the roof is as low as possible. *(Spanish.)*

Much less	When someone says: *He can't swim, much less dive,* they mean: *If he can't swim, then obviously he can't dive.* *He can't swim. How do you expect him to dive?* Also see: Let alone.
Much to one's chagrin	When someone says: *Much to Pierre's chagrin, Sophia didn't remember him,* they mean something like: *Pierre was upset, saddened, irritated, or humiliated to find out that Sophia didn't remember him.*
Muddying the waters *Origin: Sports*	Making a confusing situation even more so. Trying to take advantage of a confusing situation. Making things confusing so that the real problem cannot be identified or addressed.
Mum's the word.	Keep quiet; Keep it a secret; as in: A. *I'm going to tell you something, but mum's the word!* B. *I understand, I'll keep it to myself.* I'll keep it a secret, as in: A. *I'm going to tell you something, but please keep it to yourself!* B. *Okay. Mum's the word!*

Musical chairs	Depending on how it is used, *musical chairs* can convey various messages:
	Political instability;
	Avoiding the issues;
	Dancing around the issues; Etc.
	I'm tired of playing musical chairs with our school issues. Can't somebody give us a straight answer?
	Background: This is a game usually played by children. As the music plays, the players walk around a number of chairs. (There is always one more player than there are chairs.) When the music stops, players rush to sit on the chairs and one player is left without a chair. This player is eliminated, another chair is removed, and the sequence is repeated until there's only one player left, who wins the game.
My bad	My fault. My mistake.
My lips are sealed.	I won't say a word.

Cheap things are expensive. *(Spanish.)*

My treat	It's free. I'll pay for it.
	I just got a raise today and I want to take all of you to lunch. My treat.
	Also: It's on me.
	Compare to: On the house.
Nail biter **Nail-biter**	A tense situation. A very close ending. A situation where one starts biting one's nails out of nervousness.
	The game on Sunday was a nail-biter, with the visiting team scoring a winning touchdown in the last five seconds.

Nailing someone (down) Locating, identifying, apprehending, or controlling someone or something.

The police have nailed the suspect and are in the process of taking her to jail.

I'm happy to announce that we have nailed the heat exchanger problem down and we'll be having a quick solution in the next couple of weeks!

Also: Pinning down.

Nature calling The feeling a person has when it's time to go to the bathroom.

I was driving when I felt nature calling, so I stopped at the next luxury hotel to use their restroom.

Also: Nature's call.

Nature of the beast That's how it is.
Something that you can't change.

A. *I hate it when our supervisor looks at his watch every time he sees me.*
B. *That's the nature of the beast. Learn to live with it.*

Neck and neck
Neck-and-neck Very close.
About at the same level.

Sports

Q. *Which horse will win the race?*
A. *It's difficult to say! They're neck-and-neck.*

Neck of the woods Neighborhood.

You'll never see that kind of behavior in MY neck of the woods!

Needing persuasion When someone says: *He needs some persuasion,* they mean something like:
We have to convince him.
We have to talk some sense into him.
We have to make him see things our way.
We should probably use some force on him.

Needle in a haystack	Talking about something that's difficult to find. *It's very difficult to find your certificate here. It's like looking for a needle in a haystack.*
Need-to-know basis	If you're told that certain information is available on a need-to-know basis, then you will not be told *everything* unless you are one of the persons who need to know. When someone says: *I'll tell you things on a need-to-know basis,* then they will only tell you the things that they think are necessary for you to know.
New kid on the block	A new student. A new player on the team. A new arrival on the market. A new arrival into a neighborhood. Also: New kid in town. Johnny-come-lately.
New lease on life	New opportunity. Starting again something (which was failing) with new energy. *Getting a low interest-rate loan for my restaurant would give my business a new lease on life.*
Next to nothing	Almost nothing or very little, as in: *It costs next to nothing.* Also see: Peanuts.
Next up	Next.
Nickel and dime **Nickel-and-dime**	Small amounts of money. When someone says: *Don't nickel-and-dime me,* they mean: *Don't waste my time over small change.*

Continued on the next page.

Nickel and dime
Nickel-and-dime

Continued from the previous page.

When someone says: *This business will nickel-and-dime me to death,* they mean:

This business is going to gradually bankrupt me with all of these small expenses.

When someone says: *He nickel-and-dimed this into a big business,* they mean:

Little by little, he made it into a big business.

A large house hides large matters. *(Swahili.)*

Where there are lots of people, there will be lots of things going on.

Nine lives

This phrase is about being very tough, or being able to get out of tough situations without being really hurt.

Q. Is it true that cats have nine lives?
A. I don't know about that. But, if it is true, mine has only one left!

Q. What do you think Vincento will do after his latest scandal?
A. Oh, don't worry about him. He still has seven of his nine lives left!

Nipping something in the bud

Taking care of a problem in its early stages.

I should have nipped my accident problem in the bud before the insurance company became involved.

Nitty-gritty

The main thing.
Heart of the matter.

Okay everyone. Enough with the small talk. Let's get down to the nitty-gritty!

No can do

No way.
I can't do it.
It's impossible.

A. Let's go on a trip.
B. No can do!

No contest *Legal*	No challenge. No argument. When someone says: *She pleaded "no contest" to the charges,* they mean: *She offered no argument.* *She didn't challenge the charges.* *She didn't admit that she was guilty, but she also didn't say that she was innocent.*
No contest *Sports*	Not enough challenge. When someone says: *Did you see the match last night? It was no contest,* they mean: *It wasn't a fair match.* *The two sides were not fairly matched.* *One side was very clearly superior to the other.*
No doubt	Certainly. Without a doubt. *No doubt she'll join us for dinner.* Also: No doubt about it. No question about it.
No holds barred *Sports*	No rules. *Okay, let them fight, no holds barred. I don't care anymore. Let them fight any way they want, with everything they have.* Compare to: All bets are off. **Background:** This is originally from wrestling, before there were any sets of rules in place.
No less	When someone says: *He walked outside for a long time–in a severe storm, no less–before going back home,* they mean something like: *Even though it was a severe storm, he walked for a long time before going back home.* *Surprisingly enough, he walked for a long time, in a severe storm, before going back home.*

- What do you think of Henry?
- I've known Henry for some time. He isn't above insulting people.
- I know. He's downstairs!

For a definition, see:

- **Not being above doing something**

No love lost A lot of hatred.
A history of disagreement.

When someone says: *There is no love lost between them,* they mean something like:
They really hate each other and always have.

A big blanket encourages sleeping in the morning. *(Parts of Africa.)*
Luxury encourages idleness.

No match When one side is clearly and overwhelmingly
Origin: Sports superior to the other side, a comparison or competition between the two sides becomes meaningless and won't be fair. In such cases, the less superior side is no match for the other.

A slide rule is no match for modern calculators.

A car is no match for a truck, if we're talking about load capacity.

A bicycle is no match for a motorcycle, if we're talking about speed.

No matter what Anyway.
In any case.
Without condition.

We'll do it, no matter what, means:
We'll do it.
We'll do it anyway.
We'll do it no matter what happens.

No, sirree, Bob! No!
Never!
No, I won't do it.
No, you can't do it.
No, it's not like that.
No, it can't be done.

Also:
No way, Jose!
Not in your life!

Opposite:
Yes, sirree, Bob!

No skin off my nose	I don't care. It's not my problem. It doesn't affect me, or bother me. Q. *Why didn't you vote for the minimum wage proposition?* A. *Why should I? It's no skin off my nose.*
No sooner ... than	An example is needed: When you say: *No sooner had Tom eaten the fish than he began to feel sick,* you mean: *As soon as Tom ate the fish, he felt sick.*
No stone unturned	When someone says: *We've left no stone unturned,* they mean: *Everything possible has been done.* *We've done everything that's necessary.*
No two ways about it	There's no other way. Q. *I thought we were going to the movies first?* A. *No, we'll have dinner first, and don't argue with me. There are no two ways about it!*
No way, Jose!	See: No, sirree, Bob!
No wonder! **Small wonder!**	It's no surprise. We shouldn't be surprised that this is the case. *No wonder everybody loves the new dance show. It's very entertaining!* *With gas prices being so high, it's a small wonder that they all stayed home during the holidays!*
Nobody's breaking china.	They're not doing any damage.
No-brainer	Very clear. Easy to understand. So easy even a caveman would understand! Q. *So, you're saying that just because Jon Stewart mentioned it, we should look into it?* A. *Of course. It's a no-brainer!*

None	Zero. Nothing. Also: Zilch. Nada. Zippo. Not a one.
Nonissue **Non-issue**	Not an issue. Not a problem. An issue that's not important.
Nook and cranny	All details associated with something or some place. *I've looked in every nook and cranny in here, but I can't find my glasses.* Compare to: Odds and ends.
Not a question of "if" but a question of "when"	We know it will happen; we don't know *when!* Similar: Not a question of *why* but a question of *how.* Not a question of *when* but a question of *why.* Not a question of *where* but a question of *how.*
Not a word! **Not a word out of you!**	Don't say a word! If you say one word, you'll get in trouble! Also: If you say: *One word out of you,* in a threatening way, it means the same thing. *One word out of you, and you'll get in trouble!*
Not being above doing something	*Helen isn't above insulting people,* means: *She insults people easily;* *She doesn't mind insulting people; etc.* Compare to: Being above doing something.
Not bothering to do something	Not doing something. Not going through the trouble of doing something. When someone says: *Masako didn't bother to read the letter,* they simply mean: *Masako didn't read the letter.*

Not having a clue **Not knowing** **which end is up**	Being clueless. Being confused. Not knowing what's going on. A. *Let's ask that guy for directions.* B. *Look at him. He doesn't have a clue! Ask someone else.*
Not holding water	Flawed. Full of problems. Something that doesn't work. Not supported by evidence or facts. Q. *What's wrong with their plan? Does it hold water?* A. *No, it's full of problems, full of holes, so to speak.*

When you follow the old man, the dog will not bite. *(Thai.)*
Where there are elders, the house does not burn. *(Haitian.)*

Listen to the advice of the elders.

Not pulling **punches**	Not holding back. Speaking truthfully, without being kind or unkind. Q. *He wasn't nice to me. Does he hate me.* A. *No, he wasn't pulling any punches. He was just telling you what he thought was right.*
Not thinking much **of**	Not taking someone or something seriously. *They don't think much of me, means:* *They don't take me seriously.* *They don't think very highly of me.* *They don't think I have anything significant to offer.* *They don't think I am good enough or important enough.* Also: Not giving someone much credit.
Not to be sneezed **at**	To be taken seriously. Not to be taken lightly.

Not to mention	And. Also. When someone says: *Wendy Crewson is beautiful, not to mention sophisticated,* they mean: *Wendy Crewson is beautiful AND sophisticated.*
Nothing doing	No way. It's no use, or it's no good. It won't work. Don't waste your time. Q. *Will you pay for my ticket?* A. *Nothing doing!*
Nothing getting by someone **Nothing getting past someone**	This is best explained through examples: When someone says: *Nothing gets by her,* they mean something like: *You can't fool her.* *She doesn't miss anything.* *She notices (or understands) everything.* And an example showing sarcasm: Q. *I see you have your running shoes on. Are you going to run?* A. *You're so smart. Nothing gets by you!*
Nothing short of something	This means "something" or "a lot of something," and is best explained through examples: When someone says: *Her victory is nothing short of anticipated,* they mean: *Her victory is anticipated or strongly anticipated.* When someone says: *Eva's recovery was nothing short of a miracle,* they mean: *Her recovery was a miracle.*
Nothing to hang one's hat on	It's nothing to brag about. Nothing substantial is available. There's nothing solid or useful here. A. *Ask her to help you with some ideas.* B. *I did, but she's giving me nothing to hang my hat on! She's wasting my time.*

Nothing to it	It isn't true.
	It's very easy.
	It's not important.
	Don't worry; it doesn't mean anything.
Nothing to show for it	A waste of time or money.
	We spent a lot of time and money bidding on this project, but we lost the bid. Now we have nothing to show for it. However, our competitors DO have something to show for it: a huge contract!

A man who does not lie shall never marry. *(Parts of Africa.)*

Now, if you will excuse me!	I'm sorry, but I have to leave.
	Please excuse, me as I have another appointment.
NSA	This is an abbreviation for:
No strings attached	No Strings Attached.
	It represents no commitment, or additional obligation, and is mostly used by the younger, Internet and texting generation:
	Please try our product and, if you don't like it, you don't have to buy it; no strings attached.
	It also represents a purely physical relationship for sexual purposes without any expectation of romantic commitment.
Number is up.	Time to go.
	Time to die.
	My number is up, means something like:
	I'm dying.
	I have to go, or it's my turn.
	I don't have any more time.
Number one	I.
	Me.
	Myself.
	I'm doing this for number one! Myself.

Numbered	Limited.
	When someone says: *Your days are numbered,* they could mean any of these:
	You're finished. *You don't have a lot of time left.* *You don't have many days left (in your life, on your job, etc.)*

Someone else's rice cake always looks bigger. *(Korean.)*
The sound of drums sounds nicely from far away. *(Turkish.)*
People are never satisfied with what they have.

Objective, subjective	An objective person: Considers the facts, not emotions. Does not let his/her personal feeling influence his/her decisions.
	Opposite: A subjective person.
Odd hours	Unusual hours. Late night hours.
Odds and ends	Little things. Various pieces. Miscellaneous items.
	Q. What did you use to make this quilt? *A. Oh, just some odds-and-ends of fabric that I had lying around the sewing room.*
Of "X" persuasion	From "X." Adhering to "X" culture, beliefs, traditions, etc.
	Of Asian persuasion. *Of Republican persuasion.*
Of mine	My. Belonging to me.
	Similar: *An idea of his; His idea.* *A friend of mine; My friend.* *A book of yours; Your book.* *Flowers of hers; Her flowers.*

Of two minds	Divided.
	Undecided.

Off one's rocker	Crazy.
	Out of one's mind.
	A. *I'm going mountain climbing this weekend.*
	B. *Are you off your rocker? It's below freezing out there!*

Off base	Not on the base, as in:
Off-base	Q. *Do you live here on the base?*
Military	A. *No, sir. I live in off-base housing.*
Sports	Mistaken, as in:
	Q. *Do you agree with your opponent on the abortion issue?*
	A. *No, she's way off-base on this one. I don't think she knows what's going on at all.*

Off limits	Available to certain people.
Off-limits	Not available to everybody.
Military	When someone says: *The cafeteria is off-limits,* they mean something like:
	We don't have permission to go there.
	When someone says: *Hey, guys, the mayor's family is off-limits,* they mean something like:
	Don't photograph them.
	Don't make jokes about them.
	Don't write about their private lives.

Five fingers are brothers, not equals. *(Persian.)*

Off schedule	Late.
Off-schedule	Behind schedule.
	If you say: *The construction is off-schedule,* you mean:
	It won't be completed on time, as previously planned.

Off the beaten path	Away from the normal, usual, or familiar ways.

Off the charts **Off-the-charts**	Difficult to measure. Not within the usual limits.

Off the cuff **Off-the-cuff**	Unprepared. Without preparation.

Sir, now that you're an elected official, you should be more careful about making some of your typical, off-the-cuff remarks. You could get in trouble!

Also: Off the top of one's head.

Off the record **Off-the-record**	Unofficially. An unofficial statement.

When someone says: *I'm going to tell you this off-the-record,* they mean something like:

I'll tell you, but you can't use my name.
I'll tell you, but you can't use it against me.
I'll tell you, but I'll deny it if you tell anybody.

Off the wagon	Starting to drink alcohol again. Drinking alcohol after a period of not drinking.

Q. *Hey, Max, are you drinking again? I thought you were on the wagon.*
A. *I was, but unfortunately I fell off the wagon! I'll have to do something about it.*

Note:
This expression primarily relates to drinking alcohol, but it can also apply to other activities such as going on a diet, working out, etc.

Compare to: On-the-wagon.

Off-the-wall	Odd. Unusual. Different. Unconventional.

A. *I feel like doing something off-the-wall today.*
B. *Well, maybe you should ride a horse to your office!*

OMG	This is an abbreviation for: <u>O</u>h <u>M</u>y <u>G</u>od. It is used by the younger, Internet and texting generation. Also: OMIGOD and OMIGOSH.
On all fours	Begging for mercy. Being on hands and knees. *I hate it when he gets down on all fours. Doesn't he have any self respect?*
On behalf of	Speaking for. As a representative of. *On behalf of my family, I thank you for being here. Speaking for myself, however, I wish you'd all go home!*

Three monks have no water to drink. *(Chinese.)*
Many midwives, and child will be lazy. *(Croatian.)*
Two midwives, and the baby's head will be crooked. *(Persian.)*

On budget	A project that is completed (or is likely to be completed) at or within the estimated cost.
On cloud 9 **On cloud nine**	Feeling free. Having a good time. Being under the influence of recreational drugs. Behaving in a manner that is not considered to be normal. Feeling elated or thrilled about something wonderful that has happened.
On death row *Legal*	A person who is sentenced to die and is awaiting execution.
On location	The place, other than a studio, where a movie is made. Q. *Those were very realistic scenes. Was this movie made at the studio?* A. *No, it was made on-location, around San Diego.*

On message **Off message** *Political*	This is a political phrase and shows if someone is (or is not) in agreement with the policy or policies accepted by a group. *If a politician is expressing views that are in agreement with his party's policies, then he is on message. Otherwise, he is off message.*
On one's high horse	Arrogant. Inflexible. Condescending. Looking down on others. A. *Why don't you like my friend?* B. *He always gets on his high horse, no matter what subject we're talking about.* Related: Off one's high horse.
On one's own	Alone. Independent. Not having help from others. Because of one's own efforts. *There was no one there. I thought, Wow. I'm really on my own here.* *Son, if you stay in college, I'll help you in any way that I can. If you drop out, however, I won't be helping you. You'll be on your own.*
On par with **On a par with**	Equal. On the same level. *I'm happy to tell you that your daughter is on par with the other kids.*
On pins and needles	Nervously waiting for something or someone. A. *Let's go out for lunch.* B. *I can't. I'm on pins and needles waiting to hear about my scholarship.* Also: The tingling feeling in one's legs (due to low blood circulation) resulting from sitting in certain positions for too long.

- Boss, you've been here since early morning. Maybe you should go home with your son.
- Yes, I think I'm done. You can stick a fork in me!

For a definition, see:
- **I'm done.**
- **Stick a fork in it!**

On second thought	After review, as in: *I was thinking of going to the movies with my friends. On second thought, however, I decided to stay home.* Compare to: Second thought. Having second thoughts.
On someone's dime	Someone will pay for it. At someone else's expense. If the kids are at the movies on your dime, then you're paying for the tickets! A. *I hear your ex-wife wants to go to Hawaii.* B. *Not on my dime!* A. *Who's paying for the kids' trip then?* B. *They're traveling on my dime!*

When eating a fruit, think of the person who planted the tree. *(Vietnamese.)*

On someone's payroll	Indebted to someone. Someone's employee. When someone says: *They're on the insurance company's payroll,* they could mean either of the following: *They're the insurance company's employees. (Positive connotation.)* *The insurance company pays them to do their dirty work. (Negative connotation.)*
On the back burner	Something that: Is not a rush job. Can be done later. Is not important at this time. Has been discontinued temporarily. Q. *Are we working on the budget report today?* A. *No, we're doing the scholarships. The budget report will be on the back burner for a while.* Opposite: On the front burner.

On the chopping block	In trouble, as in:
	If she finds out, my neck will be on the chopping block.
	Other usage:
	When you put someone on the chopping block, you're making them the scapegoat, and putting the blame on them.
	If a company is laying people off, and you are on the chopping block, it could mean that you are among those being considered for termination.
On the contrary!	I beg to differ.
	Contrary to that.
	The opposite of something.
	Contrary to what you're saying.
	A. *I think huge taxes should be imposed on Japanese cars to help the Americans.*
	B. *On the contrary, that will hurt us, as our manufacturers will stop trying to improve their products.*
	Also:
	Au contraire!
	(This is French for *On the contrary,* and may be used by itself or followed by an additional explanation.)
On the defensive	Defending and/or explaining one's actions.
	I'm sorry, but once you're on the defensive, it means you'll probably lose the argument.
	Compare to: On the offensive.
On the double *Military*	Right away.
	When someone says: *Come here, on the double,* they mean: *Come here right now.*
	Background:
	This term comes from the military, where an order is supposed to be carried out at twice the normal pace.

On the eve of	On the night or day before an event, as in:
	Christmas Eve.
	New Year's Eve.
	Eve of the dance competition.

On the fence	Undecided.
	Not taking sides or making a decision.
	Q. *Do you think the others will join us?*
	A. *Joey is still on the fence about it, but Ken and Mitch are both coming with us.*

On the heels of	Immediately after.
	When someone says: *The scandal was reported on the heels of the elections*, they mean something like:
	It became public knowledge right after the elections.

On the horizon	Close by.
	Can be seen.
	In the near future.
	Practical and affordable electric cars are on the horizon. I think they'll be here soon.

On the house	This usually refers to drinks and it means the management pays for it.
	To show our appreciation for your continued business, tonight the drinks are on the house!
	Compare to: My treat.

On the lam Legal	Hiding from the police.

On the level	Frank.
	Honest.
	Someone who tells the truth.
	If you're on the level, you're being straight with people.
	Q. *What do you think of the new guy?*
	A. *I don't really know him, but he seems to be on the level.*

On the line	At risk.
	I'm risking everything, and I have to be careful. My neck is on the line, you know!
	Also:
	My ass is on the line! (Same thing, but not polite.)
On the menu **On the table**	On the agenda. Available options. The things to talk about or make decisions about.
	When someone says: *That wasn't on the menu,* they mean something like:
	I didn't know that. I didn't agree to that.
	When someone says: *What's on the table?* they mean something like:
	What are we going to talk about? What options, or choices, do we have?
On the offensive	Attacking and/or questioning someone's actions.
	Your opponents seem to be vulnerable now. It's time for you to go on the offensive, and start questioning their motives.
	Compare to: On the defensive.
On the other hand	However. Looking at it from another point of view.
On the real	Really. For real. Doing serious stuff.
On the rise	Going up. Getting bigger. Becoming more noticeable.
	As more and more banks are running into trouble, the number of banks going bankrupt is on the rise.

On the rocks	Having problems or facing certain failure, as in: *Our relationship is on the rocks.* A drink served with ice cubes, as in: *Do you like your drink straight or on the rocks?*
On the run *Legal*	Hiding. Avoiding arrest, or something, or someone. Q. *Is your husband still on the run?* A. *Yes he's hiding from the police. From me, too!*
On the same page **On the same wavelength**	Being in general agreement. When you say: *We're on the same page,* you mean something like: *We agree with each other.* *We understand each other.* *We both know what we're talking about and we're in agreement.* Also see: Seeing eye-to-eye.
On the sidelines *Sports*	Not being actively involved. *She won't be working, as she'll be on the sidelines temporarily. We won't hear from her for a while.*
On the straight and narrow.	Following the rules. Doing things in the correct way. *The new laws were intended to keep corporations on the straight and narrow, but they didn't work.*
On the up-and-up	Frank. Honest. Someone who tells the truth. *If you're on the up-and-up, you're being straight with people.* *I don't trust the politicians in Congress. I don't think they're on the up-and-up with the people.* Another meaning: Someone who is successful.

On the verge About to happen.
Close to something happening.

Q. *Why are you so quiet these days?*
A. *I think we are on the verge of another recession!*

On the wagon Not drinking.
Being, and staying, sober.

Q. *Hey Joe, you want a drink?*
A. *No, thanks. I'm on the wagon!*

Note:
Although this expression primarily relates to drinking, it can also apply to other activities, such as going on a diet, working out, etc.

Compare to: Off the wagon.

Clothes put on while running come off while running. *(Parts of Africa.)*

On thin ice On risky ground.
In a dangerous situation.

When someone says: *You're walking on thin ice,* they mean:

What you're doing is risky. Please be careful.

A. *I'm dating my boss's daughter, and he doesn't know.*
B. *You're skating on the thin ice corner of the lake, buddy!*

Also:
On slippery slopes.
On slippery or shaky grounds.

Compare to: Walking on eggshells.

On track On the correct path.
Proceeding according to the plans.

Q. *Is he on track to fix the problems?*
A. *Yes, he's going in the right direction, doing the right things.*

Once bitten, twice shy **Once burned, twice shy**	If you have a bad experience with something, you would be reluctant to try it again, or at least you'd be more careful the next time. A. *I had an accident on the roller coaster once when I was a kid, and I never rode on roller coasters again.* B. *I can understand. Once bitten, twice shy!*
Once in a blue moon	Rarely. Not often.
One down, two to go	We have finished one. We must do two more.
One for the road	One more (drink) before I go. This usually applies to alcoholic drinks, but it can also apply to food items, a hand of cards, etc.
One generation removed	One generation apart. Separated by one generation. *When my great grandparents got married, they weren't educated. One generation removed, the grandchildren were all college graduates!*
One of a kind	Unique. Very rare. Like no one else or nothing else. Also: One in a million.
One taco short of the combination plate!	Slow. Not smart. When someone says: *He's one taco short of the combination plate,* they mean: *He's not very smart.* Similar: He's not all together. He's got a screw loose. His upper floor is leaking.

Continued on the next page.

One taco short of the combination plate!

Continued from the previous page.

He hasn't got all his buttons.
He has one ore out of the water.
He's one can short of a six-pack.
The lights are out on the top floor.
There's something missing up there.
The lights are on, but nobody's home.
The upstairs unit has been rented out.
He doesn't have his head screwed on straight.

One too many

Too many.
One more than enough.
One unit more than the allowable amount.

A. *Your honor, I only committed one burglary.*
B. *Well, that is one burglary too many! Take him away.*

If you want to see a rainbow, you must first sit through the rain. *(Hungarian.)*

One's backyard

Home.
Hometown.
Neighborhood.

Nuclear waste? Never. Not in my backyard!

We don't want any sex offenders in our backyard.

One's cup of tea

Something one likes.

Q. *Do you want to come and sit here in the sun with me?*
A. *Sitting in the sun may be your cup of tea, but it's not my cup of tea!*

One's cut
One's take

One's share of the profits.

Q. *You seem very happy! What's your take?*
A. *I'm doing this for a friend. I'm not getting anything.*

Also:
One's piece of the action.
One's share of the action.

One's honor

If you say: *We're having a party in Aysha's honor or in honor of Aysha,* it means:

We're having a party to honor Aysha or to show our respect for her.

If you say: *Helga told us on her honor (or upon her honor) that she was not involved,* it means:

Helga gave us her word of honor (similar to being under oath) that she was not involved.

One's own recognizance
Legal

Personal guarantee.

When someone says: *She's free, on her own recognizance,* they mean something like:

She's free without bail, without paying anything, because they believed her when she said she'd appear when a new court date was set.

One's ship coming in

Making it.
Becoming successful, making money, etc.

When someone says: *Pay me when your ship comes in,* they mean something like:

Pay me when you can, or when you make it, or when you make your money, etc.

One's turf

One's familiar area, where one feels comfortable, protected, and at home.

This is my turf. No one can catch me here!

One's two cents' (worth)

One's humble opinion.

If you want my two cents' (worth), I don't think you should interfere in this matter.

Note:
Using this expression, you can offer your opinion with less chance of offending the other person. Two cents, a very small amount, makes it humble and less offensive.

Also, jokingly:
Hey, Johnny, what do you think of my plans? Give me your two cents.

One's undoing	One's failure. One's cause of failure. When someone says: *The jail sentence was the key to his undoing,* they mean something like: *The jail sentence ruined his life.* Another usage: One's OWN undoing. When someone says: *The jail sentence was his own undoing,* they mean: *The jail sentence was his own fault.*
One-track mind	Stubborn. A person who thinks constantly about one thing, often related to sex. A person who thinks and acts in a certain way only and is not willing to consider the alternatives.

No nuts when one has teeth, no teeth when one has nuts. *(Indian.)*
God gives nuts to those who don't have teeth, and teeth to those who don't have nuts. *(Portuguese.)*

You never get what you want.

One-trick pony	A person who is only good at doing one thing. Q. *It took you a long time to hire a new secretary, so I'm assuming she's good?* A. *Oh, absolutely. She's not a one-trick pony. She's multi-talented.*
One-upping someone	Having an advantage over someone, as in: *My competitors are finally one-upping me. I'm falling behind.* Being arrogant about having an advantage, as in: A. *I wrote my first novel when I was 45 years old.* B. *That's nothing. By the time I was 45 years old, I had written several novels!* A. *There you go again, one-upping me!*

Oops! **Whoops!**	This is an informal exclamation and is used to express admission to, or surprise at, or apology for, making (or almost making) a mistake.
	Oops, I did it again! *Oops, I didn't mean that!* *Oops, I almost ran into you!* *Oops, I didn't know you were here!*
Op-Ed	This is an abbreviation for: Opinion Editorial. Opposite the Editorial page.
	Background: Some believe *Op-Ed* is an abbreviation for *Opinion Editorial* which is an article that is written by writers who are not usually associated with the publication but are voicing their own opinion. This is different from editorials by the publication's own editors. These editorials are usually printed *opposite* the real editorial, which is where others believe the abbreviation comes from.
Open and shut **Open-and-shut**	Easy or quick. Something that won't require a lot of effort to finish.
	A. *You promised to go out tonight!* B. *This is an open-and-shut case, and won't take long. We can still go.*
Open ended **Open-ended** *Legal*	Without limits.
	I don't like open-ended contracts because I don't want to get into a situation without clear guidelines and limitations.
	An open-ended-question is a question that allows or encourages discussion.
	An open-ended-agreement is an agreement that allows future changes.
	An open-ended-discussion is an open discussion with no set limits.

At the job performance review:

I've seen your work, David. You always hit the nail on the head, and I like that! I wish everyone here could follow instructions the way that you do.

For a definition, see:

- **Hitting the nail on the head**

264 · English Idioms and Expressions for Foreigners, *Like Me!*

Open season *Origin: Sports*	A period during which certain restrictions don't apply.

Q. *Do you know that everybody's killing rats?*
A. *I know! It's open season on them!*
Q. *Speaking of open season, are Republicans still taking heat for the bad economy?*
A. *Yeah, everybody is still blaming them.*

Compare to:
Fair game.

Open secret	A secret that everyone is aware of. It's supposed to be a secret, but it's not really.

The candidate's infidelity was an open secret among his staffers.

The day a monkey is destined to die, all trees become slippery. *(Swahili.)*

Opening a can of worms	Asking for trouble. Creating, or uncovering, new problems.

A. *Let's just change the bulbs, not the fixtures. Otherwise, we'll be opening a can of worms.*
B. *Why?*
A. *Well, if you want to change the fixtures, we'll have to cut into the wall. Then we may have to change the wiring, bring things up to code, etc.*

OPM	This is an abbreviation for:

Other People's Money.

The key to real estate investment is using OPM!

Optional material	Not standard. Available at extra charge. Available but not necessary.

Q. *Do you have automatic transmission and air-conditioning on this car?*
A. *Well, yes. Automatic transmission is standard, but air-conditioning is optional.*

Or else

This is a warning and means something like:

If not, you'll be sorry.
If not, I'll do something bad to you.
If not, something bad will happen to you.

A. *Tell me where my books are, or else!*
B. *Or else what?*
A. *Or else I won't tell you who came here looking for you!*

Or otherwise

Or in other ways.
Or in ways other than that.

I don't trust him, professionally or otherwise, means something like:

I don't trust him at all! Whether from a professional point of view, or from other points of view, I don't trust him!

I'm not in a position to go on a vacation, financially or otherwise, means something like:

I can't go on a vacation! Because of financial reasons, family problems, etc., I can't go on a vacation!

He who builds with sweat defends with blood. *(Albanian.)*

OTC
Medical

This is an abbreviation for:

Over **T**he **C**ounter, medication that can be sold without requiring a prescription from a doctor.

Q. *Mr. Pharmacist, would you give me some pills for my cholesterol?*
A. *That's not an over-the-counter medication. You need to get a prescription from Dr. Pund!*

Other fish in the sea

Plenty more fish in the sea

More opportunities.
(Usually used in order to sympathize with a girl or boy who has been hurt romantically.)

Don't worry. There are plenty of other fish in the sea. There will be other (romantic) opportunities.

Other side of the tracks

The poor part of town or community. (Depending on the circumstances, it could also refer to the rich part of town or community.)

Compare to:
Wrong side of the tracks.

Too many chiefs and not enough Indians. *(English.)*
You're a master, I'm a master. Who is to milk this cow? *(Turkish.)*
When there are too many bosses, work doesn't get done.

Out of left field

Origin: Sports

Something unrelated happening.
Something happening unexpectedly.

Q. *Your promotion surprised everyone, including yourself, didn't it?*
A. *Yeah, it came so far out of left field you would need a crystal ball to see it coming.*

Background:
This has its origins in baseball. One theory comes directly from the experience of players. A runner, attempting to score at home has his back to the left field, thus a throw to the plate coming from left field can arrive as a surprise to the runner.

Out of line

Origin: Military

Out of place, as in:
You're out of line. Please step back in line.

Disrespectful, as in:
You were out of line. You should apologize.

Not in the expected place, as in:
We're way out of line with these results. Let's do the calculations again.

Inappropriate, as in:
She was out of line with that remark. It was the supervisor's responsibility to say it.

Out of sight, out of mind

If people don't see you, they'll forget you.
If you want people to remember you, stay in sight.
If you don't see something or someone, you might forget about them.

Out of the blue	Appearing or happening suddenly, as in:

We were walking when, out of the blue, my wife started crying!

Q. *Were there any rumors before they started the lay-offs at your company?*
A. *Nothing! It was totally out of the blue!*

Similar:
Coming out of nowhere, as in:

Q. *Didn't you see the policeman before you ran the red light?*
A. *No, he came out of nowhere!*

Out of the woods   Out of trouble.
Out of danger.

A. *Well, it sure looks like the economy is on its way up again.*
B. *Yes, but there's still high unemployment! We're not out of the woods yet.*

Out of wedlock   Outside of marriage.

When someone says: *Susu was born out of wedlock,* they mean something like: *She's a lovechild. Her parents were not married.*

With patience, you will see an ant's breasts. *(Haitian.)*

Out the window   When someone says: *If my demands are not met, the script goes out the window,* they mean something like:

I will not use it.
You can forget about it.
There won't be a script.

Out there   Weird.
Strange.

A. *I must say, I find your story somewhat hard to believe.*
B. *I know it sounds a bit out there but, believe me, it did happen!*

Out to get somebody	Planning to get someone. (With a negative connotation.)
	When someone says: *The police are out to get him,* they mean something like:
	They are looking for him to arrest him.

Close friends are like a double-edged knife; far away friends are money saved. *(Haitian.)*

Out to lunch	Not alert. Not paying attention. Acting in a stupid way. Not aware of what's going on around you.
	For a couple of hours, my husband and family were frightened because I was totally out to lunch. They thought I had gone crazy.
	Also see: At sea.
Outside the box	Unusual. Out of the ordinary. Not in the traditional way.
	Try to be original, and think outside the box for a change!
	Compare to: Inside the box.
Over a barrel	Not in control. At someone's mercy.
	Q. *Are you going to accept Dilliano's conditions?* A. *Hell, no! Now that we finally have him over a barrel, we should ask for more.*
Over my dead body!	No! I won't do it! I won't let it happen (as long as I'm alive).
	A. *I'm going to take your sister to the party.* B. *Over my dead body!*

Over one's head	Going outside the chain of command, as in:

Q. *I hear your supervisor is mad at you. Why did you go over his head?*
A. *Well, he kept putting off my promotion. I had to talk to the director directly*

Too difficult or complicated, as in:
Q. *Did you understand the problem?*
A. *No, it was way over my head.*

Too much to handle, if used with "in", as in:
A. *You're in over your head. You should hire someone to help you.*
B. *No, I can do it. I just need a little more time.*

Compare to:
Biting off more than one can chew.

Over the edge	Beyond help. Losing one's mind.

My friend has gone over the edge, means:

There's no hope for him; or
I believe he's lost his mind.

A priest, a doctor, and a policeman had better not enter one's house. *(Greek.)*

Over the hill	Old. Too old. Too old to do certain things. Older than one would like to be.

A. *I'd like to learn about computers, but I'm a bit over the hill for that.*
B. *Oh, stop it! You're never too old for anything, unless you want to be.*

Over the moon	Happy. Hoping for something big.

Q. *Does she know we're going over for dinner?*
A. *Oh, yes, she's over the moon with excitement.*

Over the top	Great.
	Exceptional.
	Too much. (Negative connotation.)
	Extraordinary. (Positive connotation.)
	An over-the-top performance. (Could be a great performance, or a case of over-acting.)
Over-egging the pudding	Overdoing things.
	Spoiling by overdoing, even if it's overdoing a good thing.
	Q. *What did you do? The coffee is so sweet that I can't drink it.*
	A. *I guess I over-egged the pudding.*
Over-rated, Under-rated	Over-rated. (Has a negative connotation.)
	Worse than people think.
	Not as good as people think.
	Under-rated. (Has a positive connotation.)
	Better than people think.
	Not as bad as people think.
	I hate it when I see a lot of under-rated supporting actors struggling in life, while a few over-rated ones command millions of dollars for their mediocre performances, just because!
Owning up to something	Admitting (a mistake).
	Acknowledging something.
	Taking responsibility for a mistake.
	This is something you did. You'd better own up to it, and face the consequences.
Packing a punch *Origin: Sports*	Having a powerful punch.
	Having a lot of power or influence.
	Hey, your kid brother really packs a punch. I'm still dizzy!
Page turner **Page-turner**	An interesting book or other written material that is SO interesting, you cannot wait to see what will happen next, like this one! You cannot wait to turn the page.

Pain in the neck	Annoying.
	When someone says: *He's a pain in the neck,* they mean something like:
	He's annoying; *He bothers me;* *He gets on my nerves; etc.*
	Also: A thorn in the side. A pain in the you know what. A pain in the ass, or in the butt. (Not polite.)
Painting oneself into a corner	Getting oneself into a situation that is difficult or impossible to get out of.

The dead does not know the value of white sheets. *(Haitian.)*

Funerals are for the living.

Painting someone as something	When you say: *He paints her as a good mother,* you mean something like:
	He says she's a good mother. *He talks about her (describes her) as if she's a good mother.*
Pants off	The following examples show how this phrase is used to emphasize a point.
	When someone says: *I can cook the pants off anybody,* they mean: *I can cook much better than anybody.*
	When someone says: *He scared the pants off me,* they mean: *He really scared me.*
	When someone says: *She wants to sue the pants off me,* they mean: *She wants to sue me for everything I have.*
Paper pusher	An office worker. A government official without power. One who does paper work at the office.
	Q. Is this guy a manager or something? *A. No, he's just a paper pusher, stuffing envelopes all day.*

Partisanship ends at waters edge.	When politicians travel to other countries, their political opponents should stop criticizing them. Politicians should stand in unity on controversial issues while abroad.
Party favors	Interesting little things (provided by the host) that you take with you from a party, such as hats, paper plates, plastic utensils, etc.
Pass muster	Pass the test. Meet the requirements. When someone says: *I couldn't pass muster,* they mean something like: *I didn't qualify, or I didn't meet the standards.*
Passing for	Being accepted as someone (or something) that one is not. *Hermann passed for a famous doctor for several years until he got sick!*
Passing resemblance	Little resemblance. *Soobie bears a passing resemblance to her mother,* means: *She looks a little like her mother.* *Manuchehr has MORE than a passing resemblance to Lorne Greene,* means: *Manuchehr looks a lot like Lorne Greene.*
Passing with flying colors	Passing an exam with very high marks. Doing very well, as in a test, presentation, etc.
Pat on the back	Gratitude, encouragement for a job well-done, as in: *You don't deserve a pat on the back yet. You haven't done anything!* Related: Pat oneself on the back, as in: *You guys have done such a great job. You should pat yourselves on the back!*
Patience running thin	Losing patience. Also: Patience wearing thin

Paying through the nose
Paying a huge amount for something; a very high price; etc.

Q. *Hey, do you have medical insurance?*
A. *I wish I did. I'm paying through the nose for the medical services I receive!*

He who doesn't have a brain by twenty shouldn't expect one at thirty. *(Greek.)*

Pea brain
Pea-brain
Pea-brained
Stupid.
Someone whose brain is implied to be the size of a pea.

Whose pea-brained idea was this anyway?

Who is the pea-brained moron standing in the middle of the street in rush-hour traffic?

Peanuts
Very little.

Q. *How much are you getting paid at this job?*
A. *Peanuts!*

Also see: Next to nothing.

Penny for your thoughts
This is short for *I'll give you a penny for your thoughts,* which means: *What's on your mind? What are you thinking about?*

Penny pincher
Stingy.
One who doesn't spend money easily.

Q. *Should we ask your brother to help us with the gas money?*
A. *No, he's such a penny pincher. He won't give us anything.*

Also: Tight pocket.
Tight with money.

Perception trumps facts.
This is a sarcastic expression, which implies:

Seeing is believing;
People believe what they see;
Perception is stronger than facts;
People believe their eyes without considering the facts; etc.

Perp walk *Legal*	Sometimes the police take suspects to a public place (while in handcuffs and prison clothing) in order for reporters to observe, or even interview them. The practice is called *perp walk* and the idea is to socially humiliate a *perp,* or *perpetrator,* and to discourage other potential perpetrators.
Pet project	A favorite project. Not a typical, work related project. A project that has a special meaning to a person. Q. *What is Joe's pet project these days?* A. *Oh, he's still restoring his old 1966 Mustang.*
Petering out	Diminishing, waning. Becoming less and less. Running out of something. Running short on something. Not having enough of something.

A bird will always use another bird's feathers to feather its own nest. *(Parts of Africa.)*

Picking a fight	Starting a fight, argument, quarrel, etc. Compare to: Picking one's battles.
Picking one's battles **Choosing one's battles**	Choosing fights, arguments, issues, etc., that you know you will win. *One should be picking one's battles wisely.* Compare to: Picking a fight.
Picking someone's brain	Asking someone questions. Getting ideas from someone. *After I picked her brain long enough, I knew what she was talking about.* *Hey Joe, let me pick your brain. Do you know if we ever worked on the 747 nose section?*

- I want your Number 2 sandwich with everything. The whole nine yards.

- Sorry, but we only have six-inchers and foot-longs!

For a definition, see:

- **Whole nine yards**

Picking up on something	Getting the message, usually without talking about it.
	I didn't really want to go to the party. Fortunately my wife quickly picked up on that and came up with an excuse.
Picking up steam	Getting better or stronger.
	It's only two months into the campaign, and his campaign is already picking up steam!
	Also: Gaining strength. Gaining momentum.
Picking up the pieces	Getting back, or trying to get back, to normal.
	First it was the fire, then the mudslide, and now the earthquake. We've lost almost everything! But we're picking up the pieces and moving on.
	Also see: Moving on.
Picturing something	Imagining something. Getting a mental picture of something.
	Picture this: Sicily, 1932. It's winter, there's snow everywhere, and Sophia is waiting.
Pissing someone off!	Making people angry. (Not polite.)
	Q. *Why don't you care about Kenyata? I think he's a nice guy.*
	A. *I'm sure he is, but he pisses me off! As a matter of fact he pissed me off today and he also pissed me off yesterday!*
Planting evidence *Legal*	Putting certain items in a place to make someone look guilty, or involved, in relation to a crime.
	Q. *Are you upset that your client was found guilty?*
	A. *Of course I am. He's innocent! He was found guilty because of planted evidence.*
	Related: Being set up, or being framed.

Play ball
Origin: Sports

To go along with what others are doing, especially if you don't like it.

A. *I hate those guys. They're so arrogant. I don't want to do business with them.*
B. *I want you to play ball with them. They can make your career soar.*

Similar: Be a team player.

What you wish for when you're sober, you act out when drunk. *(Greek.)*

Play it by ear.

Be spontaneous.
Act without plans.
Act according to the existing conditions.
See what happens, and act accordingly.

Q. *So, how are we going to do this?*
A. *Well, I'm going to play it by ear for a while until I see what's really going on.*

Playing a bad hand
Gambling

Having bad luck.

Also: Playing a losing hand.

Playing along

Agreeing with others.
Not arguing with others.
Going along with others.
(Mostly done for the sake of keeping peace.)

Also see: Play ball.

Playing by the rules
Sports

Obeying the rules.
Not violating regulations even if doing so would give you better results.

Also:
Falling in line.
Staying in line.
Keeping in line.
Staying in check.
Following the rules.
Observing the rules.
Playing by the book.
Listening to the rules.

Playing hardball	Being a tough negotiator. Not giving too many, if any, concessions. Acting rough, aggressive, determined, etc.
Playing Russian roulette	As an expression, playing *Russian roulette* means taking a huge, huge risk. Playing the real *Russian roulette,* however, means risking your life.

He who knows nothing doubts nothing. *(Vietnamese.)*

Playing someone like a fiddle (or violin)	Using people. Manipulating them. Q. Do you think my girlfriend is taking advantage of me? A. Well, I don't know about that, but she IS playing you like a fiddle!
Playing the heavy	Pretending to be a bad guy. Acting as a bad guy in the movies. *He's a nice guy but it doesn't show because he's always played the heavy in the movies.*
Playing to someone **Playing to something** *Political*	Catering to a certain group. Doing something to please a certain group. Satisfying (or saying something to satisfy) a certain group. When someone says: *The candidate is playing to the liberals,* they mean: *He's saying things that the liberal voters like to hear.* Similar: Playing to the unions, engineers, small businesses, manufacturers, etc.
Pleading guilty *Legal*	Accepting guilt. (This is a legal term, but it is also used in daily conversation.) Also: Guilty as charged.
Pleading not guilty *Legal*	Not accepting guilt. (This is a legal term and is not used in daily conversation.)

Pleading the Fifth *Legal*	Keeping quiet. Refusing to testify.

Q. *So, tell me about your date. What did you guys do last night?*
A. *Oh, I don't know. I guess I'm going to plead the Fifth! I'm not saying anything.*

Also: Taking the Fifth.

Background:
Refusing to testify under the Fifth Amendment is a legal term and has certain legal applications. However it is sometimes used in conversation as shown in the above example.

Pocketbook issues   Financial issues, especially those at the family expense levels.

Our candidates should be addressing pocket book issues, issues that are closer to home for the average person.

Do not sit on a basket to raise yourself; do not be boisterous while carrying goods on your head; do not lie with your head covered, waiting for good luck; do not rely on the god of mercy. *(Cambodian.)*

Poetic justice   Something bad happening to a person as a result of something bad that the same person has done in the same (or similar) way or manner or setting. An outcome in which virtue is rewarded and evil punished, often in an especially appropriate or ironic manner.

Example:
An attorney defends a murderer and helps him to escape conviction using a little known loophole. The same murderer (or maybe even another person) later murders the attorney (or maybe a member of his family) and is found not guilty by using the same loophole. This is what's called "Poetic justice."

Also see:
What goes around, comes around.

Pointing out
Showing something or someone.
Mentioning something or someone.
Bringing something or someone to someone's attention.

I'd like to talk about your mistakes and point them out to you.

I'd like to meet your father if he's here tonight. Would you point him out to me?

One will get caught if one's tail is too long. *(Korean.)*

Poker face
Gambling

An emotionless face.
A face with no expression at all.

You can never tell from her poker face if she's happy or sad or whatever!

Background:
This phrase comes from the world of poker. A good poker player has a "poker face," thus keeping his or her good (or bad) hand a secret.

Poker tells
Gambling

The subtle changes in the behavior and actions of a poker player that result from having a good or bad hand. These twitches, expressions, or mannerisms can reveal or "tell" secrets about what's in the player's cards and if they are bluffing, or truly have a good hand.

I love to play poker with Johnny because I know his tells!

Politically correct
A statement, policy, idea, action, speech, etc., that won't offend anybody or any group, is considered to be *Politically correct.*

An extreme case of *political correctness,* or maybe even a mild version of it, would be considered by some as being a powerful way of exercising *censorship.*

Popping up
Appearing suddenly or unexpectedly.

I thought he was out of town, but he kept popping up in places I frequented.

Poster girl	A symbol for something.
Poster boy	The most, the highest, or the lowest example.
Poster child	*At more than $50 billion in losses, Madoff is the poster boy for stock market fraud. If you want to learn how to cheat people out of their savings, go to him!*
Pot calling the kettle black	Hypocrite. Someone who complains about others doing certain things, although he or she is guilty of doing the same things!
	Also phrased as: *Look who's calling the kettle black!*
Potentially dangerous	Something that has the potential for being dangerous or risky at any time, even NOW.
	Related: Potentially funny, explosive, etc.
Pounding the pavement	Walking on the street. Looking for something, usually employment.
Pouring cold water on something	Discouraging something. Having a negative effect on it. Putting an end to it, or attempting to stop it.
	They haven't poured cold water on the latest rumor yet, so I guess it's true!
	Also: Throwing cold water on something.

There's butter behind his ears. *(Hungarian.)*
He is guilty of something.

Practice what you preach.	Don't be a hypocrite. Follow your own teachings. Do what you tell others to do.
Preaching to the choir	Trying to convince those who already agree with you.
	A. *We need better roads and better police protection.*
	B. *You're preaching to the choir! I'm with you. Go talk to the other members on the council.*

Pregnant pause	A long period of silence. A quiet moment before some information is revealed. A period of silence designed to give importance to what is said next. A period of silence to allow the listener to digest what has just been said.
Price of tea in China	The complete expression is actually the following question: *What does that have to do with the price of tea in China?* When someone asks this question, they're saying that they're really surprised by the listener's comments. Effectively, they're saying: *Why do you say that?* *What are you talking about?* *What does that have to do with anything?* *What does that have to do with what we're talking about?*
Pride oneself	Be proud of something. When a company says: *We pride ourselves on being number one,* they mean: *We're proud of being number one.*
Prime time	The time period between 8 pm and 11 pm, used for television programming purposes. Thus, a prime-time TV show is a show that's on approximately between 8 and 11 pm.
Promises, promises!	Empty words, often without actual action to fulfill them. Q. *I want to have lunch with you some time, okay?* A. *Promises, promises! You say that every time we meet, but we never have lunch!*
Proof is in the pudding.	This is actually short for *The proof of the pudding is in the eating,* which means: *You won't know if the food has been cooked properly until you try it.*

Continued on the next page.

Proof is in the pudding.

Continued from the previous page.

Because pudding is cooked slowly to perfection, it is also used to mean:

The results are what counts, not how you start or finish.

Pros and cons

Positive and negative aspects of something.
Advantages and disadvantages of something.
Good points and bad points about something.

A. *Here's the proposal for the new expansion project, sir.*
B. *I'll look at it later. For now, just let me know its pros and cons.*

Proverbial

Traditional.
As a proverb.
As they say in a proverb.

She was bitten by the proverbial singing bug at an early age.

Pulling a fast one

Playing a trick on people.
Cheating people or fooling them.
Making someone believe they see one thing but quickly shifting it before they can see what you've done.

Q. *How could you believe her story and give her money?*
A. *I know! She pulled a fast one on me!*

Another usage for *pull:*
When someone says: *What are you trying to pull?* They mean something like:

Are you trying to trick me?
What sneaky thing are you trying to do?

Also see: Up one's sleeve.

Pulling a rabbit out of a hat

Doing something surprising.
Delivering a surprising solution.

Q. *I give up! Do you have any ideas?*
A. *No, I've run out of rabbits to pull out of my hat! I'm ready to give up, too.*

Pulling someone's leg	Kidding someone. Saying something to someone jokingly.
	A. *I hate it when he says these things.* B. *Oh, don't mind him. He's just pulling your leg!*
Pulling something off	Accomplishing a task, especially a difficult one.
	Q. *I just found out I need your sketches by tomorrow, not next week. Can you do it?* A. *Well, I don't know if I can pull it off, but I'll try.*
Pulling strings	Getting special help (maybe from inside,) as in:
	When someone says: *I had to pull a few strings to get that job,* they mean something like:
	I couldn't have gotten that job without help from friends on the inside. A few important people helped me to get the job.
	Manipulating, as in:
	When someone says: *Other people are pulling his strings,* they mean something like:
	They're manipulating and controlling him. He's their puppet.
Pulling the plug *Origin: Medical*	Canceling something. Letting someone, or something, die.
	I think it's time to pull the plug on all these money losing projects.
Pulling the rug from under someone	Betraying someone unexpectedly. Anything happening in a dramatically unexpected way that negatively and significantly affects the person it happens to.
	The rug was pulled from under me when I got the Employee of the Year Award and then was fired two weeks later.
	She'll pull the rug from under him one of these days and leave him hurt, surprised, and maybe even suicidal!

Pulling yourself up by your bootstraps   Helping yourself without relying on others, in life, in business, etc.

> Q. *How did you manage to accomplish this? Who helped you?*
> A. *Actually, no one. I had no choice but to pull myself up by my bootstraps.*

Pumping iron
Sports

Lifting weights.
Doing heavy exercising.

Background:
Weights used to be made exclusively of iron, hence the name.

From a silly hole, a silly wind blows. (Hungarian.)
Said when the person talking is not making sense.

Pushing it
Pressing it

Pushing one's luck
Pressing one's luck

Assuming that one will continue to have good luck.

You're pushing your luck by fooling around with your boss's wife. You've been lucky so far, but it is too risky.

Related warning:
You've been lucky so far, but don't push it!

Pushing someone's buttons

Pressing someone's buttons

Making someone angry by touching on a subject that bothers them. (Could be intentional or unintentional.)

> Q. *Why can't the two of you get along?*
> A. *I don't know! Somehow he always manages to push my buttons. I don't like that.*

Compare to:
Get one's goat.

Also means turning someone on sexually.

> Q. *You like her, don't you?*
> A. *Yes I do. She knows how to push my buttons, and I like that.*

Pushing the ball down the road

Continuing the work.
Going on with what you're doing.

Pushing the limits	Attempting to exceed the existing limits. Trying to do things beyond normal (or usual, or familiar, or acceptable) standards.
	Mud wrestling on TV was once considered pushing the limits, but now it is commonplace.
	Also: Pushing the envelope.
Put it to bed. **Put it to rest.**	Settle it. Finish it. Let it go. Forget about it.
	She is putting the rumors to rest by announcing her engagement.
Put the pedal to the metal	Rush. Speed it up.
	When someone says: *Put the pedal to the metal,* they mean: *Faster, hurry up, etc.*
	Compare to: Burning rubber.
	Background: This is a reference to the fact that, in order to accelerate quickly in a car, you have to push the gas *pedal* down, maybe all the way down to the *metal* floor.
Put up or shut up!	Do something about the situation, or shut up about it! Offer an explanation (or solution, or alternative, etc.,) or stop complaining about it!
Put your best foot forward.	Do your best.
	A. *I have enough material to start a TV show, but I don't know if I'll be good at it.* B. *Just do it. I know you, and I know that if you put your best foot forward, you will succeed.*
Put your house in order! **Get your house in order!**	Organize your affairs. Take care of your problems. Put your life in proper order.

Continued on the next page.

Put your house in order! **Get your house in order!**	*Continued from the previous page.* The following is a sarcastic way of using this expression and is usually reserved for people who have problems of their own but keep advising others: *Get your own house in order before you lecture me, okay?!*
Put your money where your mouth is. *Origin: Gambling*	Let's bet on it. You want to bet? Show me some proof. You better be sure about what you're saying.
Put your thinking cap on.	Brainstorm. Use your head. Start to think (about the issue) seriously. *Okay, let's put our thinking cap on, and come up with a solution.* Also: Put on your thinking cap. Similarly, we can say things such as: *Put your running shoes on,* which means: *Start running and exercising.*
Putting a gun to someone's head	Forcing someone to do something. *You didn't have to leave your wife. Nobody was putting a gun to your head!*
Putting all of the cards on the table *Gambling*	Not holding back. Not hiding anything. Speaking your mind or saying what you mean.
Putting all of the chips on the table *Gambling*	Raising the stakes. Betting all you have.
Putting all of your eggs in one basket	Putting yourself at risk. Relying on only one source. *I know you like this company, but you shouldn't put all your eggs in one basket! It's too risky. You should also invest in some other companies, and maybe even in real estate.*

Putting it on the money *Gambling*

Taking a safe step.
Betting on a sure thing.

Putting on airs

Acting pretentious.
Feeling or acting important, superior, etc.

Q. *Who's that woman? I've heard her talk. She sounds like she's ultra-wealthy.*
A. *Oh, I know her. She's a regular housewife, like us. She's just putting on airs.*

Putting one over on someone

Tricking someone.
Cheating (or taking advantage of) people.

A. *She's trying to put one over on you.*
B. *I know, but she can't fool me. She should know better!*

Trusts a goat with a cabbage. *(Hungarian.)*
Trusts something to the wrong person.

Putting one's finger on something

Identifying something.
Identifying the reason for something.

Q. *Is something bothering you?*
A. *Well, I know there's something wrong with the design, I just can't put my finger on it.*

Putting skin in the game

Investing your own capital.
When you put (or have) skin in the game, it means you invest some of your own capital into the operation that you are conducting.

Putting someone down

Humiliating people, calling them names, and making them look (and feel) unimportant, especially in front of other people.

Putting someone on

Deceiving someone.
Joking with someone.

Are you putting me on? Means something like:

Are you serious?
You're joking, right?
Are you kidding me?
You must be kidding me!

- Did you see our new proposal?

- Yes. Your new guy showed it to me, and I think it's great. I told him to run with it.

For a definition, see:
- **Go with it.**
- **Run with it.**

Putting someone out to pasture

Retiring someone.
Forcing someone to stop working, usually due to age.

A. *I think it's time for me to retire.*
B. *Why so soon? You can still work!*
A. *Yes, but if I don't do it they will. I'll be put out to pasture.*

Putting the blinders on

Having the blinders on

Not seeing the whole thing.
Being unaware of your surroundings.
Not considering all contributing factors.
Deliberately not acknowledging something.

Q. *How can Mrs. Smith not see that her daughter is using drugs?*
A. *She has put her blinders on. She doesn't want to see the truth!*

Putting the cart before the horse

Doing things in the opposite order.
Reversing the proven or accepted order of doing things.

Also: Putting the cart before the donkey.

Putting things into perspective

Keeping things in perspective

Remembering what is important.
Looking at things in proper context.
Putting things in their proper place compared to other things.

You see the cute little umbrella, I see the big storm coming. Yes, it's beautiful but, when you put it into perspective against the storm, it won't look cute anymore!

Compare to: Seeing the big picture.

Putting to sleep
Medical

Making someone sleep, or knock them unconscious, by using drugs.
Killing an animal by injection. (Of course it's nicer to say: *Putting to sleep.*)

Q. *What should we do with my cat?*
A. *She's in too much pain. I'm sorry, but we have to put her to sleep. There's nothing else we can do for her.*

Putting up a fight Fighting.
Resisting something.

If you say: *He didn't put up much of a fight,* it means something like:
He didn't resist.
He didn't really fight.
He didn't show any confidence.

Putting up with Tolerating something or someone.

Q. *How do you like working in the desert?*
A. *Well, I'm putting up with it.*

Putting your foot down Being determined.
Being firm in your decision.
Not changing your mind or backing down.

When someone says: *I'm putting my foot down,* they mean something like: *I've made my decision and I'm not changing it.*

Similar:
It's my way or the highway.

The quiet cat also drinks milk. *(Irish.)*

Putting your foot in your mouth Saying the wrong thing.
Getting yourself in trouble because of a misguided statement.

Q. *Wasn't it insensitive of your candidate to make a racial joke on the radio?*
A. *It sure was. He really put his foot in his mouth this time.*

Compare to: Shooting yourself in the foot.

Quick study A quick learner.

Racing against time Having little time.
Rushing to meet a deadline.
Trying to do something as quickly as possible.

Similar:
Beating the clock.
Racing against the clock.

Rain check	A promise to do something in the future. An example is when you get a rain check to be able to purchase an item (which is presently not available) in a store at the current sales price.
	I'm sorry I can't go to the movies with you tonight. Can I take (or get) a rain check?
Raining cats and dogs	Raining very hard.
	Also: Pouring, or pouring buckets.
Raining on someone's parade	Ruining someone's good time. Spoiling something for someone.
	Q. Do you want to come to the party with us? *A. No, go on without me! I feel depressed, and I don't want to rain on your parade.*
Raising a point	Bringing attention to something.
	Also: Raising an issue. Raising a question.
Raising eyebrows	Surprising people. (Not a negative thing.) Making others uncomfortable. (Negative.)
	The new regulations are certain to raise a few eyebrows.
Raising the bar *Origin: Sports*	Using higher standards. Making it more difficult to do something by adding to the requirements.
	I'm not happy with the performance of our new recruits. I think we should raise the bar a few notches the next time we hire someone.
Raising the stakes *Gambling*	Increasing the risks.
	When you say: *The stakes are high,* it means: *This is a very risky situation!*
Rallying cry (cries) *Origin: Military*	Cries of support and cheer. Something to organize people around a common cause.

Rank-and-file	Majority of a group. Lower-level personnel. Ordinary members of a group, not the leaders.
	A. *All Wall Street people got big year-end bonuses.* B. *Not really. The top guys did, but the rank-and-file didn't get any!*
Rather than	Instead of.
Rattling someone's cage	Irritating someone. Making them angry.

Wine is good for men when it's women who drink it! *(Portuguese.)*

Raw deal	A bad deal. An unfair deal.
	A. *I hear you got a raw deal from your boss!* B. *Yeah, I got him a business where he made thousands of dollars, but he only bought me dinner!*
Reaching across the aisle *Political*	Offering help to (and asking help from) your opponents. (Mostly a political expression.)
Reaching for the stars **Reaching for the moon**	Being ambitious. Wanting to do or achieve great things. A. *I remember how Madonna said early on that she wanted to rule the world!* B. *I know! She's been reaching for the stars ever since the beginning.*
Reaching out	Trying to communicate, help, etc. *You must reach out to the people, and help them with their problems.*
Reading between the lines	Reading the hidden or subtle meaning. Searching for the message behind the message. *If you read between the lines, you'll know that I'm really trying to make it work.*

Continued on the next page.

Reading between the lines	*Continued from the previous page.*
	When someone says: *Inger says she hates you, but you have to read between the lines,* they mean something like:
	If you pay attention to her actions, you'll see that she actually loves you!
Reading someone	Understanding someone, mostly based on intuition or being able to pick up on subtle mannerisms and clues to what someone is thinking or feeling.
	When someone says: *I can't read Mr. Hashimoto,* they mean something like:
	I don't understand his way of thinking. I don't know (I can't tell) what he's thinking about.

The tongue steals what is in the heart. *(Swahili.)*
People talk about their feelings.

Real estate **Real property** *Legal*	A piece of property, such as a building or land, that is not moveable.
	Opposite: Personal property, such as a car or furniture, which is moveable.
Red eye	A late-night flight. An overnight flight.
	Used with "catch" or "take", it has to do with taking a late-night flight.
	Q. *When did you get back?* A. *This morning. On the way back, I took a red eye!*
Red tape	Unnecessary paperwork forced upon people who have to do official business.
	Q. *Couldn't we become just a little bit more efficient?* A. *No, not as long as we have to deal with all of this red tape. It's too much paperwork.*

Red-headed step-son, step-child, or step-daughter	A person or a group that nobody likes or who is mistreated by others. **Background:** Step-children are usually not treated as well as the biological children of both parents. On the other hand, red-headed children who are born into a family where the parents aren't red-headed, are a rarity, and it makes some people suspicious. Now, add these two features together, and you can see how some closed-minded people would react. Presently the term is applied to any person or group who is not being treated fairly by others.
Register with someone	If you say: *It didn't register with him,* you mean something like: *He didn't notice it.* *He didn't recognize it.* *He didn't understand it.*
Reinventing the wheel	Wasting one's time. Wasting time, trying to do things that have been tried before.
Rhetorical question	This is a statement to stress a point, but it is in the form of a question, to which an answer is not expected. Example: A. *Why am I so stupid?* B. *Well, there are no easy answers!* A. *Oh shut up! That was a rhetorical question.* Other examples: *Why are some people so mean?* *Why does it have to rain so much?* *What's the matter with the economy?* Compare to: Figure of speech.
Right off the bat *Origin: Sports*	Quickly. Right away. *Right off the bat, they didn't like each other.*

Right on	Amen. Exactly. Very good. As you say.
Right on the money	Accurate. Absolutely right. *My dear friend, your estimate was right-on-the-money!* Related: *Putting it on the money,* which means: *Betting on a sure thing!*
Right up one's alley	In one's field. Something that one knows everything about. Q. *Can you help me with the scheduling projections?* A. *No, talk to Tien. Scheduling is right up his alley.*
Ripping someone off	Stealing from someone. Cheating someone out of their money or belongings. Q. *What did Madoff really do?* A. *He ripped everybody off.* Related: A scheme to rip people off is called a *rip-off.* Q. *What did Madoff really do?* A. *He conducted the biggest rip-off in history.*
Ripping the scab off	Opening old wounds. When someone says: *Why rip the scab off the old wounds now,* they mean something like: *Why do you want to talk about old problems again?*
Rise and shine!	Do something. Don't waste your time. Get up and do something. Wake up or get out of bed.

Rising to the occasion
Meeting a challenging situation.
Doing what is required to succeed.
Being able to do what's necessary to handle the situation at hand.

A. *You can rely on my brother. When necessary, he's always there to help.*
B. *I know what you mean. He always rises to the occasion.*

Robbing Peter to pay Paul
Borrowing money from one source to pay another debt.
Taking care of one problem but worsening another problem.
Using money that has been set aside for a specific purpose for another purpose.

When someone is robbing Peter to pay Paul, he probably doesn't have any money of his own. He could even be using other people's money to pay his own debts.

No money, no Swiss. *(Dutch.)*
Don't expect something for nothing.

Robbing the cradle
Dating or marrying a much younger person.

He's robbing the cradle, and he should be ashamed of himself. She's half his age!

Robbing the grave
Dating or marrying a much older person.

Rocking the boat
Causing trouble.
Disturbing the balance or stability.
Causing problems in a risky situation.

When someone says: *We don't want to rock the boat just yet,* they mean something like:

If we cause any problems now, the situation may get out of control, and we might get in trouble, too.

Also:
Making waves.
Stirring things up.

Role model	A person one admires. A person one wants to be like. A person who's a good example for others. *Q. Are you happy with the way that some of our celebrities behave?* *A. No. I really think that we need better role models for our kids.*
Roll in the hay	Sexual intercourse. *Q. Do you think they've had a roll in the hay?* *A. I don't know, but they sure are spending a lot of time together!*
Rollercoaster (situation) **Roller coaster (situation)**	A wild ride. An unpredictable situation. Repeated up-and-down conditions. *It's a rollercoaster economy. One day, the market is up; the next day, it's down. One day the market is up again; the next day, it's still up! Very unpredictable.*
Rolling over in one's grave **Turning in one's grave** **Turning over in one's grave**	Expression of disapproval (by someone who's dead). When someone says: *Akira's father would turn over in his grave to see him act this way,* they mean something like: *Akira's father would be really upset if he were alive and saw this.*
Rolling the dice *Gambling*	Taking risks. Taking a chance. *Well, we'll just roll the dice on this one, and see how far we can go!*
Rubbing someone the wrong way	Annoying them. Upsetting them. Saying or doing the wrong thing to them. *Q. Why are they so upset with me?* *A. Talk to them. Find out if you said something that rubbed them the wrong way.*

- Mom and Dad are getting old. I think they're over the hill.
- No, not yet! Maybe in a few minutes.

For a definition, see:

- **Over the hill**

Ruling out	Excluding. Not considering. Eliminating (from a list). *They ruled him out as a suspect. They no longer think he did it.*
Run of the mill **Run-of-the-mill**	Ordinary. Common. Nothing special.
Run-in	Quarrel. Argument. When someone says: *I've had run-ins with the law,* they mean something like: *I've had problems with the police.* *I have police records. (Not a good thing!)*
Running a red light	Not stopping at a red light. Driving through the intersection at a red light. *Women are less likely than men to run a red light!*
Running for a position	Campaigning to become the holder of a position. Q. *Is it true that the former school principal is running for mayor?* A. *Yes, but he's not campaigning hard enough. It looks more like he's walking rather than running!*
Running for one's life	Saving oneself. Q. *Have you seen Sally's husband?* A. *Yes. He was looking for you, and he was really mad. You'd better run for your life!* Similar: Saving one's (own) skin.
Running in circles	Getting nowhere. Wasting one's time and effort. Saying (or doing) the same things over and over again.

Running on empty	Driving when the fuel tank is almost empty. Trying without resources (or money) and not giving up.
Running on fumes	Almost out of power. A car that's going to stop any second because it's out of gas. A person with no energy left, but who continues in spite of exhaustion.
Running out of something	Using up (finishing) the supply of something. When you say: *We're running out of time,* you mean: *We don't have much time left.* When you say: *We're running out of options,* you mean: *We don't have any more choices.*
Running someone down	Finding someone after a lengthy search. *The fugitive was doing okay for a while until the police ran him down.*

If you can't bite, never show your teeth. *(Vietnamese.)*

Running something into the ground	Destroying something. Making something fail. *It was my mismanagement that ran this company into the ground. I hope you'll forgive me.* Also: Driving something into the ground.
Sacrificial lamb	Something or someone (that can easily be discarded) used in order to serve a more important purpose. When someone says: *Johnny's a sacrificial lamb,* they mean something like: *He's not important to them.* *They'll get rid of him when necessary.* *They'll sacrifice him to save themselves when the time comes.*

Continued on the next page.

Sacrificial lamb	*Continued from the previous page.* Also: Fall guy. Being set up. Being left high and dry. Compare to: Deep-sixing. Being framed. Taking the fall. Selling someone down the river. Throwing someone under the bus.
Safety net	A back up plan in case something goes wrong. Q. *You have no contract, no insurance, no retirement, nothing! What are you doing?* A. *What can I say? I love working without a safety net!*
Same old, same old	There's nothing new. Everything is the same. Everything is as boring as ever. Q. *Hey, how's life treating you?* A. *Oh, you know. Same old, same old.*
Save it for later.	Save it. We'll talk (or do something) about it later.
Saved by the bell *Sports*	Saved or helped by something unexpectedly, somewhat similar to being saved by the bell at the end of a class in school. **Background:** This expression comes from boxing. Imagine that a boxer is about to get knocked out or knocked down, but is *saved by the bell* at the end of the round.
Saving face	Saving one's dignity. Keeping self-respect. *They know they can't win, but they're trying to save face by staying in the race. They don't want to be completely embarrassed.*

Saving one's breath	Not wasting one's time or efforts.
	A. *Boss, I know you're busy, but I need to talk to you about a raise.*
	B. *Save your breath. There won't be any raises this year, not even for me!*
Saving someone's skin	Saving their job, life, reputation, etc. Saving them from difficulty, exposure, embarrassment, etc.
	A. *You know, when you took the responsibility for wrecking the car, you really saved my skin!*
	B. *It's okay. That's what friends are for!*
	Also: Saving one's (own) skin. Saving someone's hide, neck, or bacon.
Say it like you mean it.	Say it sincerely. Show you are sincere. Say it from the bottom of your heart.
	Also: Do it like you mean it.
Scared sh-tless	Very scared. (This is not a polite thing to say!)
Scaring the heck out of someone	This is an exaggerated, but polite, way of saying: *Scaring someone.*
	A. *Hey, you really scared the heck out of me.*
	B. *Did I? Oh, I'm so sorry!*
	The following mean the same thing but are not polite:
	Scaring the hell out of someone. *Scaring the bejesus out of someone.* *Scaring the sh-t (or crap) out of someone.*
Scoring big *Sports*	Winning in a big way.
Scot free **Scot-free**	Free from harm, punishment, penalty, etc.
	The bank robbers got away scot free.

Scraping by	Living with the bare minimum. Living with difficulty (due to being poor). *I know a number of people who, because of the bad economy, are just scraping by.* Compare to: Living paycheck-to-paycheck.
Scratching one's head	Wondering. Thinking hard. Trying to understand something, without having much luck. A. *Hank's behavior at the party left the guests scratching their heads.* B. *I'm sure he's feeling embarrassed now.* Compare to: Raising eyebrows
Scratching the surface	Not knowing everything yet. Being at the beginning of a process. *The economy is in trouble and, with the banks beginning to fail, we're only scratching the surface.*
Scumbag	Low-life. A low person. A worthless person. Also: The scum of the earth, as in: *He stole from his own mother! He is the scum of the earth.*
Second fiddle **Second banana**	The supporting (not the main) person or group. Compare to: Top banana.
Second thought	Thinking thoroughly, as in: *I yelled at her too quickly, without giving it a second thought. I should have given the matter more consideration.* Compare to: On second thought. Having second thoughts.

Second to none **Second-to-none**	The best. Number one. Ahead of everybody else.
Second-guessing	Criticizing someone or something. Attempting to anticipate something. Doubting someone's action, especially after the results of the action are known. *I'm not here to second-guess anyone. So, let's just hope that everything will happen as planned.*
See the light of day.	Be free. Be born. Become known. Come into existence. *Q. When are you going to make your movie?* *A. The script is ready, but I don't have the money. I don't know if it will ever see the light of day.* *Q. When is the ex-prime minister going to be freed from prison?* *A. He won't see the light of day for a long time.* *Q. What about his chief of security? I understand that she tried to kill herself.* *A. Yes, she did, and she went into a coma. After that, she never saw the light of day.*
See ya. **See you.**	Good-bye. I will see you later.
Seeing eye-to-eye **Seeing eyeball-to-eyeball**	Agreeing. Being in agreement. Understanding each other. *Q. Do you see eye-to-eye with your wife about anything?* *A. Well, we used to, but not anymore!* Also see: On the same page. On the same wavelength.

Seeing red	Being very angry.
	Q. *Do you think I could ask Ray for a raise?* A. *Not a good time! His wife just left him, and he's only seeing red these days.*
Seeing the big picture	Seeing the overall view. Understanding the issue in relation to everything else.
	You see the cute little umbrella, I see the big picture. Yes, it's a beautiful umbrella, but it won't help us when the big storm hits!

An ox with a tail does not walk over the fire. *(Haitian.)*

Selling an idea	Making others believe in an idea.
	When someone says: *I can't sell my ideas,* they mean something like:
	People don't believe in them. *They don't believe what I'm saying.* *I can't make them interested in my ideas.*
	Opposite: Buying an idea.
	I'm buying this Global Warming theory. I think we should do something about it.
Selling one's soul (to the devil)	Doing anything, even immoral things, in return for something the person wants. Giving up one's moral principles in return for material wealth or some other desired thing.
	Q. *How could your friend steal from the kids' funds? He knows they're orphans!* A. *He must have sold his soul to the devil. He's not my friend anymore!*
Selling oneself short	Not giving oneself the credit deserved.
	A. *If I was a bit more handsome, a few inches taller, and a lot younger, I would ask Amy to come and live with me.* B. *Oh, come on. You're selling yourself short. You should give yourself more credit.*

Selling someone down the river	Lying to a friend. Betraying someone.

When someone says: *She's selling him down the river,* they mean something like:

She's betraying a friend.
She's lying to him, even though they're friends.

Compare to: Sacrificial lamb

Sense of urgency	When someone says: *There's a sense of urgency about something,* they mean:

It is urgent.
It's an issue with high priority.
It's something that must be addressed quickly.

Serves one right.	This is about someone deserving a punishment.

Serves you right, means something like: *You deserve what's happening to you!*

They got my son into drugs, and now they're in jail. Well, it serves them right!

Compare to: Have it coming.

Set in stone **Written in stone**	Permanent. Cannot be changed.

A. *I promised my friends to go to the party with them. I can't change my word, Mom!*
B. *If it's not written in stone, then you can!*

The guilty dog barks the loudest. (*English.*)
The thief has a feather on his head. (*Egyptian.*)
It is the hen that has laid the egg that sings. (*French.*)

It's easy to spot the guilty person.

Setting the record straight	Clarifying misinformation and misconceptions.

Just to set the record straight, I want you to know that so far I haven't been totally honest with you!

Settling a suit *Legal*	Coming to a mutual agreement without going to trial.

Seven-year itch	The desire to leave any situation, and move on, after a while. The desire to experience a new romance after being with one's spouse for approximately seven years.
Shake a leg.	Get up. Hurry up. Get going. Get out of bed.
Shake-up at the top	A rearrangement of the staff at the upper levels of an organization.
Sharpest knife in the drawer	Smartest person in the group. Also: Sharpest tool in the shed.
She made her bed, and she's got to lie in it.	She caused the situation, and now she must deal with the consequences.
She's all over him like a cheap suit.	She doesn't leave him alone. She's spending too much time with him.
She's got to go. She will be let go.	She will go. She is supposed to go. She is supposed to be fired.
Shell-shocked	Shaken. Extremely surprised.
Ship-shape	Everything being in its proper place.
Shock jock	A radio and/or television personality who shocks audiences with controversial material.
Shoe in Shoe-in Shoo-in	Winner. Likely winner. Appropriate candidate. *She's a shoo-in for the job. I'm sure she'll get it!* **Background:** To shoo-in comes from horse racing and means to direct or guide in a specific direction, maybe even in a "rigged" way.

Shoe is on the other foot.	Things are the other way around.
	I helped him as much as I could when I was the boss. However, if the shoe was on the other foot, I don't think he would do the same for me.
Shoot!	Talk.
	Talk to me.
	I'm listening.
	Go ahead, say it.
	A. *I've been meaning to tell you something.*
	B. *Okay, shoot!*
	Also, an expression of disappointment, as in:
	Q. *I'm going to watch the game tonight. Do you want to join me?*
	A. *Shoot! I can't. I have to work tonight.*
Shooting fish in a barrel	A very easy task.
	Q. *Do you think you can find me an inexpensive, but really nice, house?*
	A. *In this slow market? Sure! It'll be like shooting fish in a barrel!*
Shooting from the hip	Making honest remarks.
Origin: Military, Sports	Acting or reacting quickly.
	Saying things as they come to mind, without thinking about any consequences.
	Q. *What do you think of our new neighbor?*
	A. *I've known him for a long time and I trust him. He shoots from the hip.*
	Also see:
	Calling it like it is.
Shooting the sh-t	Casual conversation.
	Talking about unimportant things, without really thinking.
	Also:
	Chit-chat. Shooting the breeze.
	Also see:
	Small talk.

Shooting yourself in the foot	Hurting yourself. Getting yourself in trouble. Making it worse for yourself.
	Wait until you have all the facts before accusing your boss, otherwise you could be shooting yourself in the foot.
	Compare to: Putting your foot in your mouth.
Short list	Any list of the most qualified, favorites, etc.
	Short list of candidates, best books, top movies, places to visit, etc.
	Q. *Am I on your short list?* A. *You're on everybody's short list! We all want to work with you.*
Short sale *Legal*	As used in real estate: Sale of a property at a price less than the amount owed to the bank, where the bank and the seller both lose money, but both agree to do it.
Shot	Gone. Messed up. Screwed up.
	My chances of getting a job with the university are shot. I don't think they'll hire me.
Shotgun wedding **Shotgun marriage**	A forced marriage.
	Related: Shotgun bride.
	Background: It used to be that if a woman got pregnant without being married, her father, or other male relatives, would force the man who impregnated her to marry her. In some places this still happens.
Should something happen	*Should it happen* means *If it happens,* as in: *Should it rain, the roof will leak.* *Should you see her, please say hello for me.*

At the company picnic:

- Psst! The woman sitting across the table works in our office. She's so stupid she couldn't pass muster at anything.
- Tell her to pass the mayonnaise instead!

For a definition, see:

- **Pass muster**

Shouting down

Keeping someone from speaking by shouting.

When someone says: *They shouted me down,* they mean:

They shouted so loudly that I couldn't continue speaking; nobody could hear me!

Shovel-ready

Political

Ready to be started.
A project wherein all of the planning and scheduling has already been done.
A project wherein all that needs to be done is to hire the workers to get started.

Shying away from something or someone

Avoiding them.
Staying away from them.
Trying not to deal with them.

She shied away from the reporters and instead retired to her room to reflect on the ordeal.

Significant other

One's spouse, girlfriend, boyfriend.

A. *I hear that you have a new significant other.*
B. *Oh, yes, and she's a lot more significant than you think!*

Also:
Better half (primarily refers to one's spouse).

Signing on the dotted line

Legal

Agreeing to do something.
Taking the final step in making a commitment.

Have you signed on the dotted line yet? If you have, it's too late to change your mind.

Before you sign on the dotted line, please consider everything carefully.

He keeps saying that he wants my car, but he hasn't signed on the dotted line yet!

Silent treatment

Getting or receiving the silent treatment has to do with being ignored on purpose, as in:

Q. *Why wasn't your wife talking to you today?*
A. *Ever since we had our latest argument, I've been receiving the silent treatment!*

Opposite: Giving the silent treatment.

Silver bullet

A special solution.
A magical solution.
A solution that would solve all sorts of problems.

A. *We're facing a lot of problems. We need a silver bullet.*
B. *This is too complicated. There ARE no silver bullets for this!*

Also:
Magic bullet.

Silver lining

A hidden, good thing.

There's a silver lining to high gas prices: public awareness. People are finally becoming aware of some important issues.

Also see:
Blessing in disguise.

If a cat is the judge, then the rat can't win its case. *(Swahili.)*

Silver spoon

Sign of being rich.

When someone says: *He was born with a silver spoon in his mouth,* they mean something like:

Let's face it, he's been rich since he was born!

Silver tongue(d)

A liar.
A great, persuasive speaker.
One who's good at using one's speaking ability!

Sin City

This is a nickname for the City of Las Vegas.

Singing the blues

Feeling sad.
Complaining.
Talking about one's problems.

Sinking in

Becoming clear.
Penetrating the mind.

I can see now why she never returned my calls. It's finally beginning to sink in!

Also: Kicking in.

Sitting duck *Military, Sports*	An easy target. An easy victim. *You know they're looking for you. You have to ask for police protection or something. Instead, here you are, like a sitting duck, doing nothing!* Compare to: Clay pigeon. Moving target.
Sitting on one's hands	Doing nothing, especially if some action is needed or expected. *Every once in a while, I see her, sitting on her hands, even as everyone else is working hard.*
Sitting something out	Not doing something. Sitting, instead of participating, through something, as in: When someone says: *I'm sitting this dance out,* they mean: *I won't be dancing this round.* Attending an entire event, as in: When someone says: *I'm sitting this lecture out,* they mean: *I will stay throughout the lecture.*
Sitting well	Being accepted. *The new proposal by the Democrats won't sit well with the Republicans. They don't like it and won't accept it.*
Six-pack	A pack of six cans or bottles, such as beer or soda. Related: When someone says: *Steve Reeves had a perfect six-pack,* they mean something like: *He was in excellent physical shape because his ab muscles looked like a six-pack.*
Size matters.	It's important whether something is big or small! (Usually this has a sexual connotation.)

Skeletons in one's closet	Terrible secrets. Bad things from one's past that are hidden. A. *I don't like it when they ask all of those questions in an interview.* B. *Why? Are you hiding some skeletons in your closet that I should know about?*
Skin game *Origin: Sports*	An operation involving trickery. A casual game where the members of one team are not wearing shirts. (Women don't usually participate in such a game!)
Slap on the wrist	A light punishment. Q. *They gave him only two years in jail for burning down a house. Isn't that ridiculous?* A. *Yes! That's just a slap on the wrist!*
Sleeping on it	Thinking about something (overnight). Taking one's time to think about something. Q. *Can I give you my answer in a few days?* A. *Sure. I don't want you to rush. Sleep on it and let me know when you're ready.*
Slim pickins	Nothing much. Not much to choose from. Q. *Did you find anything?* A. *Well, I checked the store. There were slim pickins there!* **Background:** As used in the above context, *slim pickins* probably comes from *slim pickings*.
Slipping through the cracks **Falling through the cracks**	Being missed. Being overlooked. Something happening that (if rules are followed) shouldn't happen. *We were searching everywhere looking for your package, but it slipped through the cracks and got shipped. Nobody noticed it until it was too late! I'm sorry.*

Small potatoes Not important.
Of little importance compared to something else.

Q. *Did you ever get hired to do the school construction project?*
A. *We didn't even apply. It was small potatoes. We're doing bigger projects instead.*

Also:
Not worth writing home about.

Small talk Unimportant conversation.

Also:
Chit-chat.
Shooting the breeze.

Also see: Shooting the sh-t.

Smart as a whip Very smart.

Smelling blood Ready to fight.
Ready to take advantage (of a weakness).

When someone says: *They're smelling blood,* they mean something like:

They're getting ready to destroy us, or get rid of us, or kill us, etc.

Similar:
Out for blood.
Circling the wagons.
Getting ready for the kill.

Smelling trouble Noticing that something is wrong.

I smell trouble, means: *I think there's something wrong!*

Also:
It smells fishy.
It smells like trouble.
Something doesn't add up.
There's something fishy (about it).
There's something wrong with this picture.
Something's rotten in the state of Denmark!

Smoke screen
Origin: Military

Something used for hiding the truth.

Politicians always use smoke screens. They exaggerate about unimportant things to avoid dealing with the real issues.

Smoking gun
Legal, Military

Evidence of someone's guilt.
A piece of evidence that could solve a case.

Q. What evidence do you have?
A. Her fingerprints are on the murder weapon. That's our smoking gun. Isn't that enough?

Snow job

An attempt to deceive.
A cover-up or misrepresentation.

A. The mechanic says that the car door was dented already and that it's not his fault.
B. Oh, what a snow job!

So be it!

So what?
Let it be as it is.
What else can we do?

If it takes a gift to make her change her mind, then so be it. Get her a gift, so we can continue with the party.

So help me (God)!

I swear!
I mean it!
I'm serious!
I swear to God!

You clean your room, or you'll be in trouble, so help me!

So long.

Good-bye. See you later.

So much as

Rather, as in:
She didn't so much teach as she became a friend to the students, means: *She became the students' friend rather than their teacher!*

Even, as in:
They didn't give me so much as a ride to the airport, means: *They didn't even give me a ride to the airport!*

So to speak	In a way. One way of saying it. Q. *What's the new girl doing in your office?* A. *She keeps track of calls, files reports, makes appointments, etc. She's my secretary, so to speak.* Compare to: If you will.
SOB	This is an abbreviation for: **S**on **O**f a **B**itch. It is an insulting way of referring to a man. It is also used as an exclamation at finding out something unpleasant. Compare to: Son of a gun.
So-called	Supposedly. Wrongly or incorrectly called. *The so-called chief engineer doesn't even have an engineering degree!* *None of these so-called experts could predict the environmental disaster we're facing.*
Sock it to me!	See: Hit it.
SOL	This is an abbreviation for: **S**h-t **O**ut of **L**uck. When not abbreviated, it is an impolite way of saying: *Out of good options.*
Something as hell	When someone says: *It's hot as hell in here,* they mean: *It's very hot in here.* Related examples: *My uncle is stingy as hell.* *Your dogs are stupid as hell.* Similar: *Hot as it could be.* *Sure as one could be.*

Something else	Great. Exceptional. Extraordinary. When someone says: *The cruise was something else,* they mean they really liked it. Also: Out of this world.
Something may be in order.	It may be the right time for that something. When someone says: *Writing a book about your trip may be in order,* they mean: *It may be the right time to write a book about your trip.*
Something to it **There's something to it**	It might be true. It has credibility. It means something. It has some importance or significance.
Something worth writing home about	Something important. Something worthwhile. Something that's good to know.
Something's gotta give!	It cannot continue like this. It will work out one way or another.
Son of a gun	A guy. (Informal.) A less offensive way of saying: *Son of a bitch.* An exclamation made in anger, as in: *Son of a gun, I hurt myself.* An exclamation made in surprise, as in: *You son of a gun! When did you get back?* Note: Depending on who says it, or how it is said, it could be considered an insult.
Sorry excuse	*You're a sorry excuse for a father,* means: *Shame on you!* *You're not a good father.* *You should be ashamed of yourself.* *What kind of a father are you, anyway?*

SOS **S.O.S.**	This is an abbreviation for: **S**ave **O**ur **S**hip, or **S**ave **O**ur **S**ouls. It is an internationally recognized distress call for help. Also see: Mayday! Mayday! Mayday!

One who always tells the truth is avoided by his friends. *(Swahili.)*

So-so	Okay. Average. Not good, not bad.
Soul food	Food for the mind, such as literature, music, etc. Foods traditionally favored by African Americans. In the African American culture it means comfort food. Compare to: Comfort food.
Soul man	A nice way of referring to an African American male. Related: Soul sister. Soul brother.
Sound bite	A short portion of a speech (or movie, or program, etc.) meant to be remembered and recited repeatedly and easily. This idea is used by politicians and advertisers, among others, for promotional purposes and makes it possible for certain features to stay fresh in people's minds.
Sounding board	Someone who listens when you talk about your ideas, and may even comment on them.
Speaking to what's possible	Talking about what's possible.

Speaking volumes	Implying a lot of things. Containing great meaning behind what is being said.
	What he did yesterday speaks volumes about his love for her. I know now that he really loves her!
Speaking with a forked tongue	Lying. Being two-faced. Speaking dishonestly. Saying one thing but meaning something else.
	Compare to: Talking out of both sides of the mouth.
Spiking the ball in the end zone	Being in a celebratory mood, especially in a sporting event.
Sports	**Background:** This is a celebratory end-zone expression from American football that metaphorically says *Take that!* To the opposing team!

It's "eight" to me! *(Hungarian.)*
No skin off my nose. *(English.)*
It doesn't matter to me.

Spilling one's guts	Confessing. Saying everything one knows about something.
	A. *I was on a date last night.* B. *Really? Wow, come on, spill your guts. I want to know everything!*
	Also: Spitting it out.
Spilling the beans	Revealing a secret, maybe unintentionally. Giving away a surprise, maybe unintentionally.
	A. *The birthday party was supposed to be a surprise. Who spilled the beans?* B. *Your wife, boss! With all due respect, boss, you know how women are!* A. *Yes, I do, and here's another surprise: You're fired for spilling the beans about her!*

Spin doctor	A disc jockey (DJ) who spins records at parties. A publicist hired to give a positive appearance to ideas promoted by politicians or other public figures. Someone who paints beautiful faces on ugly facts, and makes good excuses for terrible decisions.
	I wonder what the spin is today! How are they going to spin it this time? Politicians never get tired of spinning things!
Spin the bottle.	A game of chance.
	Background: This is from a game where the player spins the bottle and gets to kiss the person that the bottle points to!
Spinning one's wheels	Not moving. Not going anywhere. Trying but not making any progress.
Spitting image	Looking alike or exactly the same.
	You're the spitting image of your grandmother.
Spitting into the wind	Going against the flow. Fighting a war that you can't win.
	If someone says: *Arguing with your boss is like spitting into the wind,* they mean:
	You might get fired. You'll be sorry for sure. You'll have to forget about any promotions in the near future.
Splitting the spoils	Sharing the winnings, the prize, etc.
Spoiling for a fight	Really wanting to fight.
Spur of the moment	Without pre-planning. Doing or saying something spontaneously, without thinking about it thoroughly.
	Something came up and I made a trip to Michigan on the spur of the moment.

- There's my new boyfriend getting out of the blue car. I love him dearly, but unfortunately, he comes with baggage.

- That's okay. It's only a thin briefcase!

For a definition, see:

- **Having baggage**
- **Coming with baggage**

Square	This word, which is sometimes used as an insult, means:

Not hip.
Not cool.
Conventional.
Old-fashioned.
A traditional person.

Background:
This word is used by young people to describe others, especially older people, who don't seem to agree with them, or are unfamiliar with some of the more modern concepts or trends.

Squeaky wheel gets the grease.	The louder you complain, the sooner you'll get attention.

If you don't complain, you won't get any attention.

Stacking cheese	Saving money.

Making lots of money.

Stacking up	Making sense.

His argument simply does not stack up. He should come up with better answers before I can trust him.

Standing on a soap box	Making a speech.

Stating your opinion as if you're making a speech.

A. *Listen to him bragging.*
B. *I know, he's always on his soap box!*

Another example:
Are you standing on a soap box again? It's just you and me here, so just tell me what's on your mind.

Background:
At one time, wooden soap boxes were most often the most readily available structures to be used as a platform for making political speeches in parks or on campuses.

Standing out

Outstanding.
Conspicuous.
More noticeable than others but in a good way.

He stood out from the rest of the crowd because he was so big.

Related: (Not a compliment.)
The way he was dressed, he stood out from the rest of us like a sore thumb!

Standing someone up

Not keeping a date.
Not showing up for a planned meeting.

Q. She stood you up again?
A. Yeah, I waited for her, but she didn't show up. Is there something I should know?

Standing the test of time

Lasting for a long time.
Making sense, being applicable, being effective, being correct, etc., for a long time.

Our company has been around, successfully and in good standing, for almost fifty years. Now, that's what I call standing the test of time!

Standing up for

Supporting, believing in someone or something.
Defending or protecting someone, their ideas, their honor, their physical well-being, etc.

I'm tired of being a quiet observer. Starting today, I'm standing up for victims of violence and their rights!

Also see:
Taking a stand.

Starter wife

A first wife.
A first wife who stays with her struggling husband, and helps him, until he succeeds in life and then leaves her (usually) for a trophy wife!

Compare to:
Trophy wife.
Gold-digger.

Starting with a clean slate	Starting over, fresh and clean. When you say: *Let's start with a clean slate,* you mean something like: *Let's forget about the past and start again. Let's start from the beginning as if nothing bad has happened.*
State of the art **State-of-the-art**	The latest, most advanced, version of something available. Having, or employing, the latest technological advancements. *We have purchased a state-of-the-art security system for our banking operations, I hope!*
Status symbol	A sign of belonging to, being associated with, or being a part of the upper class. *It used to be that driving a Mercedes-Benz was a status symbol. Well, not anymore. Nowadays everybody is driving a Mercedes, including me!*
Stay of something	A delay of something. When someone says: *The authorities agreed to a stay of execution,* they mean something like: *They agreed to delay the execution and look at new evidence.*
Staying the course	Not changing anything. Doing the same things as before. Working consistently toward a goal, as planned. Compare to: In for the long haul. Standing the test of time.
Step on it!	Faster. Hurry up. Come on, drive faster. Q. *You want me to step on it?* A. *Yeah, we don't have all day, you know!* Also: Flooring it. Also see: Putting the pedal to the metal.

Stepping into something	Getting involved in something. (Can be used in a negative or positive way.) *He stepped into it again, didn't he?* *I stepped into politics when I was very young.*
Stepping on someone's toes	Offending people. Overstepping your boundaries. Interfering with other people's affairs. Taking over other people's responsibilities without their consent or knowledge. *I'm new here, so I'm going to get acquainted with everyone first before I do anything. I certainly don't want to step on anyone's toes.*

Once bitten twice shy. *(English.)*
One who has been bitten by a snake startles at a reed. *(Swahili.)*

Stepping outside	This is about asking or wanting to fight. If someone says: *Do you want to step outside?* it usually means: *Let's step outside because I want to beat you up.* Also: Taking it outside. Continuing it outside. **Background:** If someone wants to have a fight with another person, and they want to be relatively civilized about it, then they invite the other person to go and have the fight outside. This could be outside the workplace, or a bar, or a friend's house, etc. So, asking someone to step outside is usually considered to be an invitation to engage in a physical altercation.
Stepping up to the plate	Doing it. Assuming responsibility. Giving it one's best effort. *Well, my dear, this is it. It's time for you to step up to the plate and show them that you can do it.*

Stick a fork in it!	Something having been completed. Something having been destroyed. (If destruction was the intention.) *Q. Is it done?* *A. Sure! You can stick a fork in it!*
Sticking it to someone	Hurting someone. Retaliating against someone. *Q. It wasn't clear at first, but you were really sticking it to the club owner, weren't you?* *A. I sure was. They charge too much!*
Sticking someone's head in the meat grinder	Threatening someone. Forcing someone into doing something. *A. The suspect isn't very cooperative.* *B. Stick his head in the meat grinder. He'll talk!*
Stick-in-the-mud	A stubborn person. A person who resists change. *Hey, come on, let's go to the party. Don't be such a stick-in-the-mud!* Also: Fuddy-duddy. Kill-joy.
Stiff upper lip	This has to do with: Seeming to be serious. Not showing one's emotions, and maybe even show some determination. *I want you to keep a stiff upper lip, and go back to class. For now, act as if nothing is wrong, but we'll talk about the situation later.*
Still waters run deep!	A quiet person may have deep thoughts. When it's calm on the surface, it may be stormy underneath. People are not necessarily what they seem to be on the surface. Compare to: You can't judge a book by its cover.

Stopping in one's tracks	Stopping early. Stopping suddenly. Keeping from continuing. *He was hiking along, without a care in the world, until he was met by a grizzly bear and stopped dead in his tracks!*
Stopping on a dime	Stopping quickly. *Q. Did you fix the brakes on your car?* *A. I sure did. It now stops on a dime!* Similar: Turning on a dime.
Straight from the horse's mouth	First hand. From the source. From the most reliable source. *Well, I've got the latest information, and it's straight from the horse's mouth.*
Straight shooter **Straight-shooter**	An honest person. A person who speaks openly about what's on his or her mind.
Strategic planning	Planning that will move you closer toward a desired goal. Planning that has to do with the overall situation and involves many factors. Compare to: Seeing the big picture.
Stretching the truth	Exaggerating. Overstating the facts.
Striking a balance	Reaching an acceptable middle point.
Striking a nerve	Touching on an issue that is already sensitive. Saying or doing something that, directly or indirectly, upsets people or makes them worry. *The principal's actions, combined with budget cuts, have struck a nerve in the parents.* Also: Hitting a raw nerve.

. ka

Subject of attention	Something, or someone, that everybody pays attention to, or wants to know about.
Sugar daddy **Sugar mommy**	A rich person who buys gifts for or gives money to another person to spend time together or have sex. Also see: Kept person.
Sup?	What's up? What's happening? How are you doing?
Swan song	A final action. A. *This could be her swan song.* B. *I know. It may very well be the last time she'll ever make a speech!* **Background:** A swan, some believe, doesn't sing, except one beautiful song that it sings before it dies.

Throw a stone, but hide the hand. *(Indonesian.)*

Swearing by	Vouching for, or seriously believing in, someone or something. When someone says: *I swear by warm, steamy baths for relaxing the body,* they mean: *I seriously believe that a warm bath relaxes the body!*
Sweating bullets	Being very anxious.
Sweeping something under the rug	Hiding something. Hiding something, hoping to avoid giving an explanation, or doing something, about it. *We have a corruption problem here, and they're sweeping it under the rug again instead of addressing it.*
Swing shift	Late afternoon to midnight work shift. Compare to: Graveyard shift.

Tail between the legs	An expression used when someone is: Ashamed. Embarrassed. Humiliated by defeat. Asking for forgiveness. Q. *Who was that guy standing there with his tail between his legs?* A. *It was my boss, saying he was sorry that he yelled at me. So, I asked for a raise!*

He is a fool whose sheep runs away twice. *(Parts of Africa.)*
A donkey does not bump into the same stone twice. *(Dutch.)*
> *One who makes the same mistake twice is a fool.*

Tail wagging the dog	A minor situation (or item, or person, etc.,) that affects or controls a much larger situation, as in a tail wagging the dog instead of the other way around.
Take a listen.	Listen. Listen to this.
Take a look.	Look. Look at this.
Take care.	Good-bye. Take care of yourself.
Take it with a grain of salt!	Accept what you hear, but maintain a degree of skepticism about its truth
Take note of this.	Look at this. Write this down. Pay attention to this.
Take this job, and shove it!	I'm quitting. I don't want this job. **Background:** This is the title of a country song. The song became so popular that the title is occasionally used in conversation. It could also be used with other words (such as proposal, idea, etc.) but is never a nice thing to say to your boss!

Taken out of context	Misunderstood or misinterpreted. *I said something, but it was taken out of context. That is not exactly what I meant. They're looking at it the wrong way.*
Taking a beating	Losing big. Losing a lot. Being physically beaten up. *We took a beating in the stock market today, and lost a lot of money.* Also: Suffering, as in: *She took a beating at work. Her coworkers weren't nice to her and kept criticizing her.*
Taking a chance	Taking a risk. *She's taking a big chance by quitting her job in this economy. Either she's very brave, or she's simply crazy!* Also: Risking it. Also see: Going out on a limb
Taking a potshot at	Saying something negative about someone in an unfair fashion. Compare to: Cheap shot.
Taking a powder	Leaving in a hurry. Disappearing without prior notice. *Q. Have you seen my brother?* *A. He was here a minute ago. He must have taken a powder!*
Taking a stand	Choosing a cause. Supporting someone or something. When someone says: *It's time for you to take a stand,* they mean something like: *You can't remain indifferent any more.* Also see: Standing up for.

Taking a toll	Hurting. Having a negative effect. When someone says: *If the new law is passed it will take a toll on us,* they mean something like: *It will affect us in a negative way. It will wear us out.*
Taking by storm	Occupying. Overtaking fast. Succeeding in a sudden and overwhelming way. A. *Everybody on the Internet is suddenly talking about global warming.* B. *I know. It's taken the Internet by storm.*
Taking exception to	Objecting to something. Disagreeing with something. *I take exception to what you're saying. Your assessment of my involvement in this matter is totally wrong.*
Taking flight	Rushing out. Leaving in a hurry. *He didn't wait around when he heard the woman's husband in the hallway. He took flight before she could stop him!*
Taking for granted	Not appreciating someone or something fully. Assuming they will always be there. A. *I think my secretary is upset with me.* B. *That's because you're taking her for granted.* A. *How am I doing that?* B. *She's always there, she does everything, and you don't pay her much or even thank her or compliment her for what she does!* *We've been taking cheap gas for granted.* *Don't take me for granted. I may not be around much longer!*

Taking into consideration	Considering.
	When someone says: *Don't forget to take my experience into consideration,* they mean something like:
	Remember that I have experience. *Remember that you should think about my experience.*
	Also: Giving thought to.
Taking issue with	Arguing. Disagreeing with someone's perspective, actions, or words.
	He doesn't want to take issue with her because he doesn't like speaking or going against her.
Taking it out on someone	Blaming someone. Punishing someone for something that they typically are not responsible for or didn't do.
	I took it out on him because I was mad at him, but it wasn't really his fault that I lost my wallet!
	Don't take it out on yourself. It's not your fault that he didn't listen to you!
Taking it to heart	Taking something seriously. Getting upset over something.
Taking liberty with	Using or abusing someone or something as one pleases.
	Whenever Tommy comes to visit, he goes into our refrigerator without asking. He takes his liberty with our food and acts like he lives here!
	My roommate always took liberty with my school supplies. Finally, I asked him to leave.
Taking matters into one's own hands	Making one's own decisions. Taking action when others do not take action.
	We've waited long enough for assistance from the banks. It's time to take matters into our own hands and come up with a solution!

- Can I go outside and play?
- Not today. It's raining cats and dogs.
- You always say that. *Where are they?*

For a definition, see:

• **Raining cats and dogs**

Taking measure	Getting ready. Taking the necessary steps to do something.
Taking no prisoners *Military*	Giving no mercy. Aiming to destroy. Not compromising. *They're taking no prisoners, means:* *They're destroying us.* *They want us to lose completely.* *They're not looking for a compromise.*
Taking one's time	Not rushing. *I'm taking my time because I'm mad at these guys. So, leave me alone and don't rush me!*
Taking place	Happening. *Q. When did the fight take place and where?* *A. It happened this morning right over here.*
Taking sides	Choosing sides. Choosing one side (of the issue or argument) to agree with. *I'd like everyone to know that I'm not taking sides with either Republicans or Democrats on the immigration issue. I have my own ideas!*
Taking someone for a ride	Cheating someone. Making people believe a lie. Making someone believe that something will be done or will happen that won't. *A. You know what? I'm going to buy Sammy's car.* *B. Oh, boy! He sure is going to take you for a ride. His car isn't worth a cup of coffee!*
Taking someone to the cleaners	Charging someone too much. Cheating someone by charging them too much. *Don't eat at some of these waterfront restaurants. They'll take you to the cleaners!* Similar: Highway robbery.

Taking something in stride	Taking things as they come, without getting upset about them.
Taking something lightly	Not taking it seriously. *We're talking about safety on the road and in the air. Please don't take it lightly.*
Taking something lying down	Accepting something undesirable without fighting it. *The tenants have announced that they won't take the latest rent increase lying down, and will even go to court if necessary.*
Taking stock in	Believing in something. *I took stock in his proposal and supported it, but I wish I hadn't!*
Taking the blame **Taking the fall**	Accepting the blame without accepting the responsibility for someone else's action when something goes wrong. (This is not necessarily done willingly. Maybe there's no other choice.) *Q. Why are you taking the blame?* *A. It's for the good of the company. I can always do something else.* Compare to: Sacrificial lamb. Holding the bag. Throwing someone under the bus.
Taking the bull by the horns *Origin: Sports*	Trying to solve the main problem. Taking action directly, head on, where it counts. *By addressing the manufacturing crisis, we're taking the bull by the horns because that's our most serious problem.*
Taking the edge off	Relaxing, or helping to relax. Making the situation more pleasant. Reducing the unpleasant effect of something. *A. Oh I'm very angry with her.* *B. Here, have some lemonade, and take the edge off!*

Taking the heat   Being criticized.
Tolerating criticism.

My wife is very outspoken and has taken a lot of heat for her comments.

This is my measuring bucket not yours. *(Arabic.)*
Don't sprout where you haven't been planted. *(Greek.)*
                                            Mind your own business.

Taking the high   Using the ethical way to get to your goal.
road   Being more moral, mature, or classy than another person in an unpleasant situation.

When someone says: *Sandra pretends to be taking the high road,* they mean something like:

She wants people to think that she's better than us, or that she has higher standards, or is more moral.

Taking the liberty   (Used with "of" or "to.")

Taking action on one's own authority.
Assuming to have permission, and then taking action.

Sir, I took the liberty to order some food for you. I also took the liberty of making ticket reservations for your group.

Taking the stand   Answering questions truthfully.
Legal   Going to the witness stand (in a court of law) and answering questions under oath.

As a witness, you'll have to take the stand, and answer questions truthfully! Can you do that?

Taking to task   Rebuking or censuring angrily.
Holding someone responsible for something.

The government was taken to task for the nation's high unemployment.

Also:
Telling off.
Dressing down.
Calling on the carpet.

Talking back	Arguing.
	Q. *How do you feel about kids who keep talking back?*
	A. *I don't think they're cute!*
	Also:
	Back-talking.
Talking one's way out of something	Escaping punishment.
	Getting out of a difficult situation by talking, explaining things, or making excuses.
	Q. *Is David in trouble again?*
	A. *Yes, but he's talking his way out of it. He's good at that!*
Talking out of both sides of the mouth	Saying one thing to one person, but something different to someone else.
Speaking out of both sides of the mouth	*How can I trust you when you talk out of both sides of your mouth?*
	Compare to:
	Speaking with a forked tongue.
Talking points	Important topics.
	List of important issues.
	Let's put together a list of our talking points for the meeting tomorrow.

It's easy to become a father but hard to be one. *(German.)*

Tall tales	Somewhat believable stories with unbelievable parts, similar to stories told by kids, or some folk stories, said as if they really happened (but often highly exaggerated).
Teflon president	President Reagan and, later, President Clinton.
	Background:
	This term was originally used to refer to President Reagan, as nothing negative would ever stick to him. No matter how bad a situation he got into, people still liked him. President Clinton was also given the title later.

Tell me about it!
Oh, I know.
I totally agree!
I know all about it.

A. *I was just outside. It's so cold!*
B. *Tell me about it!*

Also:
Oh, don't I know it! (Not a question.)

Tell off
Rebuke.
Angry comment.
Telling someone exactly what you think of them, their actions, or their words, etc.

If someone says: *Sue told Jane off,* they mean something like:

Sue told Jane exactly what she thought about her lies.

Tempered
Toned down.
Calmed down.

When someone says: *Her optimism is tempered by what she knows,* they mean something like: *Because of what she knows, her expectation has been toned down. She knows we cannot be too optimistic or hopeful about the situation.*

Testing the waters
Examining the situation before one actually does something.

Background:
Originates from the fact that people test the temperature of the water before they jump in for a swim or before they step into the bathtub or shower.

TGIF
This is an abbreviation for:

<u>T</u>hank <u>G</u>od <u>I</u>t's <u>F</u>riday!

Thanks to
Because of someone or something.

Thanks to her I've got a good job.
Thanks to the economy we're all in trouble.
Thanks to the rain we can't go swimming today.

That makes two of us!	I agree! Me, too!
	A. *I wish I had a lot of money.* B. *That makes two of us.*
	Related: *That makes one of us,* which means the listener doesn't agree with the speaker!
	A. *I wish I could watch TV all of the time.* B. *That makes one of us.*
That said	Now that I have said that. Now that that has been said.
	When someone says: *That said, let's leave,* they mean: *Now that I have said that, let's leave.*
	Also: That being said. Having said that. That having been said.
That's the horse you rode in on.	Those are your promises. You did it, now you're stuck with it. You made a promise, now you have to keep your word.
That's the horse you've got to ride.	That's something you have to do. These are the problems you have to tackle.
The $64,000-dollar question	The main question. An important question or issue. The question the answer to which will determine the outcome of something else.
	When someone says: *The economy is the $64,000-dollar question,* they mean something like: *It's how we handle the economy that will determine if we can be successful again.*
	Other numbers are sometimes used also, such as: *The million-dollar question.*

Continued on the next page.

342 · English Idioms and Expressions for Foreigners, *Like Me!*

The $64,000-dollar question	*Continued from the previous page.* **Background:** *The $64,000-dollar Question* was a television game show that was broadcast in the United States in the 1950s. The top prize was worth $64,000. What a surprise!
The Big Easy	This is a nickname for the City of New Orleans.
The buck stops here.	I take full responsibility. This is the end of the road (for something).
The cat is out of the bag.	It's too late. The secret is out. Everybody knows about it now. Also: It's in the water. It has hit the fan. The ship has sailed. We've already set the table. The horse is out of the barn. The toothpaste is out of the tube.

When the axe came to the forest (to cut down the trees), the trees said: The handle is one of us. (*Armenian.*)

There is no one to blame but ourselves.

The jig is up.	The truth is out. You've been caught. *Hey! You can stop acting. The jig is up!* *I was sure the jig was up, and I prepared for the worst. Fortunately, however, there was some distraction, and I survived the situation.*
The long and the short of it	The essence of something. Everything there is to know about something.
The long knives are drawn.	They're ready to fight.
The marker has been laid down.	It's all clear. These are the limits. The limits have been defined.

The powers that be Powerful people.
The government.
The people in charge.
Those whose opinions matter.
Those who control public affairs.
Those who make the important decisions.

The powers that be are interested in this casino development. I know it will happen!

Too many cooks spoil the broth. *(English.)*
More cooks make a bigger mess. *(Norwegian.)*
When there are two cooks, the soup will be either too salty or tasteless. *(Persian.)*

The works The complete package.

Q. What do you want on your pizza?
A. I want everything. Give me the works.

At the carwash:
Q. Do you want me to wash the windows only?
A. I want the works. Wash it inside and out!

The world over All over the world.

Then-something Something at that time (in the past).

She was married to then-New York Governor, means:

She was married to the man who was the governor of New York at that time.

In 1975, I met my then-future wife at a school event.

Examples: Then-professor. Then-son-in-law.

There are no atheists in foxholes.
Military

When there's danger of death, people believe in God.

Also: There are no atheists on a sinking ship.

Background:
This has its origins in days of war. When you may get killed any second, there is a tendency to believe in God!

There's more to it! **There's more to it than meets the eye!**	There's more. This is not the whole thing. They're not telling us the whole story. There's more about it that we don't know or don't understand.
There's no daylight between them.	They are the same. They are no different. There's no difference between them. Also: They are two peas in a pod. They are two sides of the same coin.
They don't "X" for nothing.	There's a reason for "X." When someone says: *They don't call him a traitor for nothing,* they mean something like: *So, that's why they call him a traitor!* *There's a reason they call him a traitor.* *There must be a reason they call him a traitor.*
They're eating our lunch.	WE should be up there. They're stealing OUR ideas. They're benefiting from OUR efforts.
Think nothing of it.	It's not a big deal. Don't think about it. When someone says: *I think nothing of going there,* they mean something like: *Going there is not a big deal.* It is also used in response to *Thank you!* A. *Thank you very much for taking me home.* B. *Oh, think nothing of it. It was a pleasure!*
Thinking highly of	Having a lot of respect for someone. *I think highly of my parents,* means: *I respect my parents very much.* *I have high regards for my parents.* *I think my parents are great people.* Also: Thinking the world of someone.

Thinking twice about something	Not making a decision right away. Thinking about something seriously. Giving something serious consideration.
	Also see: Second thought.
	Compare to: On second thought.
Third time's a charm.	The third time, it'll work. The third time you do it, you'll get it right.
	Also, for humor: The third time is "not" a charm! This is actually a play on the above expression and is meant to say: *That old expression is not going to work this time!*

The woman who doesn't wish to bake bread, spends five days contemplating. *(Greek.)*
A woman who doesn't want to cook takes all day to prepare the ingredients. *(Albanian.)*

Three sheets to the wind	Disoriented. Really drunk or high on drugs. Someone not knowing what they're talking about.
	By the time I got there, he was three sheets to the wind!
	Note: Other numbers have been used also.
Three strikes, you're out! *Origin: Legal, Sports*	This is a warning, and it basically means: If you do it one more time, you're finished. If you do it three times, you'll be in real trouble.
	Background: This is a legal term that is also used by the general public. It has its origins in baseball. If you get three strikes in a baseball game while you're at bat, you're out of the game until your next turn at bat. In law, it means that if you commit three minor offenses, you will suddenly be facing more severe punishments.

Three-dollar bill	When someone says: *Henry is as phony as a three-dollar bill,* they mean something like:

I don't trust him.
He's a con artist.
He's not trustworthy.

Background:
Because there are no three-dollar bills in print, if you see a three-dollar bill, you'll know it's fake. Hence the expression.

They said to the fox, the fox said to its tail. *(Bulgarian.)*
Tell a lazy man to do something. Listen to philosophy! *(Persian.)*
Tell a lazy man to do something. He'll give you advice! *(Turkish.)*

Through and through	Thoroughly. Completely. Throughout.

She read the report through and through.
He's an honorable man through and through.

Also: Completely through something.

The bullet hit him and went in through and through.

Through the roof	Very high, as in:

Q. *Now that the prices are coming down, are you going to buy a house?*
A. *I was hoping to, but home prices are still through the roof.*

Over-reaction or anger, as in:

When Joe finds out how bad the situation is, he will go through the roof!

Through the wringer	Gone through a lot of tough times and hardship.

We'll be put through the wringer if we screw up again.
Losing all her savings in one day, and at her old age, has put her life through the wringer.

Also: Through an emotional meat-grinder.

- I've seen you working hard on this old car for a while. Is it worth it?

- Well, actually, it's my pet project.

- Your pet must be very happy!

For a definition, see:

- **Pet project**

Throwing a wrench into something.	Screwing things up. Making something fail. *Q. Was your loan approved? A. Almost, but my ex-wife threw a wrench into the process and told them that I was broke!* Also: Throwing in a monkey wrench.
Throwing in the towel *Origin: Sports*	Giving up. *Q. What happened to the new teacher? A. Oh, she threw in the towel and quit after only two weeks at the school.* **Background:** In boxing, when one boxer is being severely beaten by their opponent, if they are so badly banged up that they cannot make a decision for themselves, often their manager or coach will throw their towel into the ring to end the match by forfeiture before the person gets too badly injured.
Throwing one's hat into the ring	Joining a group of challengers. Announcing one's candidacy, usually for political office. If someone says: *She threw her hat into the ring of candidates for the senate seat,* they mean: *She joined the other candidates who are campaigning to become a senator.*
Throwing out a question	Raising a question at random to get some ideas. Asking a general question to see what the mood is like.
Throwing someone a bone	Rewarding people. Keeping them happy. Giving someone something small to keep them going or doing what you want them to do. *A. I wonder if she's going to help us again! B. Just throw her a bone and make her happy for a while until we think of something!*

Throwing someone under the bus	Using someone as a scapegoat. Sacrificing someone for personal gain. Abandoning someone, denying everything, knowing that the person will get in trouble for something that other people did. *Samantha's not needed by the campaign bosses anymore. I have a feeling that they'll probably throw her under the bus and blame her for their failure one of these days.* Compare to: Sacrificial lamb.
Throwing something in	Adding something extra. Adding a free item into the transaction. Q. *Can I just buy the helmet?* A. *No! But if you buy the bike, I'll throw in the helmet for free!*
Throwing the baby out with the bathwater	Getting rid of the good along with the bad. Q. *Should I throw away all that stuff in the garage?* A. *Don't throw the baby out with the bathwater! Some of that stuff can be used.*
Thumbing one's nose	Being dismissive, arrogant, conceited, etc. When someone says: *They're thumbing their nose at us,* they mean something like: *They're not taking us, or our ideas, seriously.* Also: Turning one's nose up.
Ticker **Old ticker**	Heart. Q. *Are you having heart problems?* A. *Yeah, the old ticker is bothering me again.*
Ticking someone off	Making someone angry. *He's not nice to me anymore. I think I must have ticked him off!*

Continued on the next page.

Ticking someone off

Continued from the previous page.

It ticks me off, means:
I don't like it.
It bothers me.
It makes me angry.

Also:
Pissing someone off. (Not polite.)

Not everyone who chased the zebra caught it, but he who caught it chased it. (*Parts of Africa.*)

Tight as a drum

Stingy.
Sealed watertight. (Like a welded, industrial drum.)
Stretched very tight. (Like the skin on a musical drum.)

Tightening the belt

Cutting expenses.
Becoming more careful about financial decisions.

A. *These are tough times. I'm not spending as much money as I used to.*
B. *I know. I've noticed that you've been tightening your belt!*

Time and again
Time after time

Repeatedly.
Again and again.

Time is of the essence.

Legal

Time is extremely important and limited (indicating a critical deadline for accomplishing something).

I want you to know that, per our contract, time is of the essence. Therefore, if you don't meet any of the deadlines, you'll be penalized accordingly.

Time is running out.

Hurry up.
The end is near.
We don't have much time.

Time to pick a horse   *Gambling*

You must decide now.
It's time to make a decision.

Tipping point	A deciding moment. The point where, as a result of several minor things adding up, a major change takes place.
To a "T" **To a tee** **Down to a "T"**	Exactly. Properly. Precisely. To the smallest detail. *The witness described the suspect's appearance to a "T."* Related: Suits you/him/her/them to a "T." Note: *To a "T"* is believed to be the correct version, although *To a "tee"* is occasionally used.
To be sure	For sure. We're sure. It is known for a fact. *To be sure, she has openly talked about the issue,* means something like: *We know for a fact that she has talked about the issue in public.*

In a piranha-infested river, alligators do backstroke swimming, and monkeys drink water using a straw. *(Portuguese.)*

Be careful in risky situations.

To begin with	First thing. In the beginning. Before you say anything. *To begin with, I wasn't even in town when the accident took place.* *It's not that she broke up their friendship. They were never friends to begin with!*
To boot	Also. In addition. *He was driving without a license, and he was drunk to boot.*

To date	So far. As of now. As of this date. *This is the largest project of its kind to date.* Compare to: Up-to-date.
To each his own	Do your own thing. People have different preferences. One has the right to do as one pleases. People have their own way of doing things. *I'm not quitting this job, but you quit if you want. To each his own!* *I won't spend my savings on a vacation, but you're free to do so. To each his own!* *People handle grief differently and she's doing it with the help of music. To each his own!*
To no avail	Having no effect. Being unsuccessful. Not getting what you worked for. When someone says: *He tried to get a degree in engineering but it was to no avail,* they mean: *He tried but he couldn't get a degree in engineering.*
To one's credit	Deserving credit. Giving credit where credit is due. When someone says: *He was wrong but, to his credit, he quickly apologized,* they mean something like: *He deserves credit because, when he realized that he was wrong, he quickly apologized.*
To one's heart's content **To one's heart's delight** **To one's heart's desire**	To satisfy one's heart. To one's complete satisfaction. *A. Please don't let the kids eat too much ice cream.* *B. Oh, it's a birthday party! I'm going to let them eat ice cream to their heart's content.*

To one's name	Owned by one.
	Belonging to one.
	They have a lot of assets to their name, means: *They own a lot of things. They're rich.*
	I've only got three dollars to my name, means: *I only have three dollars. I'm completely broke.*
To say the least	The least I could say.
	The least that could be said.
	When someone says: *I was surprised, to say the least,* they mean something like:
	I was surprised, and then some.
	I was at least surprised, if not shocked.
	The least I can say is that I was surprised.
To the best of my ability	As well as I can.
To the best of my knowledge	As far as I know.

This is where the dog is buried. *(Hungarian.)*
This is the reason for the problem.

To the best of my recollection	As far as I remember.
To this end	So. Therefore.
To that end	For this reason.
To which end	For that purpose.
	I'll be going to Europe, to which end I need to get my passport renewed.
To top it off	To complete.
	To add on top.
	He had a high-paying job. To top it off, they gave him a bonus, too!
Toe the line.	Do one's share of the work.
	Do what is expected of one.
	Note: *Tow* the line is not the correct spelling.

Toe-to-toe	Very close.
	A very close competition.
	Republicans and Democrats are going toe-to-toe on this issue.
	Similar:
	Neck-and-neck.
	Too close to call.
Tongue in cheek	Sarcastic.
Tongue-in-cheek	Humorous.
	Not to be taken seriously.
	She's known for making tongue-in-cheek remarks.
Too good to be true	Not true.
	When someone says: *This story is too good to be true,* they're telling you that they don't believe the story.
Top dog	The main person.
Top banana	The one in charge.
	Compare to:
	Second fiddle.
	Second banana.
Topping something	Doing better than something done previously.
	I'm sure you can top his performance if you try.
Tossed out on one's ear	Expelled.
	Thrown out.
Tossup	When someone says: *Something is a toss-up,* they mean:
Toss up	
Toss-up	*It could go either way.*
	It's equally likely or unlikely.
	They're not sure what the outcome will be.
	There's a fifty percent chance that it might work.
	Also:
	Fifty-fifty.
	Fifty-fifty chance.

Touching on something	Mentioning something or talking about it briefly. Q. *Did he say anything about why he would be a better candidate?* A. *Well, he used the opportunity to touch on the subject, but he didn't go into details.*
Tough love	The tough treatment of someone because you love them, as in: *Son, you can't go to the movies tonight because you still haven't finished your homework!*
Toughing it out	Tolerating a tough situation. *Listen, son, if you want to survive in this world, you have to tough it out when times are rough.*

His opinions are like water in the bottom of a canoe, going from side to side. *(Parts of Africa.)*

Track record	Record of accomplishments. Someone's or something's established background based on past actions. A. *Make me a manager, and I'll turn this department around!* B. *But you don't have a track record in management!*
Tracking down *Legal*	Looking for something or someone (for a long time) and finding them. Also see: Running someone down.
Trading blows	Exchanging verbal or physical insults or punches. A ritual where two persons take turns hitting each other until one is left standing. Q. *Are these guys always respectful of each other?* A. *Not always. They've traded blows on occasion!*

Trick or treat?	Are you going to give me something (a treat), or do you want me to play a trick on you?
	Background: This is a question asked by kids when they go *trick-or-treating* and knock on people's doors as a part of *Halloween*. The typical response is that people give candies to the kids.
Trigger-happy *Legal, Military*	A trigger happy person is a person who:
	Likes to shoot people for fun. Is ready to fire a gun or start a fight without much justification.
	A. *Too many kids are being shot to death in street fights.* B. *The sooner we stop these trigger-happy people, the better!*
Tripping up	Causing someone to stumble.
Trophy wife	A young woman whom an old (or rich, powerful, famous, etc.,) man has married in order to make him look (or feel) good in the society.
	Compare to: Gold digger. Starter wife.
True blue	Loyal. Faithful. Really honest.
Truth or consequences?	Tell me the truth, or you'll be sorry. Tell me the truth, or you'll have to suffer the consequences. Do you want to tell me the truth? Otherwise, there will be consequences.
Turn the tide **Turn the tables**	A complete change in the situation.
	I'm waiting for the tide to turn before I make any new investments.
	The tides have turned against the Democrats as they did against the Republicans before.

Turning in	Stopping to do what you're doing, as in: If you say: *I'll be turning in now,* you mean: *That's it for me. I'm tired. I'm going to bed. I'm finished. I'm going home.*
	Submitting, as in: *I'm going to finalize my report tonight and turn it in tomorrow.*
Turning lemons into lemonade	Making a good thing out of a bad situation.
Turning on someone	Betraying someone. Turning against someone. *A. I thought they were friends!* *B. They were, but recently they have turned on each other.*
Turning one's back on people	Rejecting people. Refusing to help them. *My former boss had always said that he would help me with my job search, but when I asked him for a letter of recommendation, he turned his back on me!*
Turning out to be	Becoming someone (or something) at the end, usually with a touch of surprise. *After my doctor's visit, I received a message to call his office, which scared me, but it turned out to be nothing serious. I had merely left my jacket there!* *This guy followed me in his car for several blocks. He turned out to be an old friend, however, and we had lunch!* Compare to: Ending up.
Turning over a new leaf	Starting anew. Changing for the better. *Tell me how he intends to turn over a new leaf after spending nearly two years in prison!*

Turning someone on	Attracting someone sexually or romantically. Finding someone sexually or romantically attractive.
	Q. *Does she turn you on?* A. *Oh, yes. I find her to be very sexy.*
Turning something on its head	Changing something completely. Changing things, or the direction of things, to one's advantage.
	Also: Turning something upside-down.
Turning things around	Making improvements.
	When someone says: *He'll start to turn things around,* they mean something like:
	Things will change. He'll make things better.
	Also: Taking a turn for the better.
Turning to something	Becoming active or involved in something.
	Turning to art means: *Becoming an artist.* *Turning to God* means: *Becoming religious.* *Turning to crime* means: *Becoming a criminal.*
Twenty-four/seven 24/7	Constantly. A continuous operation. Twenty-four hours a day, seven days a week.
Twisting someone's arm	Forcing or pressuring someone to do or say something.
	If someone says: *I didn't want to take the job but my wife twisted my arm,* they could mean:
	She forced me to do it. She threatened to leave me if I didn't! She put strong pressure on me to take the job. She promised me that her mother would leave us if I took the job!
Two sides to every story	Consider all of the facts before you make a decision. Always listen to both sides of a situation before you make a judgment about it.

At the construction site:

- This is where I fell down and broke my arm. I lost my footing.
- Well, then, this is where we'll start looking!

For a definition, see:

- **Losing one's footing**

Two-timing	Not being faithful. Cheating in a romantic relationship.
	When someone says: *Sue is two-timing her boyfriend,* they mean something like:
	She's with him but she's seeing someone else, too. She's cheating on him. She's a two-timer.
Under scrutiny	Being investigated or watched.
	Wan Toe is under scrutiny. They are watching everything he does very carefully.
	Similar: Under surveillance. Living in a fish bowl. Under the magnifying glass.
	Compare to: Fine-toothed comb.
Under someone's thumb	Under someone's control.
	When someone says: *Adolpho is under Julia's thumb,* they mean something like:
	He's under her full control.
	Similar: He's her puppet. She's playing him like a violin. She has him wrapped around her little finger.
Under the gun	Facing a tight deadline. Under (a lot of) pressure.
	We are under the gun to get the play on the road by next week.
Under the hat	Secret.
	When someone says: *Keep it under your hat,* they mean something like:
	Do it quietly; Keep it a secret; Keep it to yourself; Don't tell anybody about it; etc.
	Also see: Sweeping something under the rug

Under the weather	Feeling a little sick.
	Q. How are you feeling? *A. I'm feeling a little under the weather.* *Q. Is it bad?* *A. No, I've just got a cold.*
Under water	In trouble. In financial trouble. Financially speaking, when you owe more (on a loan) than the property is worth.
	Also see: Upside down situation.
Under way	In progress. Being done.
	A medical study on the effects of third-hand smoking is under way at this very moment.
Until the last dog dies	Forever. For a very long time.
	Q. How long are you going to stay here? *A. I will be here until the last dog dies!*
Up for grabs	Available for anyone to take.
	Q. By the way, I know that your chief engineer has retired. Is his position filled? *A. No, it's up for grabs.*
Up for something	Ready, or in line, for something, as in:
	This time, I'm up for promotion. *Next year, she's up for re-election.*
	Interested in something or doing something, as in:
	Are you up for some mountain climbing today?
Up in arms **Up-in-arms**	Ready to fight. In a fighting mood. Agitated or outraged about something.
	The Republicans were up in arms about the "empathy" remark that Obama made.

Up on something

Familiar with something.
Having current information about something.

I'm afraid I'm not up on the history of my country!

Also: Up-to-speed.

Up one's sleeve

Something hidden.
A hidden thing ready to be used, maybe like a trick.

What do you have up your sleeve this time?

Up the ante
Gambling

Adding to the rewards.
Adding to the incentive.
Making it more interesting.

Also:
Sweeten the pot.

Background:
This expression comes from gambling. When you *up the ante* or *sweeten the pot,* you're adding to the amount of the bet, thus making it more interesting by increasing the potential winnings.

Up to 10 years

Maximum of 10 years.
No more than 10 years, maybe less.

Note: Other *numbers* and *units* are used also.

Up to date
Up-to-date

Current.
The most recent version.
Including the latest changes.

This report was printed last week and is our most up-to-date document. Feel free to use it in your research.

Compare to: To date.

Up to snuff
Up-to-snuff

Acceptable.
At the acceptable level.
Meeting the requirements.

Also:
Up to par.

Up to speed
Up-to-speed

Current.
Aware of, or familiar with, what's going on.

Q. *Are you up to speed with our computer system?*
A. *I've worked on similar systems, so I'm sure it'll be okay.*
Q. *What about the case? Are you up to speed with the case?*
A. *No, sir, I'll have to study the case and prepare myself.*

Also see:
In touch.
Up to date.

Up-and-coming

Promising and new.
Showing signs of success.

Q. *Why are you interested in helping her?*
A. *She's an up-and-coming singer, with potential. If I help her now, she might help ME later!*

Upper hand

Advantage.

When someone says: *We have the upper hand in the negotiation,* they mean something like:

We have an advantage over them.
We're in a better position than them.

Q. *Do you want to negotiate with Richard?*
A. *Not really. I have the upper hand here.*

Upside down situation

A money losing operation or business.

We're losing money on this building. It's been an upside-down investment for us ever since we bought it!

Urban legend

A legend that may, or may not, be true. And if true, it may be exaggerated or otherwise distorted. It is also referred to as *modern legend* or *contemporary legend* and is different from typical, old legends.

Using discretion
Origin: Legal

Being diplomatic, discreet, and tactful, and using diplomacy in one's actions. Using one's knowledge, experience, and authority to separate between courses of action, and deciding on the proper one. In other words, using one's head!

When a warning at the beginning of a television show says: *Viewer Discretion Is Advised,* it means:

The show may not be suitable for younger viewers. Adults must be ready to make a decision accordingly.

When someone says: *This is my plan, but please use discretion,* they mean:

Use this information wisely.
Don't tell the whole world about it!

Also:
Do it discreetly.
Be discreet about it.
Do it with discretion.
Use it with discretion.
Do it at your discretion.

Using one's gray cells

Thinking.
Using one's brain.

Using one's head

Using one's brain.
Thinking logically.

A. *I hear you're going back to school again. I'm glad you're finally using your head!*
B. *Yeah and I'm getting a headache, too!*

Using one's judgment
Origin: Legal

Making a decision based on one's knowledge or experience.

Q. *What do you want me to do with these books?*
A. *Use your judgment. I trust you and I trust your judgment.*

Also see: Judgment call.

U-turn	A 180 degree turn. A drastic change of mind. Making a turn on the street from going in one direction to be able to go in the opposite direction.
Vantage point	A place or position from which you can see or observe something (very well). When someone says: *From my vantage point, he's alright,* they mean something like: *I think he's okay.* Similar: *If you ask me, …* *The way I see it, …* *In my point of view, …* *From where I'm sitting, …* *As far as I'm concerned, ...*
Vertically challenged	The politically correct way of referring to a short person. The politically correct way of referring to a person who has difficulty standing up.
Village fool **Village idiot**	An idiot. A foolish person.
VIP	This is an abbreviation for: **V**ery **I**mportant **P**erson. Guest of honor.
Voicing one's opinion	Telling people what one thinks.
VP	This is an abbreviation for: **V**ice **P**resident. Also: Veep.
Wait a sec.	Wait. Wait a minute or wait a second.
Wait until the dust settles.	Wait until things are clear. Wait until we know what's going on. Wait until we know what we're doing.

Waiting for the other shoe to drop	Waiting for something else (bad) to happen.
Waiting something out	Waiting long enough for something to happen or change or end.
	We are waiting out the storm (or the elections or the recession, etc.)
	The two brothers are waiting out their 84-year-old rich uncle's death, could mean:
	They are waiting until he dies so that they may get his money!

If a child cries for a razor blade, give it to him.
He who is not taught by his mother will be taught by the world.
Advise and counsel; if he does not listen, let adversity teach him.
(Parts of Africa.)

Wake up, and smell the coffee!	This expression-like sentence could have any of the following meanings:
	You're falling behind. You don't know what's going on. Pay attention to what's happening. What are you doing? Do something. Things are changing, and you're not paying attention.
	A. *My brother still trusts his ex-wife.* B. *Really?! He needs to wake up, and smell the coffee!*
	Also: Get with it! Get with the program!
	And, on a more humorous note: Wake up, and smell the cappuccino!
Waking up on the wrong side of the bed	Being moody, cranky, or impatient.
	When someone says: *She probably woke up on the wrong side of the bed this morning,* they mean something like:
	She's not in a good mood today.

Walk the walk; don't just talk the talk.	Deliver, don't just promise. Do the things that you tell others to do. Don't just tell other people to do things but then do something else yourself. When someone says: *We walk the walk; we don't just talk the talk,* they mean: *We don't just talk! We do what we say to do.* Also: Don't be a hypocrite.
Walking a fine line **Walking a thin line**	Being careful about one's actions or statements in sensitive situations. *If you're in a situation where you have to be real careful about what you're saying or doing, you must walk a fine line.*
Walking on eggshells	Being careful with what you're saying. Being very careful in a sensitive or dangerous situation. When someone says: *I'm walking on eggshells with my wife,* it means: *I have to be very careful about what I say or do around my wife, because she's very sensitive.* Also see: On thin ice.

Blame for error always lies with those who act. *(Cambodian.)*

Walking someone through something	Explaining things. Telling someone, or showing them, how something is done. *Don't worry, I'll walk you through the instructions and show you how to assemble this ridiculous machine!*
Walking the line	Following the rules. Q. *Why did Johnny Cash walk the line for June Carter?* A. *Because he loved her!*

Wall Street	The financial community in general. The financial capital of the United States. Where the New York Stock Exchange is located. A street in New York where the headquarters of major financial institutes are located. Compare to: Main Street.

Good luck or bad luck is often followed by more of the same. (*Icelandic.*)

Wanna	This is a slang abbreviation for: *Want to.* If someone says: *We wanna take it easy today,* they mean: *We want to take it easy today.*
Waste not, want not.	If you don't waste things, you won't need more. If you don't need it, don't buy it, because then you won't waste it.
Water under the bridge	Things that have already happened. Things in the past that shouldn't really matter. A. *I don't want to see them again. They didn't treat me right at school.* B. *But it's been so long. It's all water under the bridge at this point. Let's go to the reunion.*
Water-cooler talk	Office gossip. Things about the company that the employees would talk about. *More credibility is generally given to printed material than to "water-cooler gossip."*
Watered down **Watered-down**	Something that's made to look less serious, less detailed, less costly, etc., than the actual thing. Something that has been diluted so that it's not as strong as it would be at full strength, such as a watered-down drink. *I'm serving him watered-down drinks because he gets drunk easily!*

Waving the white flag *Origin: Military*	Being open to negotiation. Wanting to hold peace talks. Showing a willingness to surrender. *A. I think you guys should try to come to a compromise.* *B. Yes, that's exactly why I'm waving the white flag by inviting you here to be a mediator.* Also: A peace offering. Compare to: Extending an olive branch.
Way back when	Long time ago.
We deliver. **We can deliver.**	We can do it. If we say we'll do it, we'll do it. *A. When we signed up with you, we weren't sure you'd provide good service.* *B. Well, as you can see, we deliver!* Also: We come through, or we keep our word.
We're outta here!	Let's leave. We are done. It's no use anymore. That's it, we're leaving. That does it, we can't take it anymore.
Wearing something on one's sleeve	Being transparent (truthful, etc.,) about something. Not being good at hiding one's emotions. *She wears her heart on her sleeve,* means: *She's open about being emotionally sensitive!* *They wore their racism on their sleeve,* means: *They were not shy about being racist.*
Wearing thin	Weakening. Becoming less effective. *Your excuses are wearing thin. They're not working on me any more.* Also: Running out of patience.

Weighing in	Expressing one's opinion, as in:
	The vice president hasn't weighed in on the situation yet.
	Having or exerting influence, as in:
	The vocal mob was eager to weigh in on the election results.
Well, I'll be!	An expression of surprise.
	A. *They were talking about a talking dog on television.*
	B. *A talking dog? Well, I'll be! What's next, a flying pig?*
	Also:
	I'll be damned!
	What do you know!
	Well, I'll be damned!
	Who would've guessed!
	Well, what do you know!
Well-to-do	Wealthy.
Wet behind the ears	Innocent. Inexperienced.
	He's young and a little wet behind the ears.
	Background: This expression apparently comes from the fact that babies, when they are born, are wet all over. The area behind the ears dries last, by which time some time has passed, supposedly allowing for maturity and experience.
What did that get you?	How did that help you? What did it do for you? What did you accomplish?
	Also: Where did that get you?
What do you make of it?	Can you figure it out? What is the meaning of it? What do you think it means?

What gives?	What is it? What's up? What's cooking? What's happening? What do you want?
What goes around comes around.	You get what you deserve depending on how you behave, good OR bad. For example, if you're nice to people, nice things will, in turn, happen to you. Also: You reap what you sow.
What is your angle?	This has positive OR negative connotation and it means: What do you think? What's in it for you? What's your point of view? What are you trying to do?

Ending up with underpants on a stick. *(Croatian.)*

Being really poor.

What it is!	How are things? What's going on?
What possessed you to say that?	Why did you say that? What made you say that?
What seems to be the problem?	What is the matter? What are you worried about? What are you thinking about?
What's done is done.	It's too late. Let's move on. Let's forget about it and start from the beginning. Also: Bury the hatchet. Let's put it behind us. Let bygones be bygones. It's water under the bridge.

What's eating you?	What's wrong? What's the matter? What's bothering you?
What's on your mind?	What do you want? What are you talking about? What are you thinking about?
What's the dealio?	What's the deal? What's going on? What do you want? Also: What's up? What's the word?
What's the idea?	What are you thinking? What are you trying to do? Q. *I see that you parked your car in the manager's spot. What's the idea?* A. *I heard he's going to be away for a while, so why not?*
What's the verdict? *Origin: Legal*	What's the penalty? What's the outcome? What do you suggest? How do you feel about it? What should we do about it? Similar: What's the word? What's your take on this?
What's up with that?	What's wrong? Why did that happen? What's wrong with that? Why was this said or done? What's the matter with that?
What's your pleasure?	What would you like? What would you like to do?
What's your point?	What are you trying to say? Also see: Get to the point.

Strike at the factory:

- It looks like the strike is off to a good start. Is everyone with us?

- Almost everyone. Johnny is still sitting on the fence.

- That's an expensive fence!

For a definition, see:

- **On the fence**

What's your story? What's your life story?
What are you all about?
What's your explanation?
What do you want to tell me?
What's your side of the story?

Whatchamacallit? This word is used in place of a word that the speaker doesn't know or doesn't remember. It can mean any of the following:

What is it called?
What is its name?
What do they call that?

A. *I met this guy in charge of the, whatchamacallit, the new project!?*
B. *I know what you mean. Go ahead. Tell me what you guys talked about.*

Interesting point:
Although people sometimes don't remember certain words while they're speaking, they always remember to say *whatchamacallit!*

Wheels are coming off the wagon. The system is about to break down.
The situation is getting out of control.

Q. *Do you think the government is losing control of the economy?*
A. *Definitely, to the point that the wheels are coming off the wagon!*

Also:
Wheels falling off the wagon.

When hell freezes over! Never!

Q. *When will you buy me a new car?*
A. *When hell freezes over!*

Also:
When pigs fly!
Not in your lifetime!
It'll be a cold day in hell before that happens!

When in Rome, do as the Romans do. Follow the local customs.
Follow the rules, wherever you are.

When push comes to shove	When things get really bad. When you have no other choice. When it becomes absolutely necessary. *When push comes to shove, I'll tell them what I really think of them!* Also: When it comes right down to it.
When the cat is away, the mice will play.	No authority means no order. When there's no control, there will be chaos.
When the chips are down	When nothing seems to be working. When one is under a lot of pressure. When the situation is difficult or dangerous. *When the chips were down, she always did the right thing.* *When the chips are down, you can always count on your real friends.* In gambling: *When the chips are down, you're losing!*
Where do you come off saying things like this?	Why do you say things like this? What gives you the right to say things like this?
Where in the world is it?	Where is it? The following are similar but are not polite: Where the hell is it? Where is the damn thing? For God's sake, where is it?
Where one gets off the train	Where disagreements begin or become too much. *This is where I get off the train,* could mean: *I don't agree with you any more.* *This is where I go my separate way.* *I'm not cooperating with you any longer.* Related: People are off the bus now.

Where the rubber meets the road!	The important thing. The thing that counts. Q. *Do you think you're going to win the election? You're ahead in all of the polls!* A. *I know, but the voting next week is where the rubber will meet the road.*

First dig a well, then steal the minaret. *(Persian.)*
Steal the minaret, but first prepare the sack for hiding it. *(Turkish.)*

About planning ahead.

Whiling away the time	Passing the time. *To while away the time, the young man talks of his childhood.* Also see: Killing time.
Whisky breath	Drunk. One whose breath smells like whisky. Similarly: Dog breath. Turtle neck. Potato head.
Whistle-stop series	A series of short stops and meetings at a number of locations. *The senator is going to South America for a whistle-stop series of meetings with South American leaders.*
Whistling Dixie	Being happy, carefree. Talking or thinking a little too positively, making things seem better than they are in reality.
White elephant	A big burden. A valuable (but expensive to maintain) item that nobody wants, or can afford, to keep. A company or property that is so costly to maintain that it is impossible to make a profit. Also see: Albatross around one's neck.

White knuckler	Really scary. A tense and nervous person. Q. *How was your flight on the small plane?* A. *It was a white knuckler! The turbulence was so bad that I thought I was going to die!* **Background:** When people are scared, they sometimes grab something (edge of the seat, the railing, someone's hand, etc.) very hard. Now, if they're really scared, they will grab it so tightly that their knuckles will turn white!
White trash **White trailer trash**	White (Caucasian), lower class, low-income, generally uneducated people. (An insult. Not a nice thing to say.)
Who cares?	I don't care. Also: Whatever. See if I care. The hell with it. I don't give a hoot. I don't give a care. I couldn't care less. I don't give a damn. Who gives a damn? I don't give a rat's ass.

It is the thief who thinks that all men steal. (*Danish.*)

Whole nine yards	The whole thing. All of something. *Our vendor got us a box suite at the baseball game! It didn't just give us the best seats in the stadium. It also included free parking, a private living room, kitchen, bathroom, and lots of food; the whole nine yards!* Also: The whole shebang. The whole enchilada.

Why don't you?	What sounds like a question is actually an invitation or an order to do something, as given in the examples below:
	Why don't you say it? means: *Say it!*
	Why don't you write about it? means: *Write about it!*
	Why don't you tell me about it? means: *Tell me all about it!*
	Why don't you come over and sit next to me? means: *Sit next to me.*
Why, of course!	This is simply a more emphatic and sympathetic way of saying: *Of course!*
	Q. *Shall I tell you what I did today?* A. *Why, of course!*
	Similar: *Why, no!* *Why, yes!*
Wild goose chase	A fake task. A task that (we know) will not produce any results. Sending someone to look for something that either doesn't exist or isn't where they say it is.
	When someone says: *I sent him on a wild goose chase,* they mean something like:
	I got rid of him. I sent him in the wrong direction.
Will fly	Will work.
	If you say: *This plan will fly,* you mean: *It will work.*
	If you say: *This plan will fly with her,* you mean: *She will like it.* *She will agree with it.*
	Opposite: Won't fly.
Windy City	This is a nickname for the City of Chicago.

Winging it	Doing something without preparation. Doing something and seeing how it works. Doing something without weighing the consequences. *I didn't have time to study for my test last night, so now I'm just going to have to wing it and hope I pass.*
Wingman	Best friend, sidekick. A person assisting others (including friends) to make connection with a potential love interest, when they can't do it easily on their own. *I'm too uncomfortable approaching a woman that I'm interested in. So, I've asked "Subtle Raul" to be my wingman!* **Background:** This word has its roots in aviation. When several airplanes are flying in formation, the pilot flying behind the lead pilot is the lead pilot's *wingman* and will take over if something happens to the lead pilot.
Win-lose (situation)	A situation where one side wins, one side loses. Compare to: Lose-lose or win-win.
Win-win (situation)	A situation where both sides win. Compare to: Lose-lose or win-lose.
Wise guy **Wise-guy**	A know-it-all. A person who is very sure of himself, and pushes his own ideas. *So he's a wise guy. He thinks he knows everything, and makes sure that everyone knows it.* Another meaning: A gangster. Connected to organized crime. *Do you see those guys over there? You'd better be careful. They're "wise guys," if you know what I mean!*

With a vengeance	With intensity.
	She came back with a vengeance from near defeat, overcame her opponent, and won the game.
With all due respect	With all of the respect that is deserved.
	When someone says: *With all due respect, sir, that's not what you said the other day,* they mean something like:
	You know I respect you, but why are you lying?
	Note: This is an expression that you can use when you want to politely disagree with someone. However, in a way, sometimes it's another way of saying that you really have NO RESPECT for the other person! So, be careful about when, how, and to whom you say it.
Within earshot	Very close. Close enough to hear (it).
	Q. *Were you close to where they were arguing?*
	A. *Yes. I was within earshot and heard the whole thing*
	Opposite: Out of earshot.
Within striking distance *Military*	Close. Close enough to strike, hit, touch, etc.
	We were told not to start firing unless the enemy was within striking distance.
Without missing a beat	Without hesitating. Responding to something without showing surprise or shock.
	Compare to: Missing a beat.
Wonder years	The time of life for younger people when things are still special, like going to an amusement park.

Wooden nickels	Fake money. Fake anything. When someone says: *Don't take any wooden nickels,* they mean: *Be careful;* *Don't trust everybody;* *Don't get taken or fooled;* *Be careful in your dealings with others; etc.* **Background:** In the olden days, *wooden nickels* were sometimes issued by businesses as a promotion and didn't have a universally accepted monetary value. The warning above has now become an expression.
Work in progress **Work-in-progress**	Work or a project that has been started but not finished yet. Work or a project that has taken a long time and is still not finished. (Sarcastic.) Q. *Did your son get his degree?* A. *Oh, that's a work-in-progress. I don't think he'll ever get it!*
Working one's butt off	Working very hard. Q. *Have you been to the movies lately?* A. *No, I don't have time. I've bee working my butt off, even on the weekends!* Also: Working one's tail off. Working one's fingers to the bone.
Working to someone's advantage	Being advantageous to someone. *This can only work to HER advantage,* means: *It won't hurt HER.* *It can only be good for HER.* *It won't help US, it'll help HER.*
Worth a mint	Valuable. Worth a lot of money.

Worth noting	Good to take notice. Good to pay attention to. When someone says: *The results of our latest study are worth noting,* they mean something like: *It's worthwhile to look at these results. You might even learn something!*
Would just as soon	Would prefer. Would rather. Q. *Would you like to go to the party with us later?* A. *No, I have to be back early. I'd just as soon go now.*
Wouldn't put anything past someone	This term implies a negative connotation about the person's character. When someone says: *I wouldn't put cheating past her,* they mean something like: *She's capable of cheating.* *If she's caught cheating, I won't be surprised.* When someone says: *I wouldn't put anything past your friend,* they mean something like: *He might do anything.* *You never know what he would do!*
Wrapping one's head around something **Wrapping one's mind around something**	Understanding (feeling, comprehending, etc.,) the issue. Also: Getting one's arms around something. *She can't even get her arms around our problems. How can you expect her to make good decisions on our behalf?*
Writing on the wall	Warning. Message of doom. Some indication of things to come. The fate of something is already determined. Q. *Why are you selling your stocks?* A. *The stocks will be losing even more value. I can see the (hand) writing on the wall.*

Writing one's own ticket	Letting one decide what one wants to do per one's own desire.
	If someone is able to write their own ticket, it usually means that they are exceptionally gifted, smart, connected to influential people, financially secure, etc., and have many options for their life and future.
	When someone says: *Write your own ticket,* they mean something like:
	Tell me what you want to do. *Tell me how much you want, and I'll go along.*
Wrong end of the stick	*I got the wrong end of the stick,* could mean:
	I was cheated. *I got a bad deal.* *I was put at a disadvantage.* *I had to do an undesirable task.* *I had to do the things I hated to do.*
	Also: The raw end of the deal. The short end of the stick. The crummy end of the stick.
Wrong side of the tracks	The poor, crime-ridden part of a town or community.
	Compare to: Other side of the tracks.
"X" dollars' worth	*Thirty dollars' worth of something,* means: *A quantity of something that costs thirty dollars.*
	Any quantity, and any monetary system could be used, as in:
	Q. *How much gas do you want?* A. *Ten dinars worth. (Ten dinars worth of gas.)*
Yanking someone's chain	Teasing someone. Irritating someone. Upsetting someone. Stringing someone along.

Yet to happen	When someone says: *It has yet to rain,* it means: *It hasn't rained yet.* When someone says: *I have yet to see her,* it means: *I haven't seen her yet.*
You are kidding!	Really? Are you sure? Are you serious? Are you kidding me? Also: You must be joking! You must be kidding! You've got to be kidding me!
You are overreacting!	Take it easy. You shouldn't get so upset. It's not as bad as you think.

Evil enters like a splinter and spreads like an oak tree. *(Parts of Africa.)*

You bet!	This is a nice thing you might say if someone says *Thank you,* or if someone asks you to do something. It is equivalent to saying: No problem. My pleasure. No, thank YOU. Don't mention it. You're welcome. Also: Sure thing!
You can eat off this floor!	This is a very clean floor!
You can see daylight through it.	It's a very thin material. It has a big crack (or hole) in it.
You can take it to the bank.	It's good. You can trust it.
You can't be serious!	See: You are kidding!

You can't get blood out of a turnip.	You can't get money from a person who doesn't have money. Also: You can't get blood out of a rock.
You can't judge a book by its cover.	Don't make decisions about a person based on their appearance alone. Compare to: Still waters run deep.
You could play marbles with his eyeballs!	He was very surprised. He was so surprised that his eyeballs were sticking out enough to play marbles with! (Not a pretty picture!)
You do the math.	Figure it out. See for yourself. You have the facts. Think about it.
You don't know the half of it!	You don't know much about it. You only know a small part of it. You don't know anything about it. Other fractions are sometimes used also, as in: You don't know one tenth of it.
You don't say!	See: You are kidding!
You don't wanna know! **You don't want to know!**	I don't want to tell you. I don't feel like telling you. I don't think you want to know. I think it's better if you don't know. You might become upset if you know.
You got it!	Exactly. That's it. That's correct. You have the right idea. Also: Right on. Bull's eye. You've got it. There you go. That's my girl. That's my boy.

You have to dance with the one who brought you.	Be loyal. They helped you, now you must help them. Also see: Don't bite the hand that feeds you.
You know what you can do with that? **You want me to tell you what you can do with that?**	It's not polite to ask either one of these rhetorical questions which imply: Get out of here! I don't like your offer! Take it, and get out of here! Similar and also not polite: Put it where the sun don't shine!
You think?	This is a sarcastic way of saying: Really?
You want to bet?	Are you sure? Are you sure enough to bet on it?

If God doesn't give you children, the devil will give you nephews. *(Spanish.)*

You'd better be right.	I hope you are right. It'll be better for you if you're right. If you're not right you'll be in trouble.
You're being watched.	Be careful. You are under surveillance. Also: I'm watching you. I'll be watching you.
You're killing me.	This is too much. I can't take it any more. I can't do this any more.
You're on.	Let's do it. Okay, I accept. I accept your challenge. I accept what you're saying.
You're the man!	You're the boss. You're the important one. You're the one everybody's talking about. You're the person people should see to get things done.

You've been had.	They lied to you. You have been cheated. Also: You have been scammed.
You'd do well to listen.	It's best if you listen. The best thing you can do is to listen.
Your money is no good here!	It's on the house. You're my (our) guest. You don't need to pay. Q. It was good seeing you again. By the way, how much do I owe you for the tickets? A. Oh, forget it. Your money is no good here!
Yours truly	I. Me. Myself. *Every time there's a problem they start blaming yours truly! Am I the only one making mistakes?*
Zeroing in on	Focusing on someone or something. Concentrating on someone or something.
Zip it!	Shut up. Don't talk. Don't say a word. Also: Keep your trap shut. Keep your mouth shut.

APPENDIX

Contact information for the professional people who helped with the publication of this book.

Mojgan Mehran
www.PhotographyByMojgan.com

Daniel Middleton
www.ScribeFreelance.com

Azita Mousavi
www.AzitaArt.com

April Nelson
Warp-Dry Proofreading
www.Warp-DryProofreading.com

Kacie Paik
http://www.facebook.com/kacie.paik

Dan Poynter
www.ParaPublishing.com

Alina Fairy
www.AleStudio.us

Reference articles for the plane crash in New York:

http://www.nytimes.com/1990/02/05/nyregion/avianca-flight-52-the-delays-that-ended-in-disaster.html

http://query.nytimes.com/gst/fullpage.html?res=9C0CE2DD103 1F936A15755C0A966958260&sec=&spon=&pagewanted=all

INDEX

This book is available in the following formats:

Softcover
Hardcover
Pocketbook
E-book
PDF

A revolutionary gift idea:

Alternate cover jackets!

Because we think this book can make a great gift, we have created a number of cover jackets with the same design, but with different titles. This allows you to give copies of this book to different people as gifts, and pick a different jacket for each one that best suits the occasion.

To view the complete array of these jackets in color, or to order, please go to:

EnglishIdiomsAndExpressions.com

Other gift ideas:

- Book of illustrations.
- Book of short folk stories from around the world.
- Desktop calendar, containing one illustration per day.
- Wall calendar with a number of illustrations, large and small.

For more up-to-date information on these items, or to order, please go to:

EnglishIdiomsAndExpressions.com

CPSIA information can be obtained at www.ICGtesting.com

263703BV00003B/1/P

9 780982 773659